THE ROUGH

MADEIRA

Forthcoming titles include

The Algarve • The Bahamas • Cambodia
Caribbean Islands • Costa Brava
New York Restaurants • South America • Zanzibar

Forthcoming reference guides include

Children's Books • Online Travel • Videogaming
Weather

Rough Guides online

www.roughguides.com

Rough Guide Credits

Text editors: Sam Thorne and Ruth Blackmore
Series editor: Mark Ellingham
Production: Julia Bovis and Andy Turner
Cartography: Katie Lloyd-Jones

Publishing Information

This first edition published October 2001
by Rough Guides Ltd,
62–70 Shorts Gardens, London, WC2H 9AH

Distributed by the Penguin Group:

Penguin Books Ltd, 27 Wrights Lane, London W8 5TZ
Penguin Putnam, Inc. 375 Hudson Street, New York 10014, USA
Penguin Books Australia Ltd, 487 Maroondah Highway,
PO Box 257, Ringwood, Victoria 3134, Australia
Penguin Books Canada Ltd, 10 Alcorn Avenue,
Toronto, Ontario, Canada M4V 1E4
Penguin Books (NZ) Ltd,
182–190 Wairau Road, Auckland 10, New Zealand

Typeset in Bembo and Helvetica to an original design by Henry Iles.
Printed in Spain by Graphy Cems.

ISBN 1-85828-727-8

THE ROUGH GUIDE TO

MADEIRA

by Matthew Hancock

ROUGH GUIDES

We set out to do something different when the first Rough Guide was published in 1982. Mark Ellingham, just out of university, was travelling in Greece. He brought along the popular guides of the day, but found they were all lacking in some way. They were either strong on ruins and museums but went on for pages without mentioning a beach or taverna. Or they were so conscious of the need to save money that they lost sight of Greece's cultural and historical significance. Also, none of the books told him anything about Greece's contemporary life – its politics, its culture, its people and how they lived.

So with no job in prospect, Mark decided to write his own guidebook, one which aimed to provide practical information that was second to none, detailing the best beaches and the hottest clubs and restaurants, while also giving hard-hitting accounts of every sight, both famous and obscure, and providing up-to-the-minute information on contemporary culture. It was a guide that encouraged independent travellers to find the best of Greece, and was a great success, getting shortlisted for the Thomas Cook travel guide award, and encouraging Mark, along with three friends, to expand the series.

The Rough Guide list grew rapidly and the letters flooded in, indicating a much broader readership than had been expected, but one which uniformly appreciated the Rough Guide mix of practical detail and humour, irreverence and enthusiasm. Things haven't changed. The same four friends who began the series are still the caretakers of the Rough Guide mission today: to provide the most reliable, up-to-date and entertaining information to independent-minded travellers of all ages, on all budgets.

We now publish more than 150 titles and have offices in London and New York. The travel guides are written and researched by a dedicated team of more than 100 authors, based in Britain, Europe, the USA and Australia. We have also created a unique series of phrasebooks to accompany the travel series, along with an acclaimed series of music guides, and a best-selling pocket guide to the Internet and World Wide Web. We also publish comprehensive travel information on our website: **www.roughguides.com**

Help us update

We've gone to a lot of trouble to ensure that this Rough Guide is as up to date and accurate as possible. However, things do change. All suggestions, comments and corrections are much appreciated, and we'll send a copy of the next edition (or any other Rough Guide if you prefer) for the best letters.

Please mark letters **"Rough Guide Madeira Update"** and send to:

Rough Guides, 62–70 Shorts Gardens, London, WC2H 9AH, or Rough Guides, 4th Floor, 345 Hudson St, New York NY 10014.

Or send email to: mail@roughguides.co.uk
Online updates about this book can be found on
Rough Guides' website (see opposite).

The author

Freelance writer and author of the *Mini Rough Guide to Lisbon*, Matthew Hancock commutes regularly to Portugal and likes nothing better than putting on his boots to walk Madeira's *levadas*. He lives in London with co-author Amanda and their two small children, Alex and Olivia.

Acknowledgements

With thanks to all the help provided by Wanda Gonçalves et al at the Madeira Tourist Board; Teresa Ventura at ICEP; the guides at Turivema; Simply Portugal; Cachet Travel; Marítimo football club; Kathryn Wilson at *Reid's*; the extremely helpful staff at Quinta Bela São Tiago and Quinta Mãe dos Homens; the driving skills of Del; the kind support of Roberta (queen of Snakes and Ladders) and Paul Dickson; Alex and Olivia, who researched the kids' section with endless enthusiasm and patience; the comments by Nic Pursey; and Mandy, without whom this book would not have happened.

Special thanks to everyone at Rough Guides: Paul Gray, Andy Turner for typesetting, Maxine Repath and Katie Lloyd-Jones for brilliant maps, Sharon Martins for picture research, Susannah Wight for proofing, and especially Sam Thorne and Ruth Blackmore for their dedicated and patient editing.

CONTENTS

Map List   viii

Introduction   x

Basics   1

The Guide   43

1 Funchal   45

2 Around Funchal   93

3 Eastern Madeira   120

4 The west coast   143

5 Northern and central Madeira   162

6 Porto Santo   192

Listings   211

7   Accommodation   213

8   Eating   245

9   Drinking and nightlife   281

10   Shopping   302

11   Sports and outdoor activities   308

12   Madeira for kids   322

13   Directory   326

Contexts   329

History   331

Wildlife and the environment   347

Music   353

Books   357

Language   360

Glossary of Portuguese terms   366

Index   369

MAP LIST

Lorano–Machico Walk	139
Rabaçal Walks	157
Levada Da Central Walk	165
Mountain Walks	186–187

At back of book

1 Madeira

2 Central Funchal & Zona Velha

3 Around Funchal

4 Eastern Madeira

5 Machico

6 Western Madeira

7 Ribeira Brava

8 Northeast Madeira

9 Porto Santo

MAP SYMBOLS

▬▬	Motorway	☥	Fortress
▭▭	Road	⊙	Statue
===	Under construction	⚲	Church (regional)
}={	Tunnel	⊞	Hospital
—	Unmade tracks	☂	Gardens
......	Path	⚑	Golf course
—	Coastline/rivers	⚱	Waterfall
......	Levada	⊜	Swimming pool
◄—	Ferry route	ℙ	Parking
---	Cable car	◉	Accommodation
—	Wall	⊠	Post office
▲	Mountain peak	ⓘ	Information office
✈	Airport	∴	Beach
♦	Point of interest	▬	Building
⌂	Cave	⊞	Church (town)
⚲	Lighthouse	⭕	Stadium
⚡	Viewpoint	▢	Market
⋀	Campsite	▦	National park

Introduction

L ying some 600km off the coast of Morocco, **Madeira** is an extraordinarily dramatic island of wild mountain scenery and fantastic walking terrain. Combining precipitous valleys and sheer cliffs – including the second-highest sea cliffs in the world at Cabo Girão – the island boasts an astonishingly diverse array of colourful semitropical vegetation and gently cultivated terraces. Understandably, Madeira's natural beauty, along with its year-round mild climate, excellent hotel facilities, gardens and extremely low levels of crime, has long attracted older visitors, and consequently the island has had a reputation as a rather fusty destination for OAPs. However, it is now also attracting a much younger crowd, who are being wooed by the excellent *levada* walks and the growing number of watersports facilities and adventure sports on offer.

Madeira and the neighbouring island of Porto Santo were uninhabited until they were discovered and colonized by Portuguese explorers in the fifteenth century. Bang in the middle of a major navigational route in the Atlantic, Madeira quickly established itself as an important trading post, linking Portugal with its colonies in Africa and the Americas. However, its economy only really took off as trade in the island's famous **Madeira wine** expanded in the seventeenth century. This trade was largely controlled by the British, Portugal's traditional commercial ally, leading to a strong **British influence** on the island's elite. There are still many Anglo–Madeiran families on the island today, while top hotels like *Reid's* maintain British customs, such as English teas. However, despite English being spoken just about everywhere, Madeira is very much a Portuguese island: the population is nearly all of mainland Portuguese descent, the signs, food and culture are Portuguese, and so are the superb pastries, powerful coffees and very drinkable table wines.

As a holiday destination Madeira is relatively cheap, though, as most products have to be imported, it is more expensive than mainland Portugal. Until fairly recently, the island was one of the poorest parts of Portugal and consequently of Europe, and there are rural communities that have only recently been connected to road transport and mains electricity. Rural traditions are still important and the islanders remain conservative in their values. However, they have embraced the **European Union** with open arms, largely thanks to its funding of a new network of roads and building projects, which have helped propel most of the island into the twenty-first century. Though ancient farming methods on hilltop terraces continue, EU subsidies are updating agriculture and firmly making tourism the number-one source of income for the islanders, especially now the airport has been extended to allow jumbo jets to land.

However, despite the rash of new development to cater for an expected increase in the number of tourists, equal efforts are being made to preserve Madeira's **natural heritage**: the island boasts the greatest concentration of virgin lauraceous forests in the world, and an astonishing 66 percent of the island enjoys protected national-park status.

Where to go

Most visitors spend the majority of their time relaxing in the classy hotels of **Funchal**, the island's historic capital and its liveliest and most attractive town. Very Portuguese in character and architecture, the town has enough museums, sights, restaurants, bars and shops to keep anyone occupied for at least a week. It is also close to many of the island's top tourist attractions, incuding **Monte**, a pretty hilltop town, famed for its dry toboggan run, and **Câmara de Lobos**, an atmospheric fishing village that Winston Churchill took to his heart.

Away from Funchal, the only settlement of any size is **Machico** in eastern Madeira, the first place on the island to be settled, a picturesque and lively seaside resort set amongst terraced slopes. The rest of eastern Madeira offers a varied landscape, from the sprawling settlements around the airport to the extraordinary rocky peninsula of **Ponta de São Lourenço** and the wooded countryside round **Santo da Serra**, home to one of the island's two top golf courses.

The island's other settlements are little more than villages, though for complete peace and quiet you could do worse than base yourself at one of the many attractive seaside resorts. A few kilometres east of Funchal, **Caniço de Baixo** is the most international of these, firmly geared to tourism, and a little further east again, **Santa Cruz** is a delightful, traditional village with a rocky beach. West of Funchal, you could try the small but bustling resort of **Ribeira Brava**, set amongst verdant banana plantations, while the main centre in the unspoilt far west of Madeira is **Jardim do Mar**, a tiny, picturesque village beneath rolling mountains, with a burgeoning surfing culture – it now even hosts a leg of the World Surfing Championships.

The **north** of the island is wilder and even more dramatic than the south, with precipitous hillsides gouged by waterfalls spilling down to the Atlantic. The main centres here are **Porto Moniz**, which boasts superb natural seapools; **São Vicente**, one of the island's prettiest villages; and **Santana**, set near towering cliffs and famed for its triangular houses.

Wherever you stay, you should not miss the opportunity to head to the unspoilt heart of Madeira. For a small island 54km long by 23km wide, Madeira boasts a surprisingly diverse landscape, from the flat, high moors of **Pául da Serra** to the deep, tree-lined valleys of **Rabaçal** in the west; and from the cool mountain village of **Ribeiro Frio** to the bucolic, wooded **Queimadas** in the centre. Highlights for most people are the peaks of **Pico Arieiro** and **Pico Ruivo**, more than 1800m high, offering fantastic views over the island's north and south coasts.

Despite the relatively short distances involved, inland travel takes time – the roads consist of a series of loops and switch-backs as they climb and descend countless valleys – but it is worth the effort. Perhaps the best way to explore the island's interior, however, is by foot on the network of **levadas** (irrigation canals), which offer great routes into the island's remotest valleys and mountain peaks.

Head down from the mountains to the **coast** and the landscape becomes more lush as the temperature rises. Although Madeira lacks long strands of sand, virtually every coastal village on the island has its own beach, albeit a rocky and wave-beaten one; most are safe to swim from, including several in and around Funchal.

However, if you crave seriously big sandy stretches, you will have to catch the daily ferry service from Funchal to **Porto Santo**, the neighbouring island, which boasts a fine nine-kilometre-long beach. Porto Santo is very different in character from Madeira: less mountainous and relatively barren. However, its capital, **Vila Baleira**, is as attractive a town as any on Madeira and makes an excellent base for a relaxing beach holiday, while for a complete chill-out you could do worse than stay at the isolated settlements further down the beach, **Campo de Baixo** and **Cabeço da Ponta**.

When to go

There is no bad time to visit Madeira (semi-permanent sunshine makes it an all-year destination), though your choice of **when to go** may depend on whether you are bothered about a bit of rain and if you have a preference for the sort of vegetation in flower.

"High" and "low" **seasons** have no clear boundaries, with each hotel and travel company seeming to set its own seasons according to its main markets – northern Europeans visit mostly in winter, the Portuguese in summer. Peak time, however, is undoubtedly over New Year, when hotels hike up their prices by some thirty percent. Other busy times coincide with school holidays, so low season, such as it is, tends to be late October to early December and late January to March.

The island is traditionally called the land of perpetual spring, with average summer **temperatures** of 22°C and winter temperatures of 16°C. Despite these apparently modest figures, don't be fooled by the sun, which is extremely intense this far south and can easily burn. Sea temperatures, too, remain balmy all year, at 22°C in summer and 18°C in winter, so it is rarely too cold to swim. However, the locals mostly avoid sea swimming in winter, when offshore diving platforms and beach gear tend to be put in storage.

Though **rain** is rare in July and August, it is always a possibility at other times of the year, especially in November and January and February – though it rarely sets in for long and the sun generally makes an appearance at some stage of the

MADEIRA'S CLIMATE (FUNCHAL AREA)

| | AVERAGE DAILY TEMP °C | | AVERAGE MONTHLY RAINFALL (MM) |
	MAX	MIN	
Jan	19	13	100
Feb	19	13	90
March	19	14	75
April	20	14	45
May	21	15	25
June	22	18	10
July	24	19	0
Aug	25	20	5
Sept	25	19	30
Oct	24	18	75
Nov	22	16	100
Dec	20	14	75

day. The island's semitropical nature means there is verdant **vegetation** all year, though deciduous trees still shed their leaves over winter – an odd sight when it feels like summer – while other plants save their blooms for spring or summer.

Madeira's **climate** can be extremely localized. The south is generally sunnier and drier than the north, while the east tends to be windier and cooler. The mountains have their own microclimates, with mists frequently descending and with more frequent rain than the coastal areas; snow also falls in winter. **Daylight hours** don't vary as much as in northern Europe: in winter it gets dark at around 6pm, while in midsummer it is dark by about 9.30pm.

The best months for **walking** are probably July, August and early September, when rain is unlikely and skies are generally clear – and high up at least, it is not too hot. June is the month most likely to have cloud covering the coasts (though it is usually clear above the cloud line in the mountains), while the rainier months can make *levada* paths waterlogged and slippery. At other times, clouds often form over the mountains in the afternoons, so an early start is the best option for good views.

Porto Santo has its own climate. Rainfall is very low and most days are dry and sunny, though it can be breezy. Low cloud, known as *capacete*, sometimes descends from the mountains at around lunch time, though this usually clears by mid-afternoon and acts as quite a handy shield against the strongest sun of the day.

BASICS

Getting there from Britain and Ireland 3

Getting there from North America 9

Getting there from Australia and New Zealand 13

Visas and red tape 16

Health and insurance 18

Information, maps and websites 22

Money and costs 25

Holidays and festivals 28

Getting around 33

Communications and the media 39

Getting there from Britain and Ireland

The simplest and often cheapest way of visiting Madeira from Britain and Ireland is on a package holiday, especially during the low season (late-Oct to March, apart from Christmas and school holidays). Good deals can also be found in the shoulder seasons (Easter–June and mid-Sept to mid-Oct). However, prices rise considerably in high season (July to mid-Sept and over Christmas, New Year and Easter), when you'll probably find it cheaper to take either one of the scheduled flights direct – or via Lisbon – from London with GB Airways or TAP Air Portugal or a charter flight, and arranging your own accommodation on the island. Flight time to Madeira from London is around three and a half hours. There are no direct scheduled flights to Madeira from Ireland – both GB Airways and TAP route via Heathrow – but you can get direct seasonal charter flights from both Belfast and Dublin.

FLIGHTS AND FARES

Only two airlines offer scheduled **flights** from Britain – TAP and GB Airways – and as flights quickly get booked up, it pays to book well in advance. If there are no direct flights available, TAP offers daily flights to Madeira via Lisbon, though the stopover will add an hour or so to your journey (see below).

GB Airways flies from Gatwick on Tuesday, Friday and Saturday in summer, and on Monday, Wednesday, Friday and Saturday in winter, with fares starting at around £200 return in low season and rising to around £260 in high season. **TAP** offers direct flights from Heathrow to Madeira on Thursdays and Sundays all year from around £200 in low season up to £300 in high season; note that the mid-week flights tend to be around £10 cheaper than those at weekends. TAP also has daily flights via Lisbon for the same fare as the direct flights, though there tends to be better availability (and hence often special deals). Low-season flights from Belfast and Dublin on GB Airways start at around £300 and IR£320/€250 respectively, rising to around £600 and IR£500/€390 in high season.

Charter operators fly to Madeira from several regional airports, including Birmingham, Glasgow, Gatwick, Luton, Bournemouth, Manchester and Newcastle; fares start at around £200 in low season rising to around £300 in high season. There is also a direct charter from Belfast run by Transsun (☎0870/444 4747), with fares starting at around £350, but it only runs certain months in the year (phone to check), and a seasonal charter from Dublin (Nov–March), run by Panorama, bookable through Joe Walsh Tours (see opposite), with fares starting at around IR£260/€205.

The best places to look for **cheap flights** are the mainstream tour operators and travel agents listed below, Teletext

(Ⓦ www.teletext.com) and the Internet; try Ⓦ www
.thefirstresort.com or Ⓦ www.cheapflights.co.uk, or any of
the tour operators' and travel agents' websites listed on p.7.
In addition, newspaper travel sections and magazines often
feature special deals.

AIRLINES

GB Airways Ⓣ 0845/773 3377;
in Ireland Ⓣ 0141/222 2345;
Ⓦ www.british-airways.com.

TAP Air Portugal
Ⓣ 0845/601 0932,
Ⓦ www.TAP-AirPortugal.pt.

MAINSTREAM TOUR OPERATORS AND TRAVEL AGENTS

Abreu Ⓣ 020/7229 9905,
Ⓔ sales@abreu.co.uk.
Portuguese-run agency
offering various packages
round the island.

Airtours Ⓣ 0870/608 1955,
Ⓦ www.airtours.co.uk. One
of the larger package
operators offering flights
from regional airports
throughout the UK.

Caravela Tours Ⓣ 020/7630
9223. Upmarket packages to
some of the island's most
exclusive hotels.

Cosmos Ⓣ 020/8464 3444,
Ⓦ www.cosmos-holidays.co.uk.
Mass-market company which

offers flights from Manchester
year-round and additional
flights from Gatwick and
Birmingham in winter.

First Choice Ⓣ 0870/750 0001,
Ⓦ www.firstchoice.co.uk.
Upmarket packages to
Madeira; also does Porto
Santo.

Joe Walsh Tours, Dublin
Ⓣ 01/872 2555 or 01/676
3053; Cork Ⓣ 021/277959;
Ⓦ www.joewalshtours.ie.
Budget travel agent, who
can book scheduled flights
from Dublin via London and
the seasonal Panorama
charter.

Magic of Portugal
ⓣ 020/8741 1181,
ⓦ www.magictravelgroup.co.uk.
Packages in some of the island's classiest hotels – including *Reid's* (see p.225).

Mundi Color ⓣ 020/7828 6021. Offers flight-only, package-holiday and fly-drive options.

Palm Air Holidays
ⓣ 01202/299299. Small operator with flights from Bournemouth.

Portugala Holidays
ⓣ 020/8444 1857 or 020/8372 2237. Offers a range of fly-drive and package holidays, staying in self-catering apartments, *pousadas*, hotels and *residencias* all over Madeira and also on Porto Santo.

Rosetta Travel ⓣ 028/9064 4996, ⓦ www.rosettatravel .com. Travel agent who can book package holidays and

flights from Belfast via London, or on the direct seasonal Transsun charter.

Simply Travel ⓣ 020/8987 6161, ⓦ www.simply-travel .com. One of the classiest and most imaginative agents, offering flights, upmarket hotels and villas, both in Funchal and in some of the best out-of-the-way locations.

Thomson Holidays
ⓣ 0870/550 2555,
ⓦ www.thomson-holidays.com. Offers a variety of packages, mostly in the larger hotels.

Traveller's Way
ⓣ 01527/559000,
ⓔ TRAVSWAY@aol.com. A small and very helpful company offering hotels and self-catering in Madeira and Porto Santo.

Unijet Travel ⓣ 0870/533 6336, ⓦ www.unijet.com. Large operator with flights from various regional airports.

PACKAGES

Package holidays can be excellent value, and can work out much cheaper than arranging separate flights, transfers, accommodation and car hire yourself. You can get all kinds of deals, from simple flight plus self-catering options to all mod cons in a four- or five-star hotel, with car hire thrown in. Many of the packages include direct charter flights from a variety of regional airports, though some use scheduled flights, either direct or via Lisbon. **Prices** start at around £300 per person for a week based on double occupancy, usually in a two- or three-star hotel. This usually includes flights, transfers and possibly car hire in low season. Expect to pay nearer £500 over New Year. Upgrades to four- or five-star hotels cost another £200 or so per person.

Though good value and the most convenient way to travel to Madeira from regional airports, package holidays are usually fairly inflexible: most are tied in to one- or two-week slots, and are restricted to accommodation in or around Funchal, though there is an increasing number of operators offering packages elsewhere on the island. The quality of package accommodation can also be hit or miss: if you are unhappy with the hotel, complain to the holiday rep who may be able to make alternative arrangements. Most of the main hotels used by package holidays are reviewed in this guide.

Numerous tour operators also promote **special interest holidays** (see below). These holidays usually work out more expensive than travelling independently, but you do have the benefit of expert guides, plus the convenience of having all your accommodation and transport arranged for you.

SPECIALIST TOUR OPERATORS

Arblaster & Clarke Wine Tours
  ℡ 01730/893344,
  Ⓦ www.winetours.co.uk.
  Upmarket company offering five-star accommodation and visits to leading Madeiran wine cellars with expert

guides; trips also include *levada* walks and garden visits.

Brightwater Holidays
  ℡ 0870/870 1333,
  Ⓦ www.brightwaterholidays .com. Scottish-based company

specializing in garden tours; they can also arrange flight-only deals from Gatwick, Manchester and Glasgow.

Cachet Travel ⊤ 020/8847 3848, ⓦ www.cachet-travel .co.uk. Small, friendly company offering accommodation in quality hotels, villas and self-catering apartments all over the island; also does walking holidays, garden and park tours and fly-drive options.

Cadogan Holidays ⊤ 0238/828313, ⓦ www.cadoganholidays.com. Package holidays in Madeira and Porto Santo, featuring garden visits.

Destination Portugal ⊤ 01933/773269. Various options including garden tours and flight-only deals.

Exodus ⊤ 020/8675 5550, ⓦ www.exodus.co.uk. Organized walks aimed at younger trekkers, with a hotel base at Camacha.

HF Holidays ⊤ 020/8905 9558, ⓦ www.hfholidays.co.uk. Walking holidays based in Funchal; also offers walking holidays combining Madeira and the Azores.

Ramblers Holidays ⊤ 01707/331133, ⓔ info@ramblersholidays.co.uk. Specializes in walking holidays based in Funchal, Porto Moniz and Ribeira Brava; walks often include studying local flora.

Style Holidays ⊤ 0870/444 4404. A good choice for its range of packages and fly-drive options, along with walking and garden tours, jeep safaris and boat trips; has a comprehensive array of accommodation options throughout the island.

Sunvil ⊤ 020/8758 4722, ⓦ www.sunvil.co.uk. Flexible holidays include combining Madeira with the Azores or mainland Portugal, walking holidays and fly-drive options, plus a range of accommodation including *pousadas, residenciais* and hotels all over the island.

Walking Women ⊤ 01926/313321, ⓦ www.walkingwomen.com. Walking holidays for women only, based at the *Pousada dos Vinhaticos* (see p.236).

Getting there from North America

here are currently no direct scheduled flights from either the US or Canada to Madeira. The options therefore are to fly via Lisbon with TAP, or via London with British Airways (the thrice-weekly London to Funchal leg is run by GB Airways, but is bookable through BA). Alternatively you may find it cheaper to get a budget transatlantic flight to London, then pick up the GB Airways flight from London Gatwick direct to Funchal, or the twice weekly direct TAP flight from London Heathrow (see "Getting there from Britain and Ireland", p.3, for further details).

Fares to Madeira depend on the season: they are highest from July to mid-September and over Christmas and New Year; they drop during the shoulder seasons (mid-Sept to Oct & mid-March to June and the ten days or so before Christmas); and you'll get the best deals during the low season (Nov to early Dec and just after New Year to mid-March). Note that flying on weekends usually adds $50–70 to the return fare.

AIRLINES IN NORTH AMERICA

Air Canada ☎1-888/247-2262, ⓦwww.aircanada.ca. Flights to London, as well as to Lisbon, via Frankfurt or Zurich.

British Airways ☎1-800/247-9297, ⓦwww.british-airways.com. Flights from many North American cities to London with connections to Funchal on GB Airways (bookable through BA). Can also book the London to Funchal section on TAP.

Continental Airlines ☎1-800/231-0856, ⓦwww.continental.com. Daily flights from Newark to Lisbon.

TAP Air Portugal ☎1-800/221-7370, ⓦwww.tap-airportugal.pt. Daily flights from several North American cities to Lisbon, with connections on to Funchal.

TWA ☎1-800/892-4141, ⓦwww.twa.com. Daily flights from New York to Lisbon with connections from many North American cities.

FLIGHTS FROM THE US

The best-value low-season flights from the **East Coast** are with British Airways, who offer New York to Funchal via London from $695 return, though you'll have to change airports in London, and may have to stay overnight. TAP's low-season fare from New York via Lisbon is $729. In high season, TAP is better value, offering New York to Funchal for $1078, while BA's high season rate is $1616.

From the **West Coast**, BA's low season fare from Los Angeles to Funchal is $945, rising to $1741 in high season, while TAP charges $1438 in low season, rising to an enormous $5206 in high season.

FLIGHTS FROM CANADA

BA flies from several cities in **Canada** via London, though you'll have to change airports in London and may have to stay overnight. BA quotes a low-season fare of CAN$1625 to Funchal from both Vancouver and Montreal via London. High season rates, are CAN$4860 from Montreal and CAN$3079 from Vancouver. Alternatively you may find it cheaper to fly to London with Air Canada and pick up the GB Airways or TAP flight from there (see p.4).

DISCOUNT TRAVEL AGENTS AND TOUR OPERATORS IN NORTH AMERICA

Abreu Tours ☎1-800/223-1580, ⓦwww.abreu-tours.com. Portugal specialists, offering Madeira as part of its holidays and flight-only deals.

Council Travel ☎1-800/226-8624 or 617/528-2091, ⓦwww.counciltravel.com. Nationwide US organization, specializing in student travel.

Homeric Tours ☎1-800/223-5570 or 212/753-1100, ⓦwww.homerictours.com. Customized tours and packages – a two-centre nine-day trip to Lisbon and Madeira, including accommodation and flights from Newark, starts at $1139.

Magellan Tours ☎1-888/962-4355 or 609/786-6969, ⓦwww.magellantours.com. Portugal specialist, who can arrange flights and accommodation in Madeira.

New Frontiers/Nouvelles Frontières ☎1-800/677-0720 or 212/986-6006; in Montreal ☎514/526-8444; ⓦwww.NewFrontiers.com. French discount travel firm with branches throughout the US and Canada.

Now Voyager ☎212/431-1616, ⓦwww.nowvoyagertravel.com. Courier flight broker and consolidator.

STA Travel ⓣ 1-800/777-0112 or 1-800/781-4040, ⓦ www.sta-travel.com. Worldwide specialists in independent travel, particularly student travel, although they offer many other services for non-students, including insurance.

Travac ⓣ 1-800/872-8800, ⓦ www.thetravelsite.com. Consolidator and broker offering a wide range of flights from North American cities to Funchal. Its website is particularly useful, giving a full run-down of the options for getting to Madeira.

Travel Avenue ⓣ 1-800/333-3335, ⓦ www.travelavenue .com. Discount travel agent.

Travel Cuts in US ⓣ 416/979-2406; in Canada ⓣ 1-800/667-2887; ⓦ www.travelcuts.com. Canadian student travel organization.

Getting there from Australia and New Zealand

There are no direct flights from Australia or New Zealand to Madeira: the most straightforward route is to fly to London on British Airways, and pick up the GB Airways flight (bookable through BA) from there to Madeira. TAP Air Portugal does not fly from either Australia or New Zealand, but you could buy a cheap flight to London from a discount agent – on Garuda, for example – then get a TAP or GB Airways flight from there to Funchal (see "Getting there from Britain and Ireland", p.3, for further details). Any of the travel agents listed below can book the London–Funchal return flight for around A$700 low season and A$800 high season, but it's usually cheaper to book the flight in London.

FARES

Fares vary according to the seasons, which break down as follows: high season (mid-May to Aug & Dec to mid-Jan); shoulder season (March to mid-May & Sept); and low season (mid-Jan to Feb, Oct & Nov). You can expect to pay about A$400–600/NZ$574–860 more for high-season fares.

Low-season fares **from Australia** (Sydney) to Madeira via London on British Airways are currently A$2500 and high season are A$2800. It is slightly cheaper to go the less direct route via Lisbon (also bookable through BA), with Sydney–London–Lisbon–Funchal costing A$2050 in low season and A$2560 in high season.

The most direct way to **fly from New Zealand** to Funchal is with BA via Los Angeles and London, though you'll have to change airports and may have to stay overnight in London. BA quotes a low-season fare of NZ$2799 and a high-season rate of NZ$3299 (prices quoted are out of Auckland, with fares from Christchurch and Wellington NZ$150–300 more).

ROUND-THE-WORLD TICKETS

It may also be worth considering a **Round-the-World** (RTW) ticket (valid for a year). They are usually priced according to the number of stopovers you make, with extra stops costing around A$140/NZ$160 each. The cheapest option is Qantas-BA's "Global Explorer", valid for three continents with up to three stopovers in each (including Funchal), from around A$3000–3500/NZ$4300–4900.

AIRLINES, AGENTS AND OPERATORS IN AUSTRALIA AND NEW ZEALAND

Airlines

Air New Zealand Australia ☎ 13/2476; New Zealand ☎ 0800/737000; ⓦ www.airnz.com. Daily flights from Sydney and Auckland to London via LA.

British Airways Australia ☎ 02/8904 8800; New Zealand ☎ 09/356 8690; ⓦ www.british-airways.com. Daily flights to London from Sydney, Perth or Brisbane with onward connections to Funchal.

Garuda Australia ☎ 1300 /365330; New Zealand ☎ 1800/128510; ⓦ www.garuda-indonesia. com. Several flights a week from major cities in Australia and New Zealand to London, via Bali or Jakarta.

Qantas Australia ☎ 13/1313; New Zealand ☎ 09/357 8900 or 0800/808767; ⓦ www.qantas.com.au. Daily flights from state capitals to London.

TAP Air Portugal Australia ☎ 02/9244 2344; New Zealand ☎ 09/308 3373; ⓦ www.tap-airportugal.pt. TAP do not fly from Australia or New Zealand, but can book flights from Lisbon and London to Funchal.

Discount agents

Anywhere Travel Australia ☎ 02/9663 0411, ⓔ anywhere@ozemail.com.au.

Flight Centre Australia ☎ 02/9235 3522; ☎ 13/1600 for nearest office; New Zealand ☎ 09/358 4310; ⓦ www.flightcentre.com.

STA Travel Australia ☎ 1300/360960 or 13/1776; New Zealand ☎ 09/309 0458; ⓦ www.statravelaus.com.au.

Thomas Cook Australia ☎ 13/1771 or 1800/801002; New Zealand ☎ 09/379 3920; ⓦ www.thomascook.com.au.

Trailfinders Australia ☎ 02/9247 7666.

Travel.com Australia ☎ 02/9290 1500, ⓦ www.travel.com.au.

Specialist agents and tour operators

European Travel Office (ETO)
Melbourne ⓣ 03/9329 8844;
Sydney ⓣ 02/9267 7727. A
wide selection of package
holidays and accommodation.
Ibertours Australia ⓣ 03/9670
8388 or 1800/500 016,
ⓦ www.ibertours.com.au.
Specializes in holidays to
Portugal, plus help organizing
study trips.

PFM Travel Australia
ⓣ 02/9550 0788. Very helpful
agent specializing in flights
and holidays to Portugal and
Madeira.
Yalla Tours Australia
ⓣ 1300/362 844. Holidays to
Portugal and other European\
destinations.

Visas and red tape

E U citizens need only a valid national identity card or passport to enter Madeira for up to ninety days. American, Canadian, Australian and New Zealand nationals can stay up to ninety days on production of a valid passport. Visa requirements do change, however, and it is always advisable to check the current situation before leaving home.

Anyone wishing to **stay longer** will need an extended stay visa, valid for a further ninety days, available for a small fee from any immigration office in Madeira (the airport is the easiest place to do this). EU citizens are also free to **work** in Madeira, though in practice work options are very limited. For non-EU citizens, work permits are only available for those with Portuguese residency, which can be obtained from a Portuguese consulate abroad (see below for addresses).

PORTUGUESE EMBASSIES ABROAD

Britain 11 Belgrave Square, London SW1X 8PP ⓣ 020/7235 5331, ⓕ 7245 1287.

Ireland Knocksinna House, Knocksinna, Fox Rock, Dublin 18 ⓣ 01/289 3375, ⓕ 289 2849.

USA 2125 Kalorama Rd NW, Washington DC 20008 ⓣ 202/328-8610, ⓕ 462-3726, ⓔ embportwash @mindspring.com. Plus consulates including New York, Boston and San Francisco.

Canada 645 Island Park Drive, Ottawa K1Y OB8 ⓣ 613/729-0883, ⓕ 729-4236, ⓔ embportugal@embportugal -ottowa.org. Plus consulates in Vancouver, Montreal and Toronto.

Australia 23 Culgoa Circuit, O'Malley ACT ⓣ 02/6290 1733. Plus consulates in Sydney (ⓦ www.consulportugalsydney .org.au), Brisbane, Adelaide and Fremantle.

New Zealand Consulates: Auckland ⓣ 09/309 1454; Wellington ⓣ 04/382 7655.

CONSULATES IN MADEIRA

Britain, Avda Zarco 2–4, Funchal ⓣ 291 221 1221 (map 2, D4).

USA, Avda Luís de Camões, Ed. Infante, Bloco B, AP. B-4, Funchal ⓣ 291 743 429 (map 2, A4).

Health and insurance

Madeira is very safe in terms of health. No inoculations are required to visit, though, as with any country, it is worth ensuring you have up-to-date polio and tetanus immunization. Mosquitoes can be an irritant in the warmer summer months, but the main danger is from the sun. Even if it does not seem particularly hot, it is very strong this far south and sun protection cream is advisable at all times.

Water is safe to drink from a tap anywhere on the island, though on neighbouring Porto Santo it is best to stick to bottled water: as the tap water is desalinated, it tastes revolting. In theory, water in *levadas* is also safe to drink on the higher mountain slopes, but should definitely not be drunk lower down as it may have passed through farm land.

MEDICAL MATTERS

For minor health complaints you should go to a **farmácia** (pharmacy), which you'll find in almost any village. Most have someone who can speak English. The pharmacists are trained to dispense suitable medication that would normally only be available on prescription in Britain or North America. Pharmacies are usually open Mon–Fri 9am–1pm & 3–7pm, Sat 9am–1pm. In the larger towns, they take it in turns to stay open out-of-hours (*fora das horas*); check in any pharmacy window for the address of the one which is open.

In an emergency, dial ☏112.

For more serious illnesses, you can visit the **English-speaking doctor** in Funchal (Dr Zino) at Avenida do Infante 26, opposite the Casino complex (map 2, A5; ☏291 742 227); or ask to see any local doctor, most of whom speak some English.

Madeira's **hospitals** are used to treating foreign visitors, particularly the elderly, and the standard of care is generally good. Funchal has several large hospitals – the main ones are Hospital Cruz Carvalho, Avenida Luís Camões (map 3, D6; ☏291 705 600), and Hospital dos Marmeleiros, Estrada dos Marmeleiros 291 (map 3, 5E; ☏291 705 730). There are smaller **health centres** (*Centros de Saúde*) dotted round the island.

INSURANCE

Travel insurance is strongly advised for non-EU citizens, especially, who must pay for any medical treatment in Madeira. With insurance, you'll have to pay for treatment on the spot, but will be able to claim back the cost of treatment or drugs purchased from chemists, as long as you keep the receipts. As an EU country, Portugal has a free reciprocal health agreement with other member states for basic treatment in local hospitals; to take advantage of this, EU

ROUGH GUIDES TRAVEL INSURANCE

Rough Guides now offers its own **travel insurance**, customized for our readers by a leading UK broker and backed by a Lloyd's underwriter. It is available to anyone, of any nationality, travelling anywhere in the world, and we are convinced that this is the best-value scheme you'll find.

There are two main Rough Guide insurance plans: Essential, for effective, no-frills cover, starting at £11.75 for two weeks; and Premier – more expensive but with more generous and extensive benefits. Each offers European or Worldwide cover, and can be supplemented with a "Hazardous Activities Premium" if you plan to engage in sports considered dangerous, such as windsurfing or trekking. Unlike many policies, the Rough Guides schemes are calculated by the day, so if you're travelling for 27 days rather than a month, that's all you pay for. You can alternatively take out annual multi-trip insurance, which covers you for all your travel throughout the year (with a maximum of sixty days for any one trip).

For a policy quote, call the Rough Guides Insurance Line on UK freefone ☏0800/015 0906, US freefone ☏1-866/220-5588, or, if you're calling from elsewhere, (☏+44) 1243/621046. Alternatively, get an online quote and buy your cover at ⓦ www.roughguides.com/insurance.

citizens need form E111, available from main post offices. Before treatment, you must present the completed E111 form, with your passport, to Serviço de Migrantes, Centro do Saúde de Bom Jesus, Rua das Hortas 67, Funchal (map 2, F2; Mon–Fri 9.30am–noon & 2–4pm; ☏291 229 161), or the local health centre if you are not in Funchal.

As well as medical expenses, travel insurance usually provides cover for baggage, money and tickets in case of **theft**; to reclaim from your insurance company, you must register theft with the local police within 24 hours (see p.328 for details of police stations in Funchal).

Before you buy any insurance, check to see if you are already covered by credit card companies, some of which offer free cover for holidays bought on their account or as a reward for using their services. You may also find medical costs are covered if you have your own private health insurance policy, whilst some personal possessions may even be covered by your home contents insurance; check the small print, and make sure you take a copy of contact telephone numbers should you need to make a claim.

If you plan to participate in water sports or dangerous sports, check the travel insurance policy which may require you to pay a premium.

Information, maps and websites

You can pick up a range of maps and brochures from Portuguese National Tourist Offices, which deal with Madeira, though most of the information provided tends to be on the superficial side. Generally a better source of information is the growing number of websites (see p.24), offering everything from photos of individual hotels and sites to details of car hire, tours and the latest news and weather.

In Madeira itself, there are **tourist offices** at the airport and in Funchal, Caniço de Baixa, Machico, Câmara de Lobos, Ribeira Brava, Porto Moniz and Santana. There is also one in Vila Baleira on Porto Santo. Full addresses and opening times are given in the text. All of the tourist offices give out maps of the local area and can help with accommodation, including rooms in private houses. In addition, they provide details of local festivities and events, and many sell local guides. If you are planning to do any walks, it is also worth asking the tourist offices about the latest conditions of the nearest *levadas*.

PORTUGUESE TOURIST OFFICES ABROAD

Britain 2nd Floor, 22–25A Sackville Street, London W1X 1DE Ⓣ 09063/640610, Ⓕ 020/7494 1868, Ⓔ iceplondt@aol.com.

Ireland 54 Dawson Street, Dublin 2 Ⓣ 01/670 9133, Ⓕ 670 9141, Ⓔ info@icep.ie.

USA 590 Fifth Avenue, 4th Floor, New York, NY 10036-4785 Ⓣ 212/719-3985, Ⓕ 764-6137, Ⓦ www.portugal.org; 1900 L Street NW, Suite 310, Washington, DC 20036 Ⓣ 202/331-8222,

Ⓕ 331-8236; 88 Kearny Street, Suite 1770, San Francisco, CA 94108 Ⓣ 415/391-7080, Ⓕ 391-7147.

Canada 60 Bloor St West, Suite 1005, Toronto, Ontario M4W 3B8 Ⓣ 416/921-7376, Ⓕ 921-1353, Ⓔ iceptor@idirect.com.

Australia and New Zealand
There are no Portuguese tourist offices in Australia or New Zealand, but the website Ⓦ www.consulportugalsydney.org.au has useful information on Portugal for Australians and New Zealanders.

MAPS

The tourist offices and most major hotels give out free **maps** of Madeira and Funchal, which are quite adequate for basic touring. However, if you're planning to do any in-depth exploration, it's worth investing in a good road map. The best one available is the GeoCentre's 1:75,000 *Holiday Map, Madeira*, which includes Porto Santo. For walkers, the best bet is the more detailed topographical maps published by the Instituto Geografica e Cadastral (IGC; Ⓣ 291 222 532, Ⓦ www.ippcc.pt), although these have not been updated to include the newest sections of Madeira's ongoing road-building programme. These maps are all on sale in Funchal's main tourist office (see p.48) and in *Pátio Livraria Inglesa* in Funchal (see p.303).

INFORMATION, MAPS AND WEBSITES

MADEIRA ON THE NET

ⓦ **www.madeiraonline.com**. The main Madeira search engine and a good first point of call, with links to countless other sites covering everything from walks to news, recipes, arts and education.

ⓦ **www.madeira-portugal.com**. Website promoting hotels on Madeira, with details of facilities and prices and pictures of the hotels themselves. Also has details of car rental and tours, which can be booked through the site.

ⓦ **www.madeira-holiday.com**. Well-designed and highly readable Net magazine run by the newspaper *Madeira Life*, with local news, features, good links and practical details of accommodation, car hire, shops and events.

ⓦ **www.madeiratourism.org**. The rather staid official tourist board site, offering limited general information, though it does have interesting sections on current events and features on ecotourism.

ⓦ **www.madeira-island.com**. Lively Net magazine with stacks of information on local news and events as well as details of accommodation, shops, car hire, etc.

ⓦ **www.Madeira-real-estate .com**. Where to go to buy up a slice of the island.

ⓦ **www.madeirawine.com**. Information on all things related to Madeira wine, with latest news and its own online wine shop.

ⓦ **www.madeira -shopping.com**. Chance to buy Madeiran produce on line, with everything from books, guide books and maps to cakes, CDs and wine.

ⓦ **www.madinfo.pt**. Information on everything from culture and news to travel and tourism.

ⓦ **www.portugal.org**. The national government-run website, with its own tourism section covering Madeira, offering very basic background information.

Money and costs

As many products need to be imported, Madeira is more expensive than mainland Portugal, but remains inexpensive by Northern European standards – certainly in terms of food, drink and entry to sights. Accommodation is likely to be the most expensive part of your stay, but though Madeira has a reputation for the quality of its hotels – and corresponding high prices – you can easily find inexpensive places in most of the main centres. Petrol is subsidized by the local government and is actually cheaper than on mainland Portugal.

CURRENCY

Portugal is one of twelve European Union countries which have changed over to a single currency, the **euro** (€). However, the transition period, which began on January 1, 1999, is lengthy: euro notes and coins are not scheduled to be issued until January 1, 2002, with the current unit of currency, the **escudo** ($), remaining in place for cash transactions, at a fixed rate of 200.482 to 1 euro, until it is scrapped entirely at the end of February 2002.

Even before euro cash appears in 2002, you can opt to pay in euros by credit card and you can get travellers' cheques in euros – you should not be charged commission for changing them in any of the twelve countries in the euro zone (also known as "Euroland"), nor for changing from any of the old Euroland currencies to any other (French francs to escudos, for example).

All prices in this book are given in escudos and the equivalent in euros rounded down to 200 escudos to 1 euro. When the new currency takes over completely, prices are likely to be rounded off – and if decimalization in the UK is anything to go by, rounded up.

Escudos are written with the $ sign in the middle: thus 250$00 is two hundred and fifty escudos. 1000$00 is often called a *conto*. Notes come in **denominations** of 500$00, 1000$00, 2000$00, 5000$00 and 10,000$00; coins as 5$00, 10$00, 20$00, 50$00, 100$00 and 200$00. Euro notes will be issued in denominations of 5, 10, 20, 50, 100, 200 and 500 euros, and coins in denominations of 1, 2, 5, 10, 20 and 50 cents and 1 and 2 euros. At the time of going to press **exchange rates** were around 305$00/€15 to the pound sterling, 217$00/€10.80 to the US dollar.

COSTS

Apart from your flight, **accommodation** is likely to take up most of your budget. Double rooms start from around £20/$28 at the lowest end of the market, with mid-range places charging more like double, going up to over £100/$140 a night for the top hotels.

You should be able to get a decent **meal** at an inexpensive restaurant for around £5/$7, and even dinner at a smart restaurant won't set you back much more than £10–15/$14–21 a head, not including wine. Local

(Portuguese) **drinks** are extremely cheap (less than £1/$1.40 for a beer or brandy, and around £6/$8.40 for a bottle of wine in a restaurant). **Entry fees** to most museums and gardens are around £1–3/$1.40–4.20, while **public transport** is very cheap (a bus ride across Funchal is just over £1/$1.40).

Accommodation apart, if you travel around by bus, buy your own picnic lunches or eat at the cheaper restaurants, you could survive on a **daily budget** of around £10–15/$14–21 a day. Allow yourself a more expensive restaurant meal and entry to a museum or two with a few drinks in the evening, and £20–30/$28–42 a day is a more realistic figure.

BANKS AND EXCHANGE

By far the easiest way to get money in Madeira is to use a **credit or debit card** to withdraw cash from any of the large number of ATMs (signed *Multibanco*) in Funchal and the larger resorts. Any card using the Cirrus or Eurocheque system will work, as will all major credit cards (Visa, American Express, Mastercard and Eurocard). Credit and charge cards charge a fee of around three to four percent on any cash advance or purchase; for debit cards the currency conversion fee is 1–2 percent. Credit cards are accepted for payment in most hotels and restaurants. Most Portuguese banks will give cash advances on cards over the counter and charge a currency conversion fee of around two percent.

It is very expensive to change **travellers' cheques** in Madeira, although it is probably worth taking a supply in case your credit card is lost or swallowed by an ATM. They are accepted by all banks in Madeira and by exchange bureaux. Current rates of commission are around 2000–3000$00/€10–15 per transaction, so it is worth changing a reasonable amount of money each time.

Normal **banking hours** are Mon–Fri 8.30am–3pm. In Funchal, some banks also open Saturday 9am–1pm. You can also use currency exchange bureaux (*cambios*), generally open Mon–Fri 9am–1pm and 2–7pm, Sat 9am–7pm. Outside these hours, most major hotels offer currency exchange, though not always at favourable rates.

Holidays and festivals

As on mainland Portugal, Madeira has a good share of public holidays, during which banks and most shops close and buses take on a Sunday timetable. However, most tourist services – including most cafés, restaurants and sites – function as normal.

Madeira also has a seemingly endless supply of **festivals**, which crop up all over the island at frequent intervals throughout the year – the biggest and best of them are listed below. Usually coinciding with local saints' days or harvests, they are occasions for the locals to let rip, and they follow a similar format: religious services in the church followed by cultural celebrations in the form of folk dancing, usually accompanied by live music. Food stalls, lots of alcohol and sometimes fireworks enliven the proceedings. The best ones to catch are the New Year's Eve festivities and Carnival.

Unfortunately, it is impossible to give exact dates for some of the festivals listed below, as they vary from year to year; tourist offices will, however, be able to provide you with up-to-date information on these, as well as the many other smaller events occurring throughout the year.

PUBLIC HOLIDAYS

1 January New Year's Day
Good Friday
25 April Revolution Day
1 May Labour Day
10 June Portugal/Camões Day
1 July Discovery of Madeira Day
15 August Assumption

5 October Republic Day
1 November All Saints' Day
1 December Independence Day
8 December Immaculate Conception
25 December Christmas Day

CALENDAR OF FESTIVALS

January
Night Festival and End of New Year Festivities (January 6). The official end of the New Year's festivities, with live entertainment – usually consisting of live music and dance – in Funchal and elsewhere.

February–March

Festa dos Compadres, Santana. The "Godfather's Festival", though not in the Mafia sense. Usually held the week before Funchal's carnival.

Carnival festivities in Funchal (see box on p.66).

April–May

Festa da Flor. The three-day Flower Festival sees Funchal's Avenida Arriaga decked out in carpets of flowers, with shop windows vying to outdo each other for the best floral display. Main events include The Wall of Hope Ceremony, in which children pin posies onto the city hall in Funchal and make a wish to start the festival. This is followed by the Great Allegorical Parade the following day, with a parade of blooms in baskets on floats, plus local music and dancers in Praça do Município.

June

Santos Populares (Popular Saints). June sees the celebration throughout Madeira of the main saints' days:

St Anthony, the patron saint of lovers (June 13). Evening festivities include the tradition of jumping over fires (it is said that the highest leapers will be lucky in love).

St John (June 24) is the big saint's day for Funchal, with shops competing to prepare the most lavishly decorated mock altar and evening festivities centred round Largo do Carmo. There is also a procession and evening entertainment on Porto Santo.

St Peter (June 29), the patron saint of fishermen. St Peter's is celebrated most enthusiastically in the fishing port of Câmara de Lobos and in Ribeira Brava; the latter's streets are decorated with flowers, and barbecues take place on the beach.

Classical Music Concerts. Annual series of concerts performed by local students along with more professional concerts performed by top international names, mostly in Funchal's Sé and the Teatro Municipal.

Vintage Car Rally. Some 60 vehicles dating back to the 1920s tour round the island, starting and finishing in Funchal.

July

Dança de 24 horas. Various folk dancing groups gather in Santana to perform over a 24-hour period; food and drink stalls are lined up to help keep them – and the spectators – going.

Machico Gastronomy Week. Along with a chance to sample regional cuisine, the town lays on various events, including a veterans' football competition, beach volleyball, a cocktail festival and live music.

August

Madeira Wine Rally (first weekend). International amateur rally drivers speed round the island's and Funchal's precipitous roads in what is considered one of the most challenging rallies in Europe.

Festival of the Assumption (August 15). This is one of the most important religious festivals on the island, with all areas celebrating with Mass and an evening procession.

The biggest celebration is at Nossa Senhora do Monte in Monte (August 14–15), the island's principal church, with two days of festivities (see p.96).

Festa do Santissimo Sacramento (Festival of the Holy Sacrament; last Sunday of August). A carnival-style procession departs from Machico, culminating in a huge bonfire on the neighbouring Pico de Facho.

September

Nossa Senhora da Piedade (third Sunday). A statue of the Virgin is taken from a chapel in the cliffs above Prainha to Caniçal by fishermen in a procession of boats.

Madeira Wine Festival. The wine harvest is celebrated with bare-foot wine treading and folk dancing in Estreito de Câmara de Lobos, and with special shows and exhibitions in Funchal. There is also a Grape Festival in Porto da Cruz.

Colombus Week. A week's festivities in honour of Christopher Colombus on Porto Santo (see box on p.199).

Festa de Senhor Jesus.
Religious festival in Ponta Delgada when a holy relic is paraded round the village (see p.172).

October
Meeting of the Regional Philharmonic Bands. Annual classical music event, with a procession ending in a series of performances outside the main church in Ribeira Brava.

November
Festa das Castanhas (Chestnut Festival). Folk displays and various dishes made of chestnuts are on offer in Curral das Freiras to celebrate the local harvest.

December
Christmas. The build-up starts on December 8, when spectacular Christmas lights are turned on in Funchal. On the 16th traditional nativity scenes are set up in churches, shops, hotels and village squares, and on the 23rd the Mercado dos Lavradores in Funchal stays open all night for shoppers. For locals, the main event is on the 24th, with Midnight Mass followed by a traditional meal of *bacalhau*. On Christmas Day itself, most hotels lay on special Christmas meals and events.

New Year's Eve. Funchal has a justifiable reputation as one of the best places in the world to see in the New Year. Virtually every house in the city puts on all its lights, the harbour is jammed with visiting cruise liners, and at midnight the whole bay becomes a riot of exploding fireworks and blasting ships' sirens. It is traditional to see in the new year with *bolo de mel* and champagne. Be aware that many hotels have obligatory New Year's Eve "gala" dinners at stonking rates, which can cost up to 22,000$00/€110 per person – check to see what you're tied to before you book.

HOLIDAYS AND FESTIVALS

Getting around

While you could happily spend a week just in Funchal, it would be a shame to miss seeing the rest of the island. Madeira has an efficient bus network, and taxis are a relatively inexpensive option, but if you're planning to see the wilder parts of Madeira, you're going to have to hire a car. Although distances on the island are small, the roads are narrow and winding so journeys can take time; nevertheless, even Porto Moniz at the furthest point of the island is less than two hours' drive from Funchal.

For information about cycling and
walking in Madeira, see p.308.

BY BUS

Madeira's **buses** serve almost every village of any size on the island from Funchal's various privately run bus terminals. **Tickets** are inexpensive – a ride from Funchal to Porto Moniz, in the far northeast of the island, costs just 860$00/€4.30. For all journeys, tickets can be bought on board from the conductor.

Though reliable and relatively rapid, the buses are geared to the needs of local people, so that day-trips are not always feasible or convenient, often departing at an unearthly hour of the morning or returning too early for you to make the most of the day. Service times vary considerably depending on the route, with some starting at around 5am and others not until 11am or so; likewise some last buses are in the late afternoon, while others run to beyond midnight. Buses don't always run on public holidays and you may find, at any time, that timetables change at short notice. It's also worth noting that the buses don't serve much of the island's best scenic and walking territory, so it is probably worth considering car hire at some stage.

**Details of buses from Funchal to specific places
on the island are given in the *Guide*. From villages
outside Funchal, look for timetables at bus stops
marked *paragem*, or ask in the local café.**

Buses in and around Funchal are served by the yellow **Horários do Funchal** (℡291 705 555 or 291 742 444; see p.49). Generally buses to the west and north west of the island are served by **Rodoeste Buses** (℡291 220 148), which leave from Rua Ribeira João Gomes in Funchal (map 2, H1). The east and northeast of the island, including the airport, are served by **SAM Buses** (℡291 229 144) from Rua Calouste Gulbenkian, Funchal (map 2, B4). Three smaller companies – **Empresa de Automóveis do Caniço** (to Caniço; ℡291 222 558); **Autocarros da Camacha** (to Camacha, Santo do Serra, Palheiro Ferreiro and Curral das Freiras; ℡291 705 555 or 291 222 762); and **São Roque do Fail** (to the north coast via Ribeiro Frio; ℡291 220 060 or 291 228 688) – all have their terminals on the Zona Velha end of Avenida do Mar in Funchal (map 2, G4).

BY CAR

Madeira's size means that nowhere is too far to visit on a day-trip from Funchal by **car**, despite the fact that journeys take a lot longer than mileage would suggest due to the precipitous terrain. Only the south and east coasts of the island have straight stretches of road on which you can build up any speed; on all other roads, take extreme care and watch out for locals' reckless overtaking habits. Be sure to familiarize yourself with the position of lights and wind-screen wipers, as roads often plunge into unlit tunnels, some of which have cascades of water at the entrance or exit, which fall over the car.

Remember to drive on the right.

Rental prices are more expensive than on mainland Portugal, though it is generally cheaper to hire a car in Madeira than through international car companies abroad. In Madeira, expect to pay at least 5000$00/€25 for a day or 30,000$00/€150 for a week in low season and 7000$00/€35 a day or 50,000$00/€250 a week in high season, though discounts may be given for longer hire periods. Third-party insurance is usually included in the price, while further insurance can be offered by the rental company at a daily rate. **Petrol** is subsidized, and, at around 200$00/€1 a litre, it is relatively inexpensive – cheaper than on mainland Portugal.

For information about driving and
parking in Funchal, see p.50.

To hire a car, you'll need a current **driving licence** from your home country or an international driving licence – as well as your passport – which you must have with you at all times when driving. Some companies will only rent out cars to drivers over 21 years of age with at least two years' experience. Seat belts must be worn and there are strict laws against drink-driving. A credit card is useful to make a security deposit. Individual car rental companies have their own systems to deal with breakdowns; make sure you are familiar with these before you leave the car rental office. There are orange telephones at fairly regular intervals along the main roads to make emergency calls if you do break down.

CAR RENTAL COMPANIES

Atlantic-Rent-a-Car, Centro Comercial Belo Sol, Caminho Velho Ajuda, Funchal ☎ 291 761 711 (map 3, D7).

Atlas, Avda Infante 29, Funchal ☎ 291 223 100, ℉ 291 741 212 (map 2, A5).

Avis, Largo António Nobre 164, Funchal ☎ 291 764 546; *Hotel Monumental Lido*, Funchal ☎ 291 764 546 (map 3, D7); and airport ☎ 291 524 392; ⓦ www.avis.com.

Bravacar, Caminho do Amparo 2, Funchal ☎ 291 764 385 (map 3, C7).

Budget, *Hotel Duas Torres*, Estrada Monumental 239, Funchal ☎ 291 766 518, ℉ 291 765 619 (map 3, D7); and airport ☎ 291 524 661; ⓦ www.budget.com.

Hertz, Centro Comercial Lido Loja 1, Estrada Monumental, Funchal ☎ 291 764 410, ℉ 291 764 452 (map 3, D7); and airport ☎ 291 523 040, ℉ 291 523 017; ⓦ www.hertz.com.

Lidorent, Edifício Alto Lido, Estrada Monumental, Funchal ☎ 291 761 420, ℉ 291 761 635 (map 3, D7).

Moinho, Estrada Monumental 28, Funchal ☎ 291 762 123, ℉ 291 766 188 (map 3, D7).

Rent-a-car do Futuro, Centro Comercial Infante, Loja G, Avda do Infante, Funchal ☎ 291 220 721 (map 3, E6).

Rodavente, Edifício Baía, Estrada Monumental, Funchal ☎ 291 758 506 (map 3, E7).

BY TAXI

If you don't fancy driving yourself, it is worth considering hiring a **taxi** for a day or half-day tour to any part of the island. Most authorized taxi drivers speak good English and they can be extremely knowledgeable as guides too. The tourist office in Funchal can book taxi tours in advance at set rates. If you want to book your own driver, make sure you agree a price beforehand. Prices start at around 8000$00/€40 for a half day to 15,000$00/€75 for a full day's tour.

BY MOTORBIKE

A couple of companies rent out **motorbikes**, which are an excellent way of getting round the island, as well as negotiating the narrow streets of central Funchal, though you'll need to hire a machine of above 100cc to be able to negotiate the mountainous interior properly. The only problem is the price, which is far higher than renting a car, starting at around 9000$00/€45 for a day and 60,000$00/€300 for a week. As with car hire, you'll need a current **driving licence** from your home country or an international driving licence, as well as your passport. You must keep these with you at all times when you are driving. A hefty security deposit is also usually required. Wearing a **helmet** is obligatory; these come as part of the bike hire.

MOTORBIKE RENTAL COMPANIES

Joyride, Centro Comercial Olimpo, Loja 210, Avda do Infante, Funchal ⓣ 291 234 906 (map 2, B5).

Magos Bike, Apt. 46, Caniço de Baixo ⓣ 291 934 818, ⓕ 291 934 819 (map 4, B7).

TOURS

Most major hotels can arrange island-wide **sightseeing coach tours**, usually with a daily changing programme. The tours are usually well organized and informative and will take you to the more obvious sites on the island. Several travel agents offer similar coach tours: try Blandy, Avda Zarco 2, Funchal (map 2, D4; ⊤291 227 699, ⓕ291 233 909), or RR Tours, Rua Dr Pita, Funchal (map 3, D7; ⊤291 764 733, ⓕ291 764 728).

For details of jeep safaris, helicopter tours, walking tours and dolphin- and whale-watching expeditions see p.308 onwards.

Communications and the media

Despite its isolated position in the middle of the Atlantic, Madeira is well connected to the outside world with a modern communications system, which embraces a fairly efficient postal system and the usual array of local and international television and radio stations.

POST

Madeira's **postal service** is reliable, though erratic, with post to Europe taking anything from a few days to over a week. The Correio Azul system is faster, guaranteeing delivery in three to four days, but you pay extra for the service; use the blue post boxes for this service.

The main central **post office** (*correio*, usually marked CTT) in Funchal is on Avenida Zarco (map 2, D4) and is open Mon–Fri 9am–1pm & 3–7pm, Sat 9am–1pm. There are smaller post offices in most of the other towns and villages around the island (usual opening hours Mon–Fri 9am–12.30pm & 2.30–5.30pm, Sat 9am–12.30pm), all of which offer poste restante. You can also buy stamps and send mail from most of the major hotels.

TELEPHONES

Nearly all hotels have their own **telephones**, but these are invariably more expensive than public phone boxes. You'll also find more expensive pay phones in bars, cafés and some restaurants, which usually take coins. Unless you have a stack of coins, it is best to make international calls using a *credifone*, a **phone card** which you can buy in denominations of 600$00/€3, 1200$00/€6 or 1800$00/€9 from post offices, some newspaper kiosks and shops with a CTT sign. The main post offices also have pay cabins (open until 10pm) charging the same rate as a *credifone*; take a token from the attendant and pay for the call at the end. The **cheap rate for international calls** is between 10pm and 8am and at weekends.

Reverse charge (collect) calls (*chamada cobrar ao destinatório*) can be made from any phone, dialling ☎099 for a European connection or ☎098 for anywhere else. If you encounter difficulties, dial the international operator on ☎171.

Most UK, Australian and New Zealand **mobile phones** will work in Madeira, though users of US-bought handsets, which use a different system, may have difficulties. If you are planning to take your phone with you, it is worth checking with your phone provider whether you need to get international access switched on (which may incur a charge), and what the call charges will be: you are likely to be charged extra for incoming calls when abroad, as the people calling you will be paying the usual rate. You'll also have to ask your provider for a new access code if you want to retrieve voice messages while you're away, as your home one is unlikely to work abroad.

TELEPHONE CODES AND USEFUL NUMBERS

To phone Madeira from abroad, dial the international access code (Australia 0011; Canada 001; Ireland 00; New Zealand 00; UK 00; USA 001) + 351 (country code) + 291 (area code) + number.

To phone abroad from Madeira, dial the country code (Australia 0061; Canada 001; Ireland 00353; New Zealand 0064; UK 0044; USA 001) + area code (minus initial zero) + number.

Useful telephone numbers
Directory Enquiries: local ℡118; international ℡179
Operator: local ℡090; international ℡171
Emergency services ℡112

INTERNET CAFÉS

Internet cafés are making slow inroads into Madeira. There are just two in Funchal: *Cremesoda*, Rua dos Ferreiros 9 (map 2, D2; Mon–Fri 9am–9pm, Sat 10am–9pm, Sun 5pm–9pm; ⓦwww.cibercafe.co.pt); and the student café *www.cyber Café*, Avenida Infante 6 (map 2, C4; Mon–Fri 8am–2am, Sat 8am–2pm & 8pm–2am; Ⓔcybercafé@netmadeira.com). Both offer Internet access at 800$00/€4 per hour. In Machico, *Mola Bico* on Praçeta 25 Abril (map 5, C7; Tues–Sun 10am–midnight; ℡291 963 127) offers Internet access for 600$00/€3 an hour. In Porto Santo, the gym club in the basement of *Hotel Torre Praia* (map 9, E5; daily 8am–noon & 4–10pm; ℡291 985 292, Ⓔcluvi@hotmail.com) offers access at 800$00/€4 per hour. Otherwise your best bet is to ask at the major hotels and post offices, many of which offer Internet access for similar fees.

THE MEDIA

Madeira has its own version of the Portuguese daily **newspaper**, *Diário de Notícias*, with details of local and international news as well as museum opening times and listings. *Madeira Island Bulletin* is a free monthly English-language newspaper aimed squarely at the ex-pat community and tourists, with basic local news, magazine-style articles, listings and gossip published in German, English and Portuguese. You can find it at the reception desk of the major hotels and in tourist offices.

Most **international newspapers** can be bought from kiosks and major hotels in Funchal and larger resorts such as Machico and Ribeira Brava, though it is usually the previous day's edition.

On the **radio**, you can pick up the BBC World Service, with hourly news (note that short-wave frequencies vary depending on the time of day). Local broadcasts, in Portuguese, consist of the usual mix of chat, news and international music.

Madeira receives just two of the main Portuguese mainland **TV channels**, RTP 1 and 2, along with its own version, RTPM, usually mingling local news with mainstream programmes from Portuguese TV, itself an eclectic mix of sport, game shows, cookery programmes, Brazilian soap operas, British series, Spanish bullfights and American films (in English with Portuguese subtitles). Most of the larger hotels also offer cable or satellite TV, with the usual range of international viewing.

THE GUIDE

1	Funchal	45
2	Around Funchal	93
3	Eastern Madeira	120
4	The west coast	143
5	Northern and central Madeira	162
6	Porto Santo	192

Funchal

FUNCHAL is Madeira's capital and its only town of any size – the 125,000 inhabitants represent half the island's population. The town is dramatically sited, overlooking the Atlantic from its natural amphitheatre, surrounded by mountains. Its range of exotic gardens, grand buildings, pedestrianized shopping streets and restaurants make it an instantly appealing place. Moreover, it has a friendly atmosphere and is virtually crime-free – a surprising fact, given that it's a working port and the island's main centre for tourism.

The **city centre** itself is small and manageable: you can walk its length in about forty minutes. Head inland for any distance, however, and you soon encounter outrageous gradients; the narrow roads veer uphill, affording stupendous views of the harbour below.

The natural magnet for visitors is the extensive **seafront** – the palm-fringed Avenida do Mar – that runs the length of the city's rough, black-stone beach. Its eastern end marks the beginning of the atmospheric Old Town, the **Zona Velha**, a largely residential area, which still has some fifteenth-century buildings. At the other end, sheltered by the large harbour, is a **marina**, the departure point for boat trips around the island and an appealing spot, with its bobbing boats and restaurants and cafés. Inland, a series of graceful, mostly pedestrianized streets, lined with shops, museums and gardens, links the main thoroughfare, Avenida Arriaga, to the **Sé** (cathedral) and the **Praça do Município**, the main square. West of the centre lies the so-called Zona Hoteleira, or **Hotel Zone**, which, as its name suggests, is where most of the town's hotels and tourist facilities are sited.

Reviews of accommodation, restaurants and bars in Funchal start on p.219, p.252 and p.288 respectively.

Some history

Funchal was named after the fennel (*funcho*) that the early Portuguese colonizers found in the area. The best-known of these early settlers, the navigator João Gonçalves Zarco (see p.57), made Funchal his base shortly after his arrival in Madeira in 1425. The earliest settlement was what is now the Old Town, at the eastern end of the city.

Funchal became the capital, superseding Machico, when Manuel I unified the three captaincies, or regions, of the island in 1497. The city began to flourish as a centre for the island's sugar trade. Sugar was an expensive commodity available only to the wealthy, and various foreign traders set up shop to take advantage of the lucrative export possibilities. Christopher Columbus was one of these traders, and the city's coat of arms still displays five sugar loaves today. By the early sixteenth century, Funchal's population had grown to 5000, swelled by slaves shipped over from Portugal's African colonies. As a remote and wealthy outpost, however, the city was vulnerable to pirate attack and was sacked several times; the worst occasions were in 1566 and 1620 when many residents were killed and numerous buildings destroyed. The **Fortaleza de São Tiago** in the Zona Velha – now a modern art museum – was built to help keep pirates at bay, as was the **Palácio de São Lourenço**, currently home to the army and the Minister to Portugal.

Changing economic conditions led to the collapse of the sugar market in the late sixteenth century. Many farms switched to planting vines, and wine replaced sugar as Madeira's main product. British wine merchants set up in the capital in the eighteenth and nineteenth centuries, establishing themselves in large estates or *quintas*, many of them set in extensive and beautiful grounds. Some of these estates have survived, such as **Quinta Magnolia** and **Quinta da Boa Vista**, and are open to the public; others such as **Quinta das Cruzes** have become museums.

By the nineteenth century, Funchal had become one of Portugal's most important cities. Impressive municipal buildings, churches and gardens were constructed around the central **Praça do Município**. The shipping trade grew after **Loo Rock**, a small fortified islet in Funchal bay, was connected to the mainland in 1895 to form a sheltered **harbour**. Set on the world's busiest shipping lanes, the city became an obvious stopping-off point not only for commercial shipping but also for leisure boats, and by the end of the nineteenth century it had established itself as a tourist destination for the rich. Visitors initially headed to the cool hillside *quintas* around the suburb of Monte, 6km to the northeast, but by 1891, Funchal had its first hotel, **Reid's**. Visitors continued to arrive by boat or seaplane in the early twentieth century, but it was not until 1964 that tourism really took off with the opening of the island's airport. This set in motion a rash of new hotel development, most of it to the west of the capital along the coast in the Zona Hoteleira.

Despite the tourist trade, under the rule of the dictator Salazar in the postwar years Funchal remained the capital of one of Portugal's poorest regions. Salazar was deposed in

FUNCHAL

1974, but it was not until Portugal's entry into the EU in 1986 that substantial fresh funds were channelled into the capital. EU money has recently funded a series of new roads to help ease the growing traffic congestion in the centre. The city was further spruced up for the start of the millennium, and Funchal looks better now than it has done for decades.

Arrival and information

Funchal's airport is some 18km to the east of the city, and is connected to the centre by SAM airport **buses** #20, #53, #78, #113 or #156; they depart every half-hour from 7.10am to 10.50pm (410$00/€2.05) and the journey takes thirty to forty-five minutes, depending on the route and time of day. The terminal is on Avenida Calouste Gulbenkian (map 2, B4), from where it's just five to ten minutes' walk to the tourist office (see below). Buses back to the airport depart every thirty minutes from the same place (7.15am–8pm). A **taxi** from the airport will cost around 3800$00/€19, and takes about twenty-five minutes.

Coming in **by car**, take the fast airport road which skirts round the northern upper slopes of the city. Signs for central Funchal take you down the steep river valley of the Ribeira de João Gomes, then to the seafront Praça da Autonomia. For the Hotel Zone, head right along the seafront then turn left at the junction where the road climbs up away from the sea.

Funchal's main **tourist office** is at Avenida Arriaga 18 (Mon–Fri 9am–8pm, Sat 9am–6pm; ☎291 211 900, ⒺInfo@madeiratourism.org). It stocks useful brochures, maps and guides, and the helpful staff can arrange tours and give advice on hotels and bus times. Some of the hotels and the casino have **information centres**, though these are of more limited use. For information about **events**, look for flyers in the tourist office or around the town. You'll also find some events listings in the free, bi-monthly *Madeira Life*, a fairly tacky paper in Portuguese, German and English, which can be picked up in the tourist office and in the receptions of most of the main hotels.

Getting around

The centre of Funchal can easily be explored on foot, though for some of the outlying sights, such as the Jardim Botânico, you might want to save yourself an exhausting uphill trek by making use of the city's reliable and inexpensive **bus** service, operated by Horárias do Funchal. You may also find buses handy if you're staying in the Hotel Zone, as the walk from here to the centre can get a bit tedious; buses #1, #2, #3, #4, #5, #6 and #35 all run along the seafront. **Tickets** can be bought in advance from one of the kiosks on the seafront; it's also possible to buy them on board, but you pay nearly twice as much. Tickets come singly or in blocks of ten, twenty or thirty. The city is divided into three zones, and prices vary accordingly. Zone 1, which extends from the centre as far as the Lido, costs 150$00/€0.75; Zone 2, which goes as far as the Jardim Botânico, costs 300$00/€1.5; and Zone 3, which covers Monte, costs 400$00/€2. If you plan to do a lot of travelling by bus, it may be worth getting a seven-day **pass**, which costs 3000$00/€15 and is available on production of a valid passport from the main **ticket office** (Mon–Fri 8.30am–8pm, Sat 8.30–6pm, Sun 9am–1pm & 2.30–6pm), located at the eastern end of Avenida do Mar, behind the Electricity Museum.

For details of tickets, bus terminals and buses out of Funchal, see p.33.

Taxis are numerous and inexpensive. A ride across the city should cost no more than 1500$00–2000$00 /€7.50–10, though tariffs double at weekends and during the night. You can either hail one down or go to one of the many **ranks**: Avenida Arriaga, Avenida do Mar (by *McDonald's*), Largo do Município, Praça do Mercado (by the main market), Largo do Phelps, Rua do Favila (by the Casino complex) and outside many of the larger hotels. A green light means the cab is occupied. Taxis can also be booked over the phone on ☎291 222 0911/291 222 000/291 222 500, though you'll pay a supplement of 500$00/€2.50 for this.

Driving through central Funchal can be a fraught experience. There is a nightmare one-way system to negotiate between the Sé and Praça do Município, while many roads are extremely narrow and lined with parked cars: it's advisable to pull in to let other vehicles pass. Your best bet as a through route and for parking is the seafront Avenida do Mar, from where it is a short walk to most parts of the city. There are several parking ticket machines here, though two hours is the usual maximum waiting time. For longer visits, try the car park beneath Galerias São Lorenço (map 2, D5).

The city

The city centre extends uphill from the marina in the west to the bougainvillaea-covered channel of the Ribeira de

Santa Luzia in the east and embraces a series of graceful municipal buildings, mosaic-paved pedestrianized shopping streets and many of the city's liveliest cafés and lunch-time restaurants. Highlights include the astonishing collection of Flemish art at the **Museu de Arte Sacra**, the solid **Sé** cathedral and the ornate state rooms in the **Palácio de São Lourenço**, along with the exhibits at the **Quinta das Cruzes** and **Casa Museu Frederico de Freitas**. Other attractions include the semi-tropical **Jardim de São Francisco** municipal gardens, located near the city's oldest wine lodges, the **Adegas de São Francisco**. One of the main draws after dark is the **marina**, with its lively bars and restaurants.

The area immediately east of the Ribeira de Santa Luzia is more workaday, the main attraction here being the **mercado**, Funchal's market, a riot of colour and activity. Further east lies the quieter **Zona Velha**, the old town, which retains an earthy, village quality despite a growing number of tourist-oriented restaurants. The eastern edge of the old town is marked by a fort – now the site of the **Modern Art Museum** – and a small lido, **Barreirinha**. Other sights in this area include the handicrafts institute, **IBTAM**, the **Quinta da Boa Vista** orchid house and the extensive **Jardim Botânico**.

The coast west of the centre has been heavily developed in recent years and is where most of the city's hotels are concentrated, among them the world-famous **Reid's**. The area's two main points of interest are the impressive **harbour** and the beautiful **Jardim de Santa Catarina**, the city's main park. Continuing further west takes you to a large **lido** and the city's nearest decent stretch of beach, **Praia Formosa**.

THE CITY

THE CITY CENTRE

Facing the seafront and gathered round the grand **Praça do Município**, the centre of Funchal is compact enough to walk around in an hour or two, though you will want to spend considerably longer to do justice to its principal sights. You certainly shouldn't miss the rich display of art in the **Museu de Arte Sacra**, while a must for anyone with an interest in the history of Madeiran wine is the **Adegas de São Francisco** wine lodge. Leave time, too, for a walk uphill to the house and gardens of the **Quinta das Cruzes**, whose collection of fine and decorative arts gives some idea of the comfortable lifestyle wine merchants once enjoyed on the island. A more eclectic collection is assembled at the **Casa Museu Frederico de Freitas**. Significant religious monuments that are worth your time include the city' Gothic **cathedral** and the **Convento de Santa Clara** with its beautiful *azulejos*.

The seafront

Funchal's main seaside drag, Avenida do Mar e das Comunidades Madeirenses – more widely known as **Avenida do Mar** – stretches from the Zona Velha in the east to the harbour in the west. On the seaward side, the wide, palm-fringed pavement, punctuated with kiosk cafés, is popular with locals and tourists alike. The city's beach itself with its ash-like black sand, boulders and twisted metal isn't especially appealing, but it's a pleasant enough place to sit and watch the crashing waves.

Opposite the central stretch of beach is the **Antiga Alfândega** (map 2, E4), the old customs house, a relic from Funchal's heady days of thriving international trade and now the seat of Madeira's regional parliament. The orginal Renaissance building was largely destroyed in the

Great Earthquake of 1748, though some features, such as a Manueline doorway at the northern end, have survived. The recent addition of two modern, white bulging extensions have done the building few favours, however.

Two of Funchal's most appealing cafés, *Café Funchal* and *Café Apolo* (see pp.289 & 253), are located on Rua Dr António Almeida, an attractive pedestrianized street, west of the customs house.

ILHAS DESERTAS

Lying some 20km southeast of Funchal, and often shrouded in cloud, are three large, uninhabited islands, known as the Ilhas Desertas. They enjoy protected status and are a haven for the rare monk seal, hunted almost to extinction, as well as dolphins, turtles and seabirds such as Cory's, Manx and Madeiran shearwater.

The largest of the three islands, Deserta Grande, 12km long and 1km wide, is the only one to have been inhabited. Settlers tried cattle farming and selling dyes extracted from lichens, but it was a tough existence. In 1802, the island was finally abandoned when houses were flattened by a tornado. Since 1990, the only residents have been scientists studying the island's wildlife.

You may catch a glimpse of monk seals and other wildlife by taking one of the many boat trips round the islands from the marina. Gavião, for example, runs trips every Thursday (weather permitting), departing at 10am and returning at 6.30pm, for 15,000$00/€75 per person (price includes lunch on the boat). For details, call ☏291 241 124 or visit their office in the marina. The only company to offer trips ashore is the Porto Santo Line (☏291 210 317). All-day trips cost around 12,500$00/€62.50 per person and run on Wednesdays and Saturdays.

THE CITY CENTRE

Just beyond the ramp to the beach stands a small stone column, all that remains of **Banger's Tower**. The original structure, some 30m high and nearly 3m in diameter, was one of the city's most distinctive landmarks. It was built in 1798 at a cost of £1350 by a British merchant, John Banger, as a kind of crane for loading goods on and off ships. Its original function became redundant when the harbour began to silt up and the sea receded, but under the ownership of the Blandy family (see p.101) it was turned into a signpost to let market traders know what goods incoming ships were bringing in. In 1939, despite strong local protest, the tower was demolished to make way for the Avenida do Mar.

Moored just beyond the tower is *The Vagrant*, more popularly known as the **Beatles' Boat**, a luxury yacht built in the USA for the millionaire Horace Vanderbilt and owned for a time by the Beatles. Its shipping career ended after it ran aground in the Canaries in 1977 under the ownership of a Greek shipping magnate. Two years later it was bought by a Madeiran businessman, and in 1982 it was moored in its present position and turned into the city's kitschiest café–restaurant, surrounded by a plethora of mini-boats cemented into a fake "harbour", each with its own table (see p.256 for review).

Further along is the attractive **marina**, with its sleek yachts and various bars and restaurants. After dark, this is one of the liveliest spots in the city and attracts an eclectic mix of tourists, family groups, hip Madeirans and elderly men. When there is a big soccer game on, locals crowd the pavements outside any place with a TV. At weekends, local folk musicians often perform at the outside tables.

For reviews of the best bars and restaurants in the marina, see p.288 and p.255.

BOAT TRIPS

The marina is lined with kiosks selling tickets for **boat trips** and excursions round the island. You can also book the ferry to Porto Santo from here (see p.194). Not all the companies operate the same trips every day, so it is worth shopping around to see what's on offer. Most half-day excursions set off at around 2.30pm, with "sunset" cruises leaving just before dusk. Most trips cost around 3000$00/€15 per person. The common routes are east past dramatic headlands to Baia de Abra (p.136) and west to the pretty villages of Ponta do Sol (p.146) or Ribeira Brava (p.144), where you are given 45 minutes or so to look around. The last two trips pass below Cabo Girão, the world's second-highest sea cliffs (see p.114). In calm weather, some boats anchor at sea so that you can swim off the boat. Specialist trips include cruises on a replica sailing ship, fishing trips and dolphin- and whale-watching. One such specialist is Katherine B, Quinta das Malvas, Rua da Levada de Santa Luzia 124 (℡291 220 334, ℻291 229 869, ⓦwww.madeira-web.com/sportsfishing); they arrange twice-weekly trips from Funchal marina along the west coast to see striped, spotted and bottle-nosed dolphins with the chance to swim with them. They occasionally spot sperm whales too. Departures are usually at 2.30pm, returning around 7pm. You can also buy tickets in advance from some of the larger hotels and travel agents.

Opposite the marina, with its entrance on Rua do Conselheiro José Silvestre Ribeiro, sits the **Casa do Turista**, "the tourist house", a traditionally furnished nineteenth-century house, former home of the German consul, now a somewhat commercialized outlet for local arts and crafts. The raised bit of pavement in front of the Casa on Avenida do Mar serves as a bus stop for many places in the city.

For more on Madeiran arts and crafts, see p.85.

Palácio de São Lourenço

Map 2, D4. Free visits on Wed at 9.30am & Fri at 3pm, but you'll need to book on ☎ 291 202 530 or at the main tourist office.

Just beyond the Casa do Turista stands the **Palácio de São Lourenço**, with its distinctive white facade and single tower. One of Funchal's most impressive and historic buildings, the *palácio* is the official residence of the Minister of the Republic for Madeira – basically Madeira's MP in the Portuguese government. The entrance, flanked by armed guards, is on Avenida Zarco. There are no guided tours: you're simply left to wander through a series of sumptuous state rooms full of priceless furniture and antiques, and it's quite likely you'll have the place to yourself, as the limited opening times put many people off.

The original palace was built by the first captains of Madeira and formed part of the city's defences. Most of the present structure was built during Spain's brief occupation of Portugal in the sixteenth century, though it has undergone several alterations since. The palace was taken over by the commissioners and governors of Madeira in 1775. In 1836, following the separation of civil and military powers, the east wing of the building became the headquarters of the Military Governor and still belongs to the army. Visitors are only allowed to visit the Minister's state rooms in the west wing.

The large entrance hall is known as the **Portrait Room**, named after all the paintings on the walls of the first captains of Madeira, including Zarco, the discoverer of Madeira, and his son.

The neighbouring **Ballroom** is extremely lavish, full of priceless antiques, including Louis XV mirrors and Louis

ZARCO

Though not internationally as well known as some of Portugal's navigators, **Zarco** is probably Madeira's most important historical figure, the founding father of the island. He gained his nickname – Zarco means "one-eyed" – after he lost an eye fighting the Moors. His real name was João Gonçalves, a knight who served under Dom Henrique – better known as Henry the Navigator – during Portugal's Golden Age of global expansion in the early fifteenth century. At this time, Portugal was turning its attention from crusades against the Moors to exploring the coast off West Africa. The king decided to entrust Zarco with a mission to explore the coast off Guinea. Zarco set off in 1418 with another captain, Tristão Vaz Teixeira, but as they headed south, their boat was blown off course. They fetched up on Porto Santo, and saw a densely wooded island beyond, which they called Ilha da Madeira – "island of wood". They reported back to Dom Henrique on their findings and two years later returned, this time with a group of Portuguese emigrants. They landed on Madeira at Machico and made the previously uninhabited island their home. Zarco became overall governor as well as administrator, or captain, of the southwest and it was he who ordered the burning of much of Madeira's native woodland. He settled in Funchal and lived in a house on the site of the current-day Quinta das Cruzes – remains of the original house can still be seen in the gardens. Zarco's descendants continued to be governors of the island until the Spanish occupation of 1580. The navigator's remains lie buried in Funchal's Convento de Santa Clara (see p.69).

XVI chairs. Just beyond here is the distinctive **turret** which dominates this end of Avenida do Mar. It is thought that the site was originally a water cistern which was later enlarged and covered over. In the nineteenth century, it became a *Casinha de Prazer*, literally a "little house of pleasure", that would have been used for writing letters or reading.

From the tower you pass into two more ornate rooms, the **Red Room** and the **Green Room**, painted in the colours of Portugal's national flag by Max Römer, a German artist and resident in Madeira during the 1930s. The Red Room houses several ornaments from the Ajuda Palace in Lisbon built by Dona Maria II and Dom Ferdinand, nineteenth-century royals who had a penchant for over-the-top, generally tasteless, artefacts.

The **Bulwark Room** is a reminder of the palace's original status as a fort before the bulwarks were converted into a meeting room during the nineteenth century. This was one of the last rooms Marcelo Caetano – the successor to the dictator Salazar – used before he was exiled to Brazil following Portugal's peaceful revolution of 1974. The residents of Funchal gave him a hard time, knowing exactly where he was and heckling him with catcalls during his brief stay.

The courtyard with its attractive **gardens** is only open to the public when the Minister is not in residence. In one corner there are some vibrant *azulejos* depicting São Lourenço, made in Lisbon during the 1930s. Seventeenth-century decorative *azulejos* adorn the small room in the corner of the courtyard, once part of a sixteenth-century turret.

The tour ends in the **Golden Room**, so named because it used to house a collection of gilded Louis XVI furniture, now on display in the ballroom. Nowadays, the simply furnished but ornate room serves as the Minister's office and is the place from which he frequently gives speeches or interviews on TV.

Avenida Arriaga and around

A short walk uphill from the palace takes you onto one of the city's main thoroughfares, **Avenida Arriaga**, the site of the **Museu Barbeito Cristovão Colombo** and the atmospheric **Adegas de São Francisco** wine lodge. A perfect place to relax after your sightseeing is the lush gardens of the **Jardim de São Francisco**.

One monument that you won't be able to miss as you walk down Avenida Arriaga is the **Monumento João Gonçalves Zarco**, a statue of the discoverer of Madeira and one of the best-known works by local artist Francisco Franco. The statue was commissioned by Salazar (see p.84), a keen fan of historical Portuguese heroes. You can see more of Francisco Franco's art in the Museu Franco (see p.84).

To the east of the Zarco statue is the *Golden Gate*, one of the city's most traditional cafés (see p.289).

Heading along the south side of Avenida Arriaga past the austere walls of the Palácio de São Lourenço, you reach a beautiful building clad in *azulejos*, depicting rural scenes of the island. Once the Chamber of Commerce, the building is now mostly given over to the São Lourenço shopping centre and a Toyota showroom, its vehicles looking rather ill at ease in their sumptuous surroundings. Next door is the wonderfully ornate **Teatro Municipal Baltazar Diaz**, the city's main theatre, which was founded in 1888 and regularly puts on musicals and the occasional opera or ballet, as well as occasional art-house films.

The theatre café is one of Funchal's livelier places to drink (see p.288 for a review).

Museu Barbeito Cristovão Colombo
Map 2, C4. 48 Avda Arriaga. Mon–Fri 9.30am–1pm & 3–7pm, Sat 9.30am–1.30pm; 200$00/€1.

The basement of Diogos Wine Shop hides one of Funchal's quirkier museums, the **Museu Barbeito Cristovão**

Colombo, the private collection of Mário Barbeito de Vasconcelos, a local who had a passion both for Madeira and all things to do with Christopher Columbus. The rather rambling collection consists of paintings, poems, operas and books relating mostly to Columbus's first voyage to America but also to his time in Madeira and Porto Santo. Among the displays are a copy of the first work written on Columbus in 1576, as well as a series of portraits of the explorer dating from the seventeenth to the twentieth centuries. Unless you are a fan of Columbus, of more interest is the collection of old maps, historical prints, postcards of and books about Madeira itself, including an 1840 *Invalid's Guide to Madeira* written by a surgeon, William White; William and Alfred Reid's 1891 guide to Madeira; and *An Historical Sketch of the Island of Madeira* dating from 1819.

Jardim de São Francisco
Map 2, C4.

Continuing east down Avenida Arriaga brings you to the leafy expanse of the **Jardim de São Francisco**, also known as the Municipal Gardens. The gardens were once part of the Convento de São Francisco, and some of the convent ruins are still visible amid the jungle of frangipani, agapanthus, tulip trees and ferns. The gardens also have a delightful series of ponds and fountains. To the north of the park there is a good kiosk café (see p.288), set next to a concrete amphitheatre that occasionally hosts live concerts. To the other side of the café and set in its own cat-filled grounds lies the so-called **Scottish Kirk**, an attractive wooden church built in 1861 and still serving the local Presbyterian community.

Adegas de São Francisco
Map 2, D4. Avda Arriaga 28. Mon–Fri 9am–7pm, Sat 10am–1pm; free.

The **Adegas de São Francisco** is Funchal's oldest wine

lodge, where you can sample some of the big names in Madeira wine: Blandy, Miles, Leacock and Cossart Gordon. Parts of the building date from a sixteenth-century Franciscan monastery which stood here before the order was banned from Portugal in the nineteenth century. The present structure is mostly seventeenth century. Incorporated into the grounds is one of Funchal's oldest streets, dating back to the fifteenth century, and along which casks would once have been taken to the harbour.

Tours of the Adegas de São Francisco take place at 10.30am & 3.30pm Mon–Fri, 11am on Sat; 600$00/€3.

Though you can wander round a series of atmospheric shops and tasting rooms at will, it is worth joining one of the entertaining and informative hour-long **tours** which include lots of free tastings. Furthermore, the tours take you round rooms otherwise closed to the public, including the Vintage Room, stashed high with hundreds of dark bottles of Madeira, and a series of low-ceilinged rooms where top Madeiras mature in vast wooden barrels, some as high as three metres and holding up to 9000 litres of wine. The visit gives a detailed and interesting insight into how the history of wine and the island are interlinked. Guides explain the processes behind making the best Madeiran wines, such as the 1908 Bual, which spent 76 years ageing in a cask and which will now cost you 102,000$000 a bottle (about €510 or £300). There is also a small wine museum containing old order books, nineteenth-century labels, label printing blocks and old wine-making equipment. The tour ends back in the bar where you get the chance to sample the various wines you have seen maturing.

The Sé

Map 2, E4.

A couple of minutes' walk up Avenida Arriaga from the Adegas is Funchal's cathedral, the **Sé**, built between 1485 and 1514. Its dark basalt-stone exterior and narrow windows are typical of southern European Gothic architecture, though it also has a number of home-grown features, most notably its conical, chequered tiled roof and clock. Around the back of the church are twisted conical turrets, typical of Manueline architecture. The most striking feature of the interior is the geometric patterned wood and ivory ceiling, of unmistakable Moorish inspiration and somewhat at odds with the heavy Baroque decoration imposed on the rest of the interior.

Museu Cidade do Açucar

Map 2, E4. Mon–Fri 10am–12.30pm & 2–6pm; free.

The **Museu Cidade do Açucar**, on the north side of attractive Praça de Colombo, is devoted to the history of the island's sugar trade. The building occupies the site of what is popularly known as "Columbus's House", though it's believed that Columbus only stayed here briefly in 1498 as a guest of the owner, a sugar merchant, João Esmeraldo, before he set sail for the Americas.

For more on Columbus see box on p.199.

The house was demolished in 1876, then excavated in 1986, revealing several important archeological finds, including the house's original well, given pride of place in the museum. Most of the collection, however, is fairly dull and consists mainly of artefacts connected with the sugar trade, such as fifteenth-century sugar moulds, plus sixteenth-century ceramics and religious icons.

The restaurants on narrow Rua Queimada
Baixa, Rua Queimada Cima and Rua do Bispo
are popular lunch-time spots (see p.252).

Praça do Município and around

Map 2, E3.

Praça do Município, the main square, is very much the focus of the city centre. It is certainly one of Funchal's prettiest, with red-flowering tulip trees in one corner and in another some fine examples of the extraordinary kapok tree, the pods of which explode into giant cottonwool balls in spring. The terracotta-tiled, solid, white municipal buildings set around a fountain will be familiar to anyone who has visited provincial Portuguese towns on the mainland.

The east side of the square is dominated by the **Câmara Municipal**, the town hall, built in the eighteenth century for a local landowner, the Conde de Carvalhal. The guard will happily let you stroll into the central courtyard, beautifully lined with *azulejos*. Behind the town hall lies another impressive building, the classical **Palácio da Justiça**, the city's law courts. Behind here, with its entrance on the busy Rua 5 de Outubro, a faded yellow building with a red-faced tower marks the **Instituto do Vinho da Madeira**, designed by eccentric British consul Henry Veitch (see p.74) in the nineteenth century. Despite the building's rather shabby appearance, it does house an important institution, which declares the vintage years for all Madeira wine. The institute also has a small **Wine Museum** (Mon–Fri 9.30am–noon & 2–5pm; free; ☎291 204 600), accessed via the central courtyard. For the most part, it contains a random and only mildly interesting collection of grape-picking baskets, barrel scales and corking machines.

There are, however, some evocative black-and-white photos of the *borracheiros*, the so-called "drunken" men, whose job it was to carry the hefty goatskins of wine across the island from the farms to the capital; unsurprisingly, they drank a little of their burden to keep them going on the way.

Heading back to the Praça do Município you pass the **Igreja do Colégio**, a rather dour-looking seventeenth-century church at the north end of the square. Inside, however, you'll find beautiful *azulejos* dating from the seventeenth and eighteenth centuries and a ceiling painted with figures peering over balconies draped with fruit and flowers. The church is adjacent to the **Universidade de Madeira**, the city university, originally a Jesuit college. The Jesuits arrived in Madeira from mainland Portugal in the sixteenth century and were extremely influential in the early development of Madeira, owning some of its most important vineyards. They were banished from the island, however, in 1760, after the Marquês de Pombal – king José I's powerful right-hand man – saw the Jesuits' influence as a threat to the country.

Museu de Arte Sacra

Map 2, E3. Rua do Bispo 21. Tues–Sat 10am–12.30pm & 2.30–6pm, Sun 10am–1pm; 450$00/€2.25.

Backing onto the Praça do Município, the **Museu de Arte Sacra**, occupying three floors of an eighteenth-century former Bishop's Palace, has one of the finest collections of art in Portugal, let alone Madeira, thanks to its priceless collection of Renaissance Flemish paintings. Trading links with Flanders were strong in the fifteenth and sixteenth centuries and there was a ready market for Flemish art among church and government officials and sugar-plantation owners, keen to decorate their chapels. Indeed, wealthy landowners even commissioned their own works of art from Flanders. These artworks remained unprotected and often neglected in private lodgings, chapels and churches around the island until the 1930s, when a restoration programme was undertaken in the Museu de Arte Antiga in Lisbon. After completion of the project it was decided that the works should be housed together in Funchal, and the Museu de Arte Sacra was inaugurated in 1955.

The Flemish paintings are displayed on the top floor. Many are acclaimed for their size and for the detail of their landscapes. A number of Dutch masters feature, though many paintings remain unattributed. Some of the most powerful works include the triptych *Descending from the Cross*, attributed to Gerard David (1460–1523), and *The Annunciation*, by Joos Van Cleve (1508–45). Another valuable work is the *Triptych of Santiago Menor and São Filipe*, by Pieter Coecke Van Aelst; in one of the wings of the painting sits Simão Gonçalves de Câmara, grandson of Zarco (see p.57). Other highlights are the sixteenth-century wooden sculpture of Christ – its oak form looking amazingly modern – believed to be from the Flemish or German school; and a painting of St Jerónimo pensively fingering a skull, attributed to Marinus Van Reymers.

The rest of the top floor is given over to some less interesting Portuguese Mannerist paintings, while on the first floor you'll find a fairly mundane collection of embroidered liturgical vestments, church silver and gilded-wood sculptures, including a well-worn seventeenth-century Persian carpet originating from the Convento de Santa Clara (see p.69). The most valuable exhibit here is a silver-gilt processional cross, attributed to Gil Vicente and donated as a gift by Manuel I in the sixteenth century. The ground floor houses temporary exhibitions.

CARNIVAL

Carnival in Funchal, at the end of February and beginning of March, is one of the most important events of the year on Madeira; preparations get underway a good week before, with shops stocking up with colourful masks and costumes. The carnival used to have much in common with Venice's, with people dressing up in disguise and going to a series of masked balls, but recently it's been more influenced by Rio, and Brazilian music and risqué outfits are more common.

The festivities kick off on the Friday with children from the local primary schools parading in fancy dress – neat rows of little kids in nurses' or doctors' uniforms or dressed as fruit or vegetables. As darkness falls local lads borrow their sisters' or mothers' garb before hitting town for "Transvestite Night".

Saturday evening is when the main parade takes place; people flock to the restaurants early and the coloured lights draped on the trees along the route are switched on. At around 9pm, a parade of floats weaves from outside the *Savoy* down Avenida do Infant to Avenida Ariaga and the Sé, before passing up Avenida Zarco and ending up on Praça do Município, the venue for the rest of the evening's music and partying. The

Rua da Carreira and around

Map 2, D3–B3.

One of Funchal's most historic and interesting streets, **Rua da Carreira** was once the site for riderless horse races, a far cry from today when traffic often grinds to a halt behind parked delivery vans. It was also a traditional venue for carnival celebrations (see box above). No. 43 is the site of Portugal's first ever photographic studio, set up by Vicente Gomes da Silva in 1865. It was turned into a museum, the **Museu Photographia Vicentes**, but has been closed for parade route is lined with expectant spectators, though it is rarely so full that you can't get a decent look at the floats. These are entertaining enough, even if not quite up to Rio's lavish standards, and the streets around, lined with stalls selling *bolo de cacao* and coloured balloons, are highly atmospheric.

Sunday and Monday have more low-key events, with live music in Praça Município during the evening, but things really get going again on Tuesday with the Great Allegorical Parade. The parade is a satirical event in which anyone can participate, though the traditional messy ritual of pelting people with rotten tomatoes and eggs seems to have died out in the last couple of decades in favour of a more tourist-friendly amateur parade at around 4pm, usually processing from the market to the Jardim de São Francisco. Most people wear fancy dress, with everyone from old men to tots dressing in anything from silly wigs to elaborate costumes of cellophane, make-up and tinsel. The whole of Funchal takes on a party atmosphere and coloured streamers cover the streets along the parade route. At around 6pm, there is a farewell to carnival show in Praça do Município, with prizes given to the best carnival costumes.

some time now and shows no sign of reopening. However, you can still go into the balconied courtyard, which contains some good English-language bookshops and a reasonable café–restaurant (see p.255). As a pioneering photographer, da Silva had access to an extraordinary range of people. His clients included Empress Elizabeth of Austria and the Empress of Brazil, and he managed to photograph nearly every person of note who visited the island at the end of the nineteenth century. Some of the most interesting of his astonishing collection of 380,000 negatives, however, are those which display island life as it was:

sailing ships visiting the harbour, society figures and bul-
lock carts acting as public transport. He also photographed
ordinary Madeiran people, his pictures recording changing
fashions and lifestyles on the island. You can still see some
of his photographs on the stairway at the back of the
courtyard, and many of his works pop up from time to
time at temporary exhibitions round the island, such as in
the exhibition hall by the top of Cabo Girão (see p.114).
There are also his evocative portraits of embroiderers at
IBTAM (see p.85).

Museu Municipal do Funchal

Map 2, C3. Tues–Fri 10am–6pm, Sat & Sun noon–6pm;
ⓔmmf@mail.telepac.pt; 300$00/€1.50.

The **Museu Municipal do Funchal** is mostly given over
to a natural history collection, the highlight of which is
what's referred to as an aquarium, though in fact it's just a
small room containing a collection of sea creatures native to
Madeira's shores, including crabs, lobsters, giant snails,
octopus and hermit crabs. The huge eels and groupers are
probably the most exciting, while the sight of the green sea
turtles wedged into a tank barely larger than themselves is
positively depressing. The upstairs rooms present a series of
skeletons and stuffed animals native to Madeira, including
huge rays, giant monk seals and whales. The lepidoptery
collection gives you a good idea of the range of butterflies
on the island, but otherwise the fusty assortment of insects,
fossils and birds is uninspiring.

Casa Museu Frederico De Freitas

Map 2, C2. Tues–Sat 10am–12.30pm & 4–6pm, Sun
10am–12.30pm; 350$00/€1.75.

A much more engaging museum, the **Casa Museu
Frederico De Freitas**, occupying the attractive eighteenth-century Casa Calçada, contains miscellaneous objects

collected by twentieth-century lawyer and veteran traveller, Dr Frederico de Freitas, as well as an impressive display of *azulejos*, housed in an adjoining annexe. The Casa Calçada has been renovated in the style of a nineteenth-century *quinta*. Most of the furnishings come from De Freitas's private collection and include oriental carpets, antique furniture from Britain and Portugal and religious paintings. Particularly attractive are the nineteenth-century watercolours of Madeiran landscapes by H.B. Windrush in the dining room, and the collection of drawings and illustrations in the Library, including works by twentieth-century Portuguese artist Botelho. The tiny pantry contains De Freitas's collection of Chinese porcelain, as well as German, English and Portuguese ceramics, and an impressive – if not particularly attractive – display of toby jugs and mugs. Outside the Casa Calçada there is a temporary exhibition space and an attractive courtyard garden with a small summer house.

Beautifully presented in the adjoining **Casa dos Azulejos** is a small collection of tiles from all round the world. On the ground floor are some well-preserved examples from medieval times and a short video in Portuguese about the history of tile production and painting. Successive floors display exquisitely decorated tiles from Persia, Turkey and Syria dating from the fourteenth to the nineteenth centuries; Portuguese *azulejos* which have been rescued from demolished buildings on the island; and some particularly fine mosaics taken from the Convento de Santa Clara, next door.

Convento de Santa Clara
Map 2, C2. Daily 10am–noon & 3–5pm; free.

The **Convento de Santa Clara** was founded in 1496 by Zarco's grandson, João Gonçalves de Camara, whose sister Dona Isabel was the first Abbess. Most of the original

PORTUGUESE AZULEJOS

Madeira has some fine examples of *azulejos*, the distinctive Portuguese glazed tiles, used to decorate everything from the outside of houses, walls and fountains to the interiors of churches and cafés. The craft was brought over by the Moors in the eighth century – the word "azulejo" derives from the Arabic *al-zulecha*, "small stone". The Moors were forbidden by the Koran to depict human or animal figures, so they developed abstract geometrical designs. Early Portuguese tiles were influenced by these designs, examples of which can be seen in the Convento de Santa Clara (see above). Portuguese *azulejos* developed their own style around the mid-sixteenth century when tile-making techniques were improved. Wealthy Portuguese began to commission large *azulejos* panels displaying battles, hunting scenes and fantastic images influenced by Vasco Da Gama's voyages to the east. Later, new Dutch Delftware techniques made it possible to add much more detail to each tile. Large *azulejos* panels were also commissioned by churches – these often covered an entire wall and became known as *tapetes* (carpets) because of their resemblance to large

convent was destroyed in a pirate attack in 1566, and the nuns fled to Curral das Freiras (see p.118). The present building was constructed in the seventeenth century and is still a working convent, with 26 nuns in residence; if you ring the bell during visiting hours (see above) someone will show you round. Up until the nineteenth century, the order was closed, and the young girls sent here by their parents were permitted no contact at all with the outside world. You can still see the thick wooden grille between the church and the nuns' private quarters behind which the girls were confined. During the nineteenth century, conditions

Persian rugs; there's a fine example in Funchal's Igreja do Colégio (see p.64).

In the late seventeenth century, blue and white tiles, influenced by Dutch design, were especially popular with Portugal's aristocracy, and their favoured images were flowers and fruit. The church also began to use this style to portray the lives of the saints, such as St Francis, who is depicted in Quinta Vigia's chapel (see p.75). The early eighteenth century saw trained artist "masters" producing highly decorated, multi-coloured ceramic mosaics in the Rococo style.

After the Great Earthquake (see p.338) many buildings were rebuilt with more prosaic tiled facades, as it was realized that *azulejos* protected against rain and fire and were good insulation devices. By the mid-nineteenth century, *azulejos* were being produced in factories to decorate shops and workplaces; Funchal's Chamber of Commerce (see p.59) and the city market (see p.83) show how this tradition has continued to the present day. But though there are individual artists who carry on the hand-painted tradition, the majority of today's tiles continue to be mass-produced items, pale imitations of old figurative or geometric designs.

were relaxed slightly and the nuns were allowed to make and sell sugar sweets to the congregation. The sisters soon became famed for their confectionery skills, and the sweets became popular tourist souvenirs.

There are two cloisters – one now contains a children's playground, while the other is particularly peaceful and beautiful, filled with plants and orange trees. Adjacent to the cloisters, the church, spared the pirate attack in 1566, and lined with *azulejos*, contains the tomb of Zarco (see p.57).

Quinta das Cruzes

Map 2, C2. Calçada do Pico 1. Tues–Sun 10am–12.30pm & 2–6pm.
Gardens Tues–Sun 10am–6pm; 350$00/€1.75. Bus #15a from Praça
da Autonomia.

With its stunning views over Funchal and the harbour,
Quinta das Cruzes and its gardens form one of the most
tranquil spots in the city. This seventeenth-century estate
was once the private home of a Genoese wine-shipping
family, the Lomelinos, and the mansion bears testimony to
the wealthy lifestyle wine-merchants enjoyed on Madeira at
that time and to the importance of Portuguese traders glob-
ally. The house overflows with art and silks from India and
China, Flemish paintings (including Jean de Mabuse's *Three
Magi*), French tapestry, English furniture and nineteenth-
century jewellery. The upstairs rooms are arranged themati-
cally; room 6 is particularly impressive for its fine Meissen
and Sèvres porcelain, including pieces made for Louis XVI
and Marie Antoinette. Some intricate examples of
Madeiran embroidery are displayed in room 10, while
downstairs, in room 14, is a particularly fine sixteenth-
century Hispano-Arabic chest inlaid with ivory and gold.
In room 12, you can see some early examples of recycling,
including a seventeenth-century chest made out of planks
taken from old sugar packing cases. The final room downstairs contains a large collection of silver and china pieces,
mostly dating from the eighteenth and nineteenth centuries, when the Portuguese shipped porcelain from China
to Europe on a large scale. Many of the pieces were made
to order and decorated with family coats of arms, or biblical
and mythological themes.

Outside, the estate's gardens are also outstanding, a verdant array of flowers and dragon trees forming a superb
backdrop to a somewhat esoteric gathering of tombstones
and statues that have been rescued from various demolished buildings throughout the island, and laid to rest here

on the lawns. Some of these are remnants of Zarco's house, which stood on this site before the current *quinta* was built. The most prominent item is a particularly fine Manueline stone window frame in the centre of the garden. The grounds are also home to a small, austere chapel built in 1692.

See box on p.150 for more on Manueline architecture.

The British Cemetery and around

Map 2, B3. 235 Rua da Carreira. Open daily 10am–5pm; ring bell for entry.

Although British traders had been resident in Madeira virtually since it was first colonized, a Protestant cemetery was only allowed in 1887. It's known as the **British Cemetery**, but shelters the remains of Protestants from other countries, too. It's the final resting place of some of the expats who made a mark on Madeira's trade and industry, including Blandys, Hinton and Leacock.

If you have any puff left, climb the hill to **Fortaleza do Pico** for stunning views back over the city. The fort was built under Spanish rule and is now used by the navy; the only part open to the public is a room showing photographs of the building over the years.

The English Church

Map 2, C3.

Heading back downhill along Rua da Carreira, look out for cobbled Rua do Quebra Costas. A hundred metres or so up on the right, at No. 18, you'll come across the small domed **English Church**, whose attractive gardens contain a bust of Philippa of Lancaster, daughter of John of Gaunt and wife of João I – a union that helped to establish the British–Portuguese alliance in 1387.

THE CITY CENTRE

Despite the trade alliance, the British were not allowed to build a church on the island until 1810. The design of the church was entrusted to the British Consul, Henry Veitch, and the work was funded by levies on wine exports to London. Completed in 1822, the Neoclassical building that resulted was quite controversial in that it was so unlike a traditional place of worship, with no spire or conventional arched windows. Some say this was due to constraints imposed by the Catholic church, others that the Consul just wanted a modern building.

Legend has it that Veitch buried a stack of gold coins under the church. What is known is that he received a large sum of *louis d'or* from Napoleon, who stopped at Madeira en route to exile on St Helena and took on board 418 litres of vintage wine. In the event, Napoleon never drank the wine because of his poor health, so Veitch demanded its return. It was duly sent back to Madeira in 1822, but Veitch declined to return the money that Napoleon had given him, declaring that it was a "gift" and not a payment. Veitch is then supposed to have buried the coins under the church. As for the returned wine, it was later sold to Blandys who put it in demijohns in 1840. Churchill drank one of these in the 1950s and celebrated its superb quality. "Napoleon's wine" is still sold at auction, though it is unlikely that much of it is really the same stuff that Napoleon had.

WEST OF THE CENTRE

West of the centre lies the **Hotel Zone**, the area where the majority of visitors to Funchal stay, it is made up of a sprawl of shops, restaurants, cafés and modern hotels, ranging from high-rise blocks to state-of-the-art hotel complexes. Here and there, however, a few nineteenth-century *quintas* have survived, and there's also the venerable **Reid's**, one of the world's best-known hotels. One of the main attractions in the area is the **Jardim de Santa Catarina**, the city's largest and liveliest park, bordered by the president's house, **Quinta Vigia**, to the north and the **harbour** to the south. Further west lies an enormous **lido** and Funchal's only proper beach, **Praia Formosa**.

Jardim de Santa Catarina and around

Map 2, B5–C5.
Set on a high bluff overlooking the harbour is the city's largest park, the **Jardim de Santa Catarina**, a wonderful swathe of breezy parkland. Laid out between 1945 and 1966, it contains a couple of sights worth checking out near the main entrance: a small statue of Christopher Columbus and the **Capela de Santa Catarina**, an attractive (but usually locked) seventeenth-century chapel which sits on the site of an old wooden church commissioned in 1425 by Zarco's wife. A wide area of coarse grass above this makes a good picnic spot, with superb views back over the city.

A network of paths leads uphill past plants and succulents and beautiful trees, including red-flowering tulip trees. On the seaside path, enormous cacti, *Euforbia Gigante*, reach some 15m high. At the top end of the park, a fenced-off area next to two rusting old traction engines marks a children's **playground**, complete with slides, swings and climbing frames, a must for anyone with kids. Just below the playground there is a small lake and a park **café**, *Esplanada do Lago*, where you can enjoy cold drinks or ice cream surrounded by palms, bamboos and shady trees.

Quinta Vigia

Map 2, B5. Mon–Sat 9am–5pm; free.
The president's house, **Quinta Vigia**, sits just north of the

Jardim de Santa Catarina. There is a set of gates above the café to the *quinta*, but these are usually kept locked; the main entrance is on Avenida do Infante. The eighteenth-century *quinta* is an attractive but surprisingly modest pink building formerly known as Quinta Angústias. The original Quinta Vigia was controversially demolished to make way for the neighbouring *Carlton Park Hotel* in the 1960s, so the deserted Quinta Angústias took up the role and name of the former building. The current Quinta Vigia was the home of the Empress of Brazil during the 1850s. Visitors are only allowed to visit the beautiful eighteenth-century chapel, lined with superb *azulejos* depicting the life of Saint Francis, and the attractive gardens, which contain peacocks, a parrot enclosure and more sweeping views over the harbour.

Hospício da Princesa

Map 2, B5. Gardens: daily 9am–6pm; free.

Downhill from the Quinta Vigia stands another impressive historic building, the **Hospício da Princesa**, a hospice founded in 1859 by the Empress of Brazil in memory of her daughter, Princess Maria Amélia, who died of TB in 1853 at the age of 22. The empress couldn't bear to have much do with the hospice and entrusted its running to her sister Josephine, Queen of Sweden. Its luxuriant gardens, full of spiny dragon trees and towering palms, are open to the public.

Casino

Map 2, A5. Over-18s only, Mon–Thurs & Sun 4pm–3am, Fri & Sat 4pm–4am; free.

Just north of Quinta Vigia lies Funchal's **casino**, part of a complex designed by Brazilian Oscar Niemeyer, the architect of Brasilia. Like the Brazilian capital, the park is not everyone's cup of tea. The circular casino building resembles a concrete wart and is only marginally less offensive than the park's vast hotel on stilts, the *Carlton Park Hotel* (see p.223). The casino is a little slice of Las Vegas, flashing lights luring you into a room of glittering slot machines. From 8pm daily, there are games of roulette and black jack, along with cabaret and musical performances, all sufficiently tacky to have James Bond run a mile.

Cutting through the casino park you reach Rua Imperatriz Dona Amélia. Around this road, wedged into a corner between high-rise hotels and the harbour, a small number of streets have managed to retain some of their traditional atmosphere, with a few remaining old villas and houses, most of them turned into bars and restaurants (see reviews on p.292).

The harbour and Loo Rock

Map 2, A7–E7.

Offering some of the best views of the city, the **harbour** is a bustling area of colourful fishing boats, container ships loaded with vast crates of bananas, and giant cruise ships which dock early morning most days. It's also the departure point for the daily ferry to Porto Santo (see p.194). Surveying all is the fortress on top of **Loo Rock**, which juts out into the harbour. The rock was where Madeira's first settlers spent their first night, feeling more secure here than on the mainland. In 1656, a small fortress was built on the rock, and a chapel to Nossa Senhora da Conceicão, currently closed for restoration, was added in 1682. Between 1757 and 1762, the rock was joined to the mainland, the harbour wall was gradually extended and, in 1866, a lighthouse was added. In 1992, the rock passed from the military to the local council, and the fort now houses a café and pricey restaurant, *Restaurante O Molhe* (see p.263 for review), reached by a lift. It's worth having at least a drink in the café to enjoy the views of the city and sea.

Quinta Magnolia

Map 3, D7. Daily 9am–7pm. City bus #5, #6, #8 or #45 from opposite the Marina.

Set in an attractive park and formerly the site of the British Country Club, the leisure complex **Quinta Magnolia** is an oasis of tranquillity in a busy part of the city. It's a great resource if you're staying somewhere without a pool or gardens. Facilities include a children's playground, tennis courts and a large freshwater swimming pool (pay at the main gate; 300$00/€1.5).

The low, attractive building that used to house the British Club itself is now a library, the **Biblioteca de Cultural Estrangeiros** (Mon–Fri 9am–5.30pm; ☎291 233 164 ⓔamericanccorner@mail.telepac.pt), containing a small but good stock of American, English, South African, German and French books; anyone can borrow books for free after filling out a membership form.

Reid's

Map 3, D7.

Voted the fourth best hotel in the world by the UK's *Daily Telegraph* newspaper in 1999, **Reid's** is something of a living legend, one of the world's truly great hotels. Though a night here – or, come to that, a meal at one of its many restaurants – is beyond many people's means, you can get a glimpse of the hotel's lavish interior and enjoy the terrace views by taking afternoon tea (3–6pm daily; 3800$00/€19); you'll need to book a day in advance (☎291 717 171).

The hotel was founded by William Reid, the son of a Scottish crofter, born in Kilmarnock in 1822 and one of twelve children. William was a sickly child and was advised to go to warmer climes to improve his health. In 1836, he earned his passage on a ship to Madeira via Lisbon. Once in Funchal, he got a job as a baker and later in the wine trade which allowed him to establish a decent lifestyle. A natural entrepreneur, he soon set up an agency catering to wealthy tourists who wanted to stay in local *quintas*, in those days the only places to stay in comfort. Spotting a market, Reid saved enough to buy his own place, *Quinta das Fontes,* and converted it into a hotel. The venture had a powerful backer: the conversion was financed partly by the Duke of Edinburgh and was appropriately renamed the *Royal Edinburgh Hotel* (which has subsequently been demolished to make way for the Marina shopping centre). Reid soon acquired further hotels and guesthouses, but his ambition was to own a purpose-built hotel, and eventually he managed to buy Salto do Cavalo, a five-acre British-owned estate on a clifftop, 50m above sea level. Sadly, Reid died in 1888, three years before his dream was realized. *Reid's* was completed in 1891, designed by George Somers, architect of the *Shepherd's Hotel* in Cairo.

By the early 1900s, *Reid's* had established itself as the centre of Madeira's gay social life, but it was forced to close during World War I. William Reid's sons continued to run the hotel until they ran into financial difficulties in 1925. In 1936, it was taken over by the Blandy family, who expanded the hotel, adding new wings and seawater swimming pools. In 1996, it passed to an international hotel chain and is now owned by Orient Express Hotels, who have undertaken further renovation of the building and its gardens.

In the early twentieth century, guests arrived at the hotel's own landing stage by boat or seaplanes. Nowadays, celebrities slip in quietly by car. The list of guests reads like a who's who of the last century, including Captain Scott of the Antarctic (1901); Edward VIII; Lloyd George (1925); Churchill (see p.110); George Bernard Shaw (1924), who met resident tango instructor Max Rinder and called him "the only man that ever taught me anything"; pioneer flyer Amy Johnson (1933); General Batista of Cuba, fleeing from Castro's revolution in 1958 (and who took over an entire floor of the hotel); Gregory Peck and John Huston, who stayed here while filming *Moby Dick*'s whale-hunting scenes; Portugal's dictator Salazar; James Bond AKA Roger Moore; novelist Frederick Forsyth and countless heads of state and members of European royalty.

The Hotel Zone

From *Reid's* the main coast road, Estrada Monumental, heads west through the **Hotel Zone**, a strip of modern hotels, shops, holiday homes and leisure facilities, including a municipal **lido**. One of the few remaining old buildings on this stretch is the **Barbeito Wine Lodge** (Mon–Fri 9am–1pm & 2–5.30pm), a short stroll beyond *Reid's*. Visitors are welcome to look round the lodge and free tastings are usually on offer.

For reviews of accommodation in the Hotel Zone see p.223.

The lido

Map 3, D7. Daily 9am–6pm; 270$00/€1.35. City bus #1, #2, #3, #4, #5 or #6 from opposite the Marina.

Just off the Estrada Monumental on Rua Gorgulho is the entrance to the municipal **lido**, with a rather chilly, Olympic-sized seawater pool; when the sea is rough, the waves literally break into it; when it is calm, you can also swim in the Atlantic from here. At the far end there is a smaller children's pool, complete with water slides and stepping stones. Built into the cliff face above are cafés, restaurants and shops. The whole place gets pretty packed at weekends, but it's a great place to hang out for an afternoon.

Praia Formosa

Map 3, C7. City bus #1, #2, #3 or #35 from Praça da Autonomia on the seafront.

Beyond the lido sprawls a rash of high-rise development, including hotels, fast-food outlets and car-rental offices, but it is worth heading a little further out to reach Funchal's nearest stretch of proper beach, **Praia Formosa**, a long expanse of stony shore dotted with sun shades made of palm fronds. In 1566, the beach was the landing stage for Bertrand de Montluc, a French pirate, whose band of men went on to ransack Funchal (see p.335).

Backed by a Shell petroleum plant (due for demolition in 2002) and overlooked by a lurid high-rise development, the beach doesn't win any beauty prizes. Nevertheless, it has a refreshingly local feel to it. The best part of the beach is at the western end, where there is a stretch of fine black sand, a summer go-cart track, five-a-side soccer pitch, children's playground and changing facilities. The beach's promenade is popular with locals on weekends, out to take the sea air or on their way to the cafés and excellent restaurants (see reviews on p.255). In summer, there are also watersports, including jet skiing and canoeing.

EAST TO RIBEIRA DE JOÃO GOMES

To the east of the city centre, a small river, the Ribeira de Santa Luzia, runs along a concrete channel beneath bougainvillea and disappears under Avenida do Mar close to the mouth of another small river, the **Ribeira de João**

Gomes. The area between the rivers is largely given over to bustling shopping streets, including busy **Rua Dr Fernão Ornela**, as well as offices and a growing number of hotels. It also contains the **Mercado dos Lavradores** – the central market – one of Funchal's liveliest and most characterful spots, along with a few museums of note: the **Museu de Electricidade**, which traces the history of the island's sources of energy; **IBTAM**, a handicrafts centre and museum; and the **Museu Franco**, dedicated to the excellent works of two local artists.

Museu de Electricidade

Map 2, F4. Rua Dom Carlos 1. Tues–Sun 10am–12.30pm & 2–6pm; 400$00/€2.

Set in the high-ceilinged, former Central Power Station of Funchal, the **Museu de Electricidade** is a surprisingly engaging museum charting the history of power and lighting in Madeira through exhibits of dials, generators, photos, illustrations and real street lamps. None of these is particularly interesting in its own right, but the exhibits do help record some interesting facets of island life: how olive oil was used to light people's houses until 1846 when the first petroleum oil lamps appeared; how the British ran the first electricity supply in 1897 (it was not until the end of the World War II that power was literally in the hands of the local council); and how during the war, power shortages made it necessary to develop water-powered generators, leading to HEP in the 1950s, still one of the primary sources of energy on the island today. It gives a fascinating insight into how modern technology has slowly filtered into and influenced lifestyles on the remote Atlantic islands. Neighbouring Porto Santo only received its own electricity in 1954. Upstairs there is a more general exhibition, interesting for its insights into the harnessing of alternative energy.

Mercado dos Lavradores

Map 2, F3. Mon–Thurs 7am–4pm, Fri 7am–8pm, Sat 7am–2pm.

Housed in a yellow building faced with *azulejos*, Funchal's main market, the **Mercado dos Lavradores**, on Rua Brigadeiro Oudinot, sells a colourful array of fish, exotic fruits and local crafts. It was designed in the 1930s by Edmundo Tavares, one of Portugal's best-known twentieth-century architects, and was completed in 1941. Much of its appeal lies in Tavares' design, which consists of layered arcades set around a central, plant-filled courtyard. The design gives the whole place a theatrical air, with the upper tiers thronged with tourists and locals surveying the activity below. The lower tier, set at the back of the market, con-tains counter after counter of scabbard fish, vast octopi, tuna steaks the size of frisbees and other weird-looking Atlantic fish. The main ground-floor area is a medley of stalls selling vegetables, exotic fruit and wickerwork. The upper floor has more fruit and vegetables, along with dried chillies, clothes and pet budgies. Fridays and Saturday mornings are the busiest times, when local farmers visit to sell their produce, though it remains pretty lively all week.

Rua Dr Fernão Ornelas and around

Map 2, F3.
Rua Dr Fernão Ornelas is one of the busiest shopping streets in the city, an odd medley of traditional stores and designer clothes shops. Turn right at the end of the street past orchid sellers and head up the arcaded Rua Cooperativa Agricula which takes you to Praça do Carmo, an attractive square full of outdoor café tables and surround-ed by another warren of narrow pedestrianzed shopping streets. The square is dominated by the **Igreja do Carmo**, a seventeenth-century Baroque church which contains the

tomb of the Conde de Carvalhal, the original owner of Quinta Palheiro Ferreiro (see p.100).

Museu de Francisco Franco

Map 2, F2. Tues–Sat 10am–12.30pm & 2–6pm; 300$00/€1.5.

On the corner of Rua de João de Deus and Rua Alferes Veiga Pestana is one of Funchal's smallest but most interesting art museums, the **Museu de Francisco Franco**. Set in a distinctive 1940s building with a circular patio and conical roof fronted by tree ferns, the museum is dedicated to Francisco Franco, Madeira's most important modern artist. Franco was born in Funchal in 1885. His career took off after he exhibited with Picasso in Boston in 1927, the year he created his Monument to João Gonçalves Zarco (see p.59). Black-and-white photos show the proud unveiling of the statue on Avenida Arriaga in 1934. The monument attracted the attention of Portugal's dictator Salazar, who was well known for his rampant nationalism. Salazar commissioned Franco to create statues of great Portuguese heroes: kings, bishops and, of course, himself. Many of the statues are now in mainland Portugal, though the museum displays the plaster moulds that the artist used, along with Salazar's bust cast in bronze (1934–36). What is most impressive about Franco's works is his wide range of styles, which vary from classical to distinctly modern; he was heavily influenced by Rodin, as is seen for example in *Monument to the Victims of the Bombing 1916*, an expressionist work showing a despairing figure, arms flung in the air, inspired by the German bombing of Funchal in 1916, during which French warships were sunk in the harbour. The museum also contains works by Franco's brother, Henriques, a highly respected painter himself, known for his portrayal of scenes from Madeiran everyday life, and whose work is characterized by distinctive bright colours and clear lines.

EAST TO RIBEIRA DE JOÃO GOMES

IBTAM

Map 2, G2. Rua do Visconde de Anadia 44. Mon–Fri 10am–12.30pm & 2.30–5.30pm; 400$00/€2.

A minute's walk away from the Museu de Francisco Franco is the Instituto de Bordados Tapeçaria e Artesanato de Madeira (Institute of Embroidery, Tapestry and Craftsmanship of Madeira), or **IBTAM**, set up in 1978 to monitor standards of Madeira's longstanding handicrafts industry and provide training. The tradition of embroidery, in particular, goes back a long way, a continuation of a skill practised in Portuguese convents since the Middle Ages.

Of most interest to visitors is the institute's handicrafts **museum** on the upper floor. The varied exhibits and photographs give some insight into the importance of crafts to the island's art and culture. Perhaps the most interesting exhibit – if only for its size – is an enormous tapestry entitled *Allegory of Madeira*, hung in the main hallway, halfway up the stairs. It was created by Gino Romeli and took over three years to complete, from 1958 to 1961. Three girls were employed to sew the seven million stitches that make up a Madeiran landscape. Other highlights include an Irish linen cloth embroidered by Madeirans for Queen Elizabeth II's visit to Lisbon in 1957; a bedchamber as it would have looked in the nineteenth century, when British eighteenth-century furniture and Madeiran embroidery was all the rage; and rather saucy handkerchiefs from 1935 to 1940 embroidered with scantily clad women. Many of Madeira's embroiderers have been captured in evocative black-and-white photographs by Vicente Gomes da Silva (see p.66), whose images of workers around the island in the early twentieth century are perhaps the highlight of the collection.

EAST TO RIBEIRA DE JOÃO GOMES

THE ZONA VELHA AND AROUND

The most historic and gritty part of Funchal is the **Zona Velha**, or Old Town, east of the centre, an atmospheric area of cobbled streets, dotted with yellow-flowering mimosa trees and lined with former fishermen's houses, some of which date back to the first colonization of Funchal in the fifteenth century. Once rather run down, much of the district has been spruced up recently, and a number of restaurants, firmly geared to tourists, has appeared. Its residential population is still predominantly working class, however, and forms quite a distinct community; in the evenings, locals chat on the doosteps and children play in the street.

The focal point of the area is Largo do Corpo Santo, a cobbled square, on one side of which sits the small **Capela do Corpo Santo**. It is believed to be one of the oldest chapels on the island, dating from the sixteenth century, and is dedicated to São Pedro, the patron saint of fishermen.

From the chapel, it's a short walk down the cobbled Rua do Portão de São Tiago to the **Forte de São Tiago**, fomerly the city's main fort and now a modern art museum. Beyond is the popular **Barreirinha Lido** and the Baroque **Igreja de Santa Maria Maior**.

The newly opened cable car at the eastern end of Avenida do Mar is the quickest way up to the hilltop suburb of Monte. More details are given on p.95.

Museu do Club Sport Marítimo

Map 2, G4. Mon–Fri 9am–noon & 2–7pm; free.

Near the market end of Rua Dom Carlos, at No. 14, a small gold plaque marks the **Museu do Club Sport**

Marítimo, a museum dedicated to the exploits of the city's most successful soccer team (see box on p.318). You can also buy tickets for matches at the downstairs desk. Anyone interested in soccer will enjoy a quick look round the upstairs room, full of row upon row of glittering – and not so shiny – trophies, pennants and photographs, with pride of place given to the cup that the team won at the 1925–26 Portuguese Championship.

Forte de São Tiago and the Museu de Arte Contemporânea

Map 2, H5. Mon–Sat 10am–12.30pm & 2–5.30pm; 350$00/€1.75.
Set on a little rocky outcrop overlooking the sea is the **Forte de São Tiago**, with its distinctive ochre walls. Built in 1614 to defend the city from pirate attack, the structure later became what must have been a cramped home to 3500 British troops stationed in Funchal during the Napoleonic wars. Britain was keen to protect its commercial interests in Madeira from the French, who briefly occupied mainland Portugal before the British pushed them back. In 1803, the fort was again occupied when it became a temporary shelter to the thousands of locals made homeless by the devastating floods which hit the capital. The army continued to use the fort until 1922. It now houses a couple of small and rather uninspiring museums, though it is worth the admission price just to wander round its rambling ramparts.

Overlooking the courtyard is the **Military Room**, containing a tiny, rather dull collection of military maps, illustrations and weapons. You're better off following the arrows to the former military governor's house which since 1992 have been occupied by the **Museu de Arte Contemporânea**, a rather hit-and-miss collection of contemporary Portuguese art from 1960 to the present.

The top floor contains some interesting photographic works by Helena Almeida (1971), a controversial black panel by Fernando Calhau (1994) and some powerful, Dali-esque skulls by Miguel Branco (1992). The floor below, its ancient stone decor contrasting nicely with the modern art, contains some attractive work by Pedro Cabrita Ries, notably *Naturália Parte 6* (1996), along with Rui Sanches' cracked tile effects in pale blue and white. Finally, the bottom floor displays some colourful works by Eduardo de Freitas, one of the few Madeiran artists on show.

The Barreirinha Lido

Map 2, I5. Daily 9am–6pm; 200$00/€1, extra charges for use of chairs and sun umbrellas.

Beyond the Forte de São Tiago and set into the cliffs, the **Barreirinha Lido** is a much more modest and laid-back version of the lido complex to the west of the city (see p.80). The lido comprises a gym, café, changing rooms and a seawater pool, just about deep enough to submerge yourself in and certainly great for kids. You can also swim off a small stony beach. There are lots of attentive staff and the place attracts a friendly, local crowd.

Igreja de Santa Maria Maior and Rua de Santa Maria

Map 2, I5.

On Sunday mornings the focus of activity switches from the lido to the Baroque eighteenth-century **Igreja de Santa Maria Maior** opposite, one of the most attractive churches in the city. The church was built on the site of an earlier chapel constructed to commemorate the plague of 1538. There is still a procession every May 1 in honour of the plague victims. Outside, the little courtyard with its lofty palm has great views over the sea.

From the church, the narrow **Rua de Santa Maria** leads back into the city. This is one of Funchal's oldest streets and is lined with atmospheric shops and little workshops, such as No. 237, a tiny hat workshop where the owner patiently assembles straw boaters.

The middle section of Rua de Santa Maria is where you'll find some of the Zona Velha's best-known **restaurants**: *Arsénio's, O Jango* and *Marisa* (see reviews on p.257).

JARDIM BOTÂNICO (BOTANICAL GARDENS) AND AROUND

A kilometre or two inland from the seafront lie the leafy suburbs of Rochina, Bom Sucesso and Boa Vista, containing some wonderful parks and gardens. The most popular is the **Jardim Botânico**, boasting a superb collection of native and rare plant species, as well as a parrot and tropical-bird garden. Just below the botanical gardens lies the **Jardim Orquídea**, a small orchid farm, where you can see a dazzling display of these exotic flowers nearly all year round. Orchids also grow in abundance amid the colonial-style splendour of the **Quinta da Boa Vista**. All the gardens lie on an incredibly steep hillside, so it's best to get a bus or taxi up. The walk back down, however, will only take you twenty minutes.

The Jardim Botânico and Jardim Orquídea are served by **buses** #29 and #30 from Praça dos Lavradores or #31 from opposite the marina.

Jardim Botânico

Map 3, F5. Caminho do Meio. Daily 8am–6pm.

The **Jardim Botânico**, or Botanical Gardens, consists of a series of lawns, woods and grottoes, ideal for a walk or a picnic. Furthermore, the views back over the city make it an unmissable spot, even if you don't know your roses from your rhododendrons. The grounds were once part of a private estate, the Quinta do Bom Successo, owned by the Reid family (see p.79), who laid out the gardens as a private park. It was opened to the public in 1960 and is now run by the regional government as a research and conservation station. The gardens contain some 2000 exotic plant species from five continents, including the papyrus grass, anthurium and bird-of-paradise – although most plants are either indigenous or from the Azores, Cape Verde or the Canaries.

Entry to the Jardim Botânico costs 350$00/€1.75 and includes entry to the Museu de História Natural and Loiro Parque; free on 21 March, 30 April, 1 July and 27 September; ⓦ www.madinfo.pt/organismos/botanico.

Close to the park entrance is the **Museu de História Natural** (daily 9am–12.30pm & 1.30–5.30pm; free), a rather quaint collection of pickled fish, dusty stuffed birds, mammals and fossils which have been collected from round the island. The highlight is a giant, ten million-year-old fossilized tree heather, found in an underground cavern that was discovered during tunnelling for one of Madeira's new roads; the cavern was found to be full of similar fossils, but most have been left *in situ*.

Behind the museum paths wind uphill through laurel woods and past a small lake to the garden's café, a pleasant enough spot, though selling somewhat over-priced cakes, ice creams and soft drinks. Below the café, the gardens are more formal and heavily cultivated, including vibrantly coloured bedding plants resembling a patchwork quilt.

Back near the natural history museum is an extraordinary collection of **cacti and succulents**, which range from tiny, flowering cacti to enormous spiky ones, their spines draped in cobwebs. Continuing down past the odd open-air amphitheatre, you come to a series of palm trees, a good place to sit and cool off in the shade.

From here, you can hear the distinctive squawks of the **Loiro Parque** (hours as for the Jardim Botânico; 350$00/€1.75), entered from the Botanical Gardens, or via a separate entrance on Caminho do Meio. This bird garden has a colourful array of tropical birds, including macaws, green and crimson parakeets and salmon-crested cockatoos, as well as less glamorous ducks and geese. Children will particularly enjoy chasing the peacocks which roam about at will, or stumbling across the giant tortoise.

Jardim Orquídea

Map 3, F6. Rua Pita da Silva 37. Daily 9am–6pm.

A couple of hundred metres below the parrot park in the suburb of Bom Sucesso lies the **Jardim Orquídea**, or orchid farm. Some 50,000 plants are grown here, representing around 4000 varieties of orchid. The main flowering season is from November to April, though there are usually some species in bloom at other times. The farm is based in an ordinary-looking suburban house, with spectacular views of the city from its terrace. True orchid-philes will be interested in the technicalities of orchid cultivation, which is explained here in great detail. You can see the laboratory where the orchids are cultivated in sterile conditions before being planted out in the soil, then look round the greenhouses where the different varieties of flower are in bloom. Each stage of the cultivation procedure is clearly explained, and if you want to buy a plant (packaged in easily transportable glass jars), those suitable for growing in colder climates are well labelled.

Quinta da Boa Vista

Map 3, F6. Rua Lombo da Boa Vista. Mon–Sat 9am–5.30pm; 400$00/€2.

More attractive than the Jardim Orquídea, but with few labels and little information about the plants, the **Quinta Boa Vista** boasts one of Madeira's most important collection of orchids. This attractive eighteeth-century *quinta* is owned by the family of Cecil Garton, former Honorary British Consul to Madeira. Now he and his wife Betty manage the *quinta*'s orchid collection which features many rare species. Covered areas under green gauze shelter row upon row of potted orchids in a spectacular range of shapes and colours. It's best to come early, as it can get rather crowded. Look out for the Common Dumb Cane, so-called because of its milky sap which makes it hard to speak if you drink it. The sap is used in the Caribbean as a contraceptive; indeed, the Nazis considered using it as a mass sterilization tool against the Jews until it was realized how many of the plants would be needed for the operation. Visitors can buy more conventional orchids from reception; you can get them delivered to your hotel the day before your departure.

Just below the orchid houses there is a lovely lawned area set out with tables and chairs in front of the old *quinta*; tea and cake is sometimes served on the lawns, which have superb views over the city.

Bus #32 runs to the Quinta da Boa Vista from Avenida do Mar or Rua dos Profetas, near the Mercado dos Lavradores. Take the bus to the end of the line, then walk downhill to the *quinta*.

Around Funchal

Whilst you could easily spend a week in Funchal itself, it would be a shame not to explore the surrounding area, which contains some of Madeira's best sites. The most absorbing of these – and the most accessible – is **Monte**, a hilltop town right above Funchal, containing Madeira's holiest church and spectacular gardens. Getting to and from Monte is half the fun: up on the cable car from Funchal and down on an exhilarating dry toboggan run. A short bus ride east of Funchal, **Quinta do Palheiro Ferreiro** – more popularly known as Blandy's – is a must for garden lovers, with a riot of tropical and more familiar plants set in extensive grounds, as well as being the starting point of an easy *levada* walk back to Funchal. East of here, the wealthy hilltop village of **Camacha** enjoys great views over the south coast, and is now very much given over to a thriving wickerwork trade. A more down-to-earth face of Madeira is revealed at **Câmara de Lobos**, a little to the west of Funchal, one of the few traditional working-class fishing villages on the island; its claim to fame is that Winston Churchill often came to paint its pretty harbour. The village sits near **Cabo Girão**, one of the world's highest seacliffs, and a dizzying sight from above or at sea level from the tropical farm-estate at **Fajã dos Padres**. Finally, heading inland from Funchal, the picturesque village of **Curral das**

Freiras, set in a valley surrounded by the island's highest peaks, gives a taste of the extraordinary mountainous interior of Madeira and offers great walking possibilities.

Reviews of accommodation, restaurants and bars around Funchal start on p.227, p.264 and p.294 respectively.

MONTE AND AROUND

Map 3, E4. Funchal city buses #20 and #21, from Praça da Autonomia, and #48, from the Hotel Zone (every 10min); also by cable car from the Zona Velha (see below).

The attractive hilltop town of **MONTE** lies a 6km climb northeast of Funchal. At 550m above sea level, its wooded slopes, cool air and dramatic views established it in the mid-nineteenth century as a healthy retreat for the island's wealthy residents and as a popular base for transatlantic passengers stopping off in Madeira. Numerous *quintas* were built in and around the town to put people up before the first hotel appeared in Funchal at the end of the nineteenth century. In 1893, a rack and pillion railway was constructed to serve the town, terminating at Terreiro da Luta (see p.98). Unfortunately, the steam-boilers that powered the trains proved alarmingly prone to exploding – four people were killed in one explosion in 1919 – and though the service struggled on until 1939, people lost faith in its safety and it was finally discontinued. After World War II, Monte's fortunes diminished as Funchal took over as the main centre for tourism, though it has remained one of the most popular excursions from the capital.

Though Monte is dominated by the church of **Nossa Senhora do Monte**, Madeira's prime pilgrimage destination for Catholics, it has become more popular with tourists for its secular attractions. First of these is the **cable**

car, which whisks you up on a hair-raising ride from Funchal, but even more famous is the exhilarating **toboggan run**, which propels people back down the hill towards the capital; you'll see the dapper-looking drivers lined up on the street beneath the church in pristine white trousers and shirts, with straw boaters and goatskin boots. Before you head off down the run, however, there are a number of sights other than the church worth exploring: notably the extraordinary **Jardins Tropicais do Monte Palace**, Madeira's most spectacular park – part gardens and part museum – and the monument at **Terreiro da Luta**, a short detour to the north.

The cable car

Daily: May–Sept 8.45am–8.30pm; Oct–April 8.45am–6pm;
Ⓦ www.madeiracablecar.com; 2500$00/€12.50 return,
1500$00/€7.50 single.

Opened in September 2000, the **cable car from Funchal** is quite a feat of engineering, its glass bubbles sliding between huge green metal pillars erected between Funchal's buildings. The ten-minute ride is every bit as exhilarating as the toboggan run as you ascend (or descend) over Funchal's rooftops from or to the Zona Velha at the seafront, with superb views over the harbour en route. The cable car arrives in Monte at Largo das Barbosas, a minute's walk from the Caminho das Barbosas entrance to the Jardins Tropicais do Monte Palace; to reach the main square, Largo da Fonte, continue down Caminho das Barbosas for around 200m.

Largo da Fonte and around

Buses from Funchal stop just in front of **Largo da Fonte**, Monte's leafy main square, a small cobbled expanse shaded

MONTE AND AROUND

by trees, where you'll find a taxi rank, a couple of nice cafés and numerous stalls selling woolly hats and other tourist tack. The square is centred round a little bandstand, overlooking the verdant **Parque do Monte** public gardens, which spread down the gully below. The park is bordered to the east by parts of the old viaduct of the defunct rack and pillion railway, whose arches are covered in vegetation. To the east of the square is the **Fonte da Virgem**, a little fountain with a shrine to Nossa Senhora do Monte.

Nossa Senhora do Monte

If you take the steps winding up behind the Fonte, you'll come to the twin-towered **Nossa Senhora do Monte** (Our Lady of the Mountain), the island's most important church, whose terrace offers superb views over Funchal. The church stands on the site of one of Madeira's first chapels, built in 1470 by the appropriately named Adam Gonçalves Ferreira, one of a pair of twins (his sister was called Eve) who were the first children born on the island. The original chapel was levelled in the 1748 earthquake and was replaced by the current Baroque structure in 1818, an attractive building with low-hanging chandeliers and a ceiling painted with religious images.

The church is considered to be particularly holy because of a tiny **statue of the Virgin**, which now sits amid lavish ornamentation on the central altar. The statue was found by a shepherdess in Terreira da Luta (see p.98), a little to the north of Monte, in the fifteenth century; *azulejos* panels on the front of the church depict the moment of discovery. Today, during the Feast of Assumption on August 14–15, the church forms a pilgrimage site for the devout, who climb its 74 rough basalt steps on their knees to pay homage to the statue – a feat which looks as painful as it sounds – before the statue is taken out to form the head of a procession. Far less solemn is the *romaria* in the evening, a festival with music and fireworks.

The church also has a second claim to fame: it is the final resting place of Emperor Karl I of Austria and King of Hungary, the last Hapsburg monarch, who was deposed in 1918 at the end of World War I after just two years in power. Karl was married to Princess Zita, the granddaughter of Dom Miguel I of Portugal and, when in 1921 Karl was banished from his homeland, he came to Madeira with Zita in the hope that the warm climate would improve his health. He first stayed at *Reid's* before moving to the Quinta Gordon in Monte, hoping that the mountain air would be a tonic. Instead he died of pneumonia a year later aged 35. Today his **tomb** sits on the left side of the altar in a rather spartan side room.

Jardins Tropicais do Monte Palace

Mon–Fri 9am–6pm, Sat 9am–5pm; 1500$00/€7.50.

From the foot of the church steps, it is a short walk left along Caminho das Babosas to the entrance of the **Jardins Tropicais do Monte Palace**. The park tries to justify its hefty admission fee with a "free" wine tasting – a ploy to get you into the park café as much as anything else – but it is worth paying: the park is as much museum as simply gardens, filled with fountains, statues and works of art, as well as a spectacular range of plants, all spilling down seventeen acres of verdant ravine towards the eighteenth-century home of the park's owner, José Rodrigues Berardo, a local tobacco magnate and one of Portugal's leading artistic benefactors. As well as setting up the park's imaginative range of exhibits, his Berardo Foundation for Art, Culture, Technology and Science has introduced to the gardens rare cycads – prehistoric tree ferns from southern Africa (there are now more of this species here than anywhere else in the world) – azaleas and heathers from northern Europe and indigenous plants from Madeira.

The park entrance lies above an **Art and Minerals Museum** (same hours as park; free), displaying semi-precious stones and temporary exhibitions, which often feature some of Berardo's modern art collections. From the entrance, paths descend past koi fish ponds down a series of steps into the ravine. One path is lined with a row of 40 decorative modern *azulejos* panels, each showing key moments in Portugal's history – the most dramatic is the one of the Great Earthquake in Lisbon in 1755, which is followed by a series showing the rebuilding of the capital. Just beyond here, a formal Japanese-style garden shelters 166 colourful glazed panels tracing the 450-year trading alliance between Portugal and Japan.

Further down the slope spectacular plants form the back-drop to large, flamboyant stone Manueline doors, which date back to the Golden Age of Portuguese navigation. Near the doors, just in front of the park's main lake, you can't miss the world's largest ceramic vase, which stands at 5.345m high and weighs 555 kilos.

Southeast of the lake, a path leads down to the park **café**, where you can claim your free glass of Madeira; it also sells the usual range of snacks and cold drinks. Heading back along the path, you'll see the (closed) Monte Palace itself, which dominates the front of the park and offers great views from its terrace. Enclosed arches behind the *quinta* shelter glass cabinets displaying porcelain.

Terreiro da Luta

Map 3, F4. São Roque do Faial bus #103 from Monte (Mon–Sat 4 daily, Sun 2 daily) or bus #138 (Mon–Fri 2 daily, Sun 1 daily).

Before heading back to Funchal, it's worth considering a short detour 3km north along the EN103 to the impressive hillside monument of **Terreiro da Luta**, which marks the spot where a shepherdess found the statue of the Virgin (see p.96). It's a steep climb to get there, so if you don't have a car it's best to take a bus (ask for Terreiro da Luta and you'll be dropped 200m or so from the statue) or a taxi, but the walks back down are great. You can descend down the road you came up on, or take the steep, zigzagging stone steps which start just before the junction between the E201 and E103 just below the monument.

Composed of a 5.5m column supporting a statue of the Virgin, the **monument** was built in 1927 as a memorial to the end of World War I. At the height of the war in 1916, Madeira came under attack from German submarines, during which a French ship was hit, killing several people. The Madeirans prayed at the altar of the church in Monte and vowed to build the statue if the war was stopped. This they duly did and today, at the foot of the statue, you can still see the anchor chains from the French ship that was destroyed in the bombardment. Just by the statue is the station building which formed the terminus for the short-lived Funchal–Monte railway line (see p.94). Opened in 1912, it now acts as a restaurant and reception room for functions laid on by cruise ships.

The toboggan run

Daily 9am–6pm; 1800$00/€9 for the 10min ride to Livramento; minimum of two people.

For most people, the most memorable experience to be had in Monte is a ride on the **toboggan run**, which departs from the bottom of the steps to the church on Caminho das Barbosas. The toboggans are basically giant wicker baskets, known as *carros de cesto* (basket cars), attached to wooden runners, which are oiled using a greasy rag. Until the mid-nineteenth century, similar baskets were pulled up and down the slopes by horses and bullocks, but in 1850 they were adapted so that two drivers could control their descent to carry produce to the town's market, as well as carrying local landowners into town. They quickly became popular with visiting tourists, and Ernest Hemingway, who had his fair share of adventures, described the ride as one of the most exhilarating experiences in his life.

Today this means of transport continues for tourists alone. The drivers seat you in the baskets, then get you going with the aid of ropes, hopping onto the back as you pick up speed. With the drivers behind you, it can be pretty scary as you plummet downhill, though in fact you are not going as fast as it feels, and the baskets are easily stopped if a car approaches: the drivers' goatskin boots have special rubber-treaded soles that act as brakes. The drivers manoeuvre the baskets over manhole covers and past potholes in the road, though it feels most alarming when the sleds occasionally start to veer down at an oblique angle when either of the runners needs extra oil. Most rides end up a couple of kilometres downhill in the suburb of Livramento, where there are a couple of cafés, a bus stop and usually a taxi waiting to take people back into Funchal. Previously, rides continued all the way into Funchal, and you can still negotiate a ride into town, but as the roads become busier and less appealing the closer you get to the centre, it's probably best to opt for the shorter ride.

QUINTA DO PALHEIRO FERREIRO (BLANDY'S)

Map 3, G5. Horários do Funchal city bus #36 (8 daily) or #37 (Mon–Fri 10 daily, Sat & Sun 6 daily) from Praça da Autonomia. Mon–Fri 9.30am–12.30pm; 500$00/€2.50.

Better known as Blandy's, the estate of **Quinta do Palheiro Ferreiro** lies just 8km northeast of Funchal and is a must for those into formal gardens, as well as being the starting point of one of the easiest and most accessible *levada* walks on the island – the **Levada dos Tornos**. It is also the site of one of Madeira's two excellent **golf courses**.

Buses to the gardens are fairly infrequent; as the gardens close at 12.30pm, your best bet is to aim for the 8.50am or 9.45am services.

The gardens

The 30-acre estate of Quinta do Palheiro Ferreiro was founded by the Portuguese Count of Carvalhal in the early nineteenth century, when a *quinta* and the Baroque chapel were built in the middle of formal gardens and grounds stocked with deer. Later that century, the Count was forced to flee Madeira to England during the Miguelite uprising (see p.340), and when he returned to the island, he introduced some of the gardening techniques he had encountered in England – at 550m in altitude, the cool climate is similar to Britain's, allowing trees such as oaks, beech and chestnuts to thrive. He also introduced ornamental ponds, and planted camellia trees as wind breaks. The mature, vivid red-flowering camellia trees are now a highlight when they flower from December to around April.

However, the Count of Carvalhal's descendants lacked the financial clout of the founder, and in 1884 the estate was bought out by the powerful Blandy family, who had settled in Madeira after the Napoleonic wars and stayed on to set up Blandy's Madeira Wine Company in Funchal, amongst numerous other concerns. At Quinta do Palheiro Ferreiro, the Blandys established their family home and added plants from round the world – the family continue to run the estate today.

QUINTA DO PALHEIRO FERREIRO (BLANDY'S)

THE LEVADA DOS TORNOS

From Quinta do Palheiro Ferreiro you can easily join the central section of the **Levada dos Tornos**, one of Madeira's newer *levadas*, which you can follow back towards Funchal – about a ninety-minute walk, if you don't stop at either of the two tea houses en route. Though not one of Madeira's prettiest *levadas*, it is the most accessible from Funchal and a good taster for other *levada* walks; it also offers great views over the capital.

To reach the *levada*, turn right out of the Quinta do Palheiro Ferreiro and head uphill until you come to a junction (by two small cafés), where you turn left. Follow the road for 100m, after which the *levada* is clearly signposted on the left. At first, the *levada* passes close by the busy EN102 road above an unattractive block of council houses – you'll see the golf course on the hill to the left and distant views of Funchal harbour ahead of you – but it soon plunges into shady, sweet-smelling eucalyptus woods, all the time running roughly parallel to the road, and crossing it at one stage.

After about twenty minutes you come to a sign on the left to *Jasmine Tea House* (see p.295). This makes for a pleasant place to stop and refuel, though if you want more of a Portuguese flavour, continue for another ten minutes along the

Buses drop you at the entrance to the gardens, from where a cobbled track leads down to the left past the back of the old *quinta* building to a coach and taxi rank. Just in front of the *quinta* you will see the original **chapel**, with stained-glass windows in the turret casting coloured light over the bright walls. Beyond here, the public areas consist of a series of formal flower beds, topiary, ponds and lush lawns, which combine the formal English style with a tropical exuberance, epitomized by the mingling of blackbird song with the hum of cicadas.

levada to the *Hortensia Gardens Tea House* (see p.296).

If you feel you've come far enough, you can catch bus #47 from either tea house back to Funchal (Mon–Sat 6 daily, Sun 5 daily). Alternatively, continue along the *levada*, which follows the contours of the valley away from the road beneath more towering eucalyptus trees. Eventually you will cross a steep road and pass a small weir just before another *quinta* building, Quinta do Pomar. Here, the path leads up to the right away from the *levada*, then left, skirting the back of the *quinta* and a distinctive chapel, before rejoining the *levada*. Just past here the path leads through a gate and arrives at a road.

Turn left onto the road and follow it steeply downhill. The main road veers left after 150m or so, but continue straight on down a very steep, semi-stepped cobbled track. After five minutes you will reach a junction with two restaurants on your right. If you have strong knees, you can continue straight on down the steep Caminho do Meio, which will bring you out in front of the Botanical Gardens after another 5–10 minutes (see p.89). Alternatively, turn right at the junction along the busier Caminho das Voltas, which winds more gently downhill – bus #29 (2 hourly) passes along this stretch on its way into Funchal – and after ten minutes you will come out by the Botanical Gardens' entrance.

Less formal is the untended, overgrown ravine to the west of the gardens, known as Inferno. A path leads down into a valley full of giant ferns and trailing morning glory vines before snaking back up to the entrance.

The golf course

To the east side of the gardens you will see the buggies serving the neighbouring 18-hole golf course, **Balancal Palheiro Golf** (☎291 795 161). Opened in 1994, the

QUINTA DO PALHEIRO FERREIRO (BLANDY'S)

course was designed by Cabell Robinson and is one of the most spectacular in Europe, with exhilarating views over the coast and Funchal. It lies adjacent to the grounds of the exclusive **hotel** belonging to the estate, the *Casa Velha do Palheiro* (see p.228). If you don't mind paying through the nose, you can take tea or drinks in the hotel bar or on the lawns in front.

CAMACHA

Map 3, H4. Autocarros da Camacha bus #29 (Mon–Fri 1–2 hourly, Sat & Sun 1 hourly); also bus #77 (5–6 daily).

Set in the heart of the island's willow plantations some 14km northeast of Funchal, **CAMACHA** is the centre of

THE LEVADA DA SERRA CHOUPANA

The gentle ninety-minute walk along the Levada da Serra Choupana from Vale Paraíso to Camacha takes you through some delightful woodland, with occasional striking views of the south coast. To get to the start, ask a taxi driver to take you to the Levada da Serra Choupana just beyond the village of Vale Paraíso on the ER102, 1.5km southwest of Camacha; the ride should cost around 600$00/€3. Alternatively, you could take bus #29 from Camacha, but only to Vale Paraíso itself – you would then need to walk for an extra twenty minutes up the ER203 road to the start of the *levada*.

For the first hour or so of the walk the *levada* is often more like a narrow stream as it follows the contours of wooded valleys of pine, oak and mimosas. Occasionally the landscape opens up to reveal the coast and the distant shape of the Ilhas Desertas.

After around an hour and a quarter you turn a corner to see the rooftops of the small village of Achadinha below you on

Madeira's money-spinning wicker industry and is home to one of the island's largest handicrafts centres – an ideal place to hunt down souvenirs. Even if you have no enthusiasm for such commercialism, there are other things to enjoy about the place, such as its wonderful views over the south coast and a couple of *levada* walks nearby.

The centre of the village is dominated by the wide **Largo da Achada**, an open cobbled square the size of a football pitch – probably because it used to be one. It is said that Harry Hinton, one of the wealthy Hinton family, who once owned the Ilhas Desertas (see p.53), brought a football back from a trip to England, which led to Portugal's first ever game of soccer being played out on Camacha's main square; to one side of the square, by a children's

your right. Here the path is lined with agapanthus, nasturtiums and broom bushes. After another five minutes you will join a road by a bus stop. Turn left on the road and follow the *levada* downhill through the village for a couple of minutes until it disappears under the road. Here you'll find *Snack Bar Moisés* (Mon–Sat 7am–11pm, Sun 8am–8pm), a surprisingly trendy little bar with rock music, an outdoor terrace and bottles of Murphys.

Past the café, the *levada* reappears next to the road. Follow the *levada* down the road for five minutes, then along a narrow path under trees. In another five minutes you reach another road, Caminho Municipal da Portela, where a wooden sign points downhill saying "Caminho da Portela Camacha". Turn right on the road here and head steeply downhill then up past a couple of concrete water tanks. Then it is downhill for another five minutes or so, past the soon-to-open *Quinta Levada da Serra* hotel, to the main road. Turn right here and it's a short walk past Camacha's church and down to the main square.

CAMACHA

playground, a sign reads "Aqui se jougou futebal pela primeira vez em Portugal 1875 Camacha" (Here football was played for the first time in Portugal, 1875 Camacha). The opposite side of the square is still given over to a five-a-side pitch, though nowadays Camacha's main team plays in a small stadium out on the Caniço road. The square also boasts a kiosk **café**, with outdoor tables and an outdoor jukebox, while around it are the village's taxi rank and bus stop, various shops and cafés and the small **Capela de São João**. Next to the chapel is a *miradouro* offering views over the south coast.

There's not a lot to Camacha away from the main square. A sign next to the *miradouro* points the way to the Levada dos Tornos (see p.102), which continues all the way to Quinta do Palheiro Ferreiro (around two hours' walk away) and beyond. To the north of the square, the Portela road heads uphill past the post office to the village's traditional **church**, a slightly run-down-looking Baroque building that seems to have been neglected in favour of the ungainly modern church by O Relógio (see below), whose thunderous chimes ring out every quarter of an hour. A hundred metres beyond the church, another sign to the right points you to the Levada da Serra Choupana (see box on p.104) for more attractive walking possibilities.

O Relógio

Shop: Mon–Fri 8.30am–8pm, Sat & Sun 8.30am–9.30pm.

The south side of Largo do Achada is dominated by the white **O Relógio** building, which has become the tourist nerve centre of the whole village. The building was once the home of a British merchant's family and was named after the *relógio* (clock) which was brought to Madeira from the parish church of Woolton near Liverpool by local

THE WICKER TRADE

Though **wicker** baskets had long been made in Madeira, the craft did not take off until the nineteenth century, when the same Hinton family that brought soccer to Madeira (see p.105) managed to persuade local farmers to diversify into wicker-weaving so as not to be over-reliant on the wine trade. At first the farmers sold the wicker products to local hotels, but soon they began to export: at that time there was a healthy demand for wicker – especially cane furniture – in Britain's former colonies. Demand has slumped somewhat since then, but better production techniques have helped craftsmen to make a wider range of products, and tourist demand helps the industry to employ around 2000 workers in and around Camacha.

Wicker comes from willows, which thrive in the damp ground around Camacha. The larger branches of the trees are used like conventional wood, while the narrower flexible branches are harvested in spring, then soaked, stripped of bark and dried to form wicker. Depending on the length of the branches, the wicker is then woven into baskets, furniture and other products.

doctor Michael Grabham in 1896. Though the distinctive nineteenth-century clocktower still exists, the building has since been considerably altered, and today consists of a **café** (see p.294), **restaurant** (see p.264) and shop. It also holds a regular slot for the island's most famous folk group, the Grupo Folclorico da Casa do Povo da Camacha, who play in the restaurant every Friday and Saturday night at 9.15pm (unless the group is away on tour).

The **shop** offers just about any possible souvenir you could wish for from Madeira: ceramics, ranging from tasteful traditional Portuguese pottery from Alcobaça on the mainland to downright tack; place mats inlaid with *azulejos*; individual *azulejos* tiles; liqueurs; Madeira wine; and rugs.

CAMACHA

●

But the shop is best known for its wicker (see box on p.107). Just about anything that could be made out of wicker is sold here: baskets, chairs, seats, umbrella stands, shelving units, toys, plant holders, trays and hats. Bigger items are to be found on level -1, including a giant wicker boat and a menagerie of wicker animals, among them a ten-foot giraffe. If you should find such quirky objects irresistible, they can be delivered abroad. A workshop can be found on level -2, in which you can watch the stuff being woven.

CÂMARA DE LOBOS

Map 3, B6. Rodoeste buses #1 or #96 (Mon–Fri 1–2 hourly, Sat & Sun hourly).

CÂMARA DE LOBOS, 8km west of Funchal, is one of the island's most atmospheric fishing villages, and is heavily promoted as Winston Churchill's favourite spot for painting. If you have a car, the nicest approach is on the old coast road: head through the Hotel Zone and the road winds up and down to the village in around twenty minutes – take the highway and the journey time is only ten minutes.

Despite the rash of new development spreading up the slopes around it, the central section of the village remains instantly likeable and charismatic, made up of a cluster of whitewashed houses, shops and bars strewn round a stony beach which doubles as the harbour.

The village was named after *lobos de mar* – monk seals ("sea wolves" in Portuguese) – who were frequent visitors to the harbour when it was first settled by Gonçalves Zarco in 1420, and who have since become the symbol for Madeira. There are no monk seals here nowadays, however (they are one of the most endangered species in the world, forced to the remoter shores of the Ilhas Desertas), and the local fishermen who hastened their departure now make their living out of catching *espada*, scabbard fish. Judging by the local poverty, this isn't a lucrative business (indeed the village is the only place you're likely to encounter begging on the island, usually in the form of children asking for sweets or coins), though the 7am **fish market** (Mon–Sat) in a concrete harbourside building is an animated affair. Usually it is over within an hour or so, with the proceedings usually moving to the nearest bar.

Largo da República and around

Buses drop you off at **Largo da República**, a little square to the west end of town centred round an iron bandstand. Here you'll find a cluster of cafés, bars and restaurants (see p.265 and p.295 for reviews) and the modern **tourist office** (Mon–Fri 9am–12.30pm & 2–5.30pm; ℡291 942 108), which can provide information about private *quartos* if you wish to stay the night. On the square opposite the tourist office, a bougainvillea-lined *miradouro* offers fantastic views over the cliffs of the nearby Cabo Girão (see p.114).

If you want to sample some of the local **wine**, from the square head up Rua de Santa over a bridge where you'll see huge barrels in the glass-fronted modern wine lodge, **Henrique e Henrique** (Sítio de Belém; ℡291 941 551; Mon–Fri 9am–1pm & 2.30pm–5.30pm). The produce here is every bit as good as you'll find in Funchal but the tours are usually quieter, and there are free tastings of the different types of Madeira wine, all of which are for sale.

However, the most interesting part of the town is the harbour. From Largo da República, the best approach is along the seafront **Rua Nova da Praia**, which skirts a rocky escarpment. As you approach the central section of the road, you'll see rows of crumbling houses, their windows draped in flapping washing, some of the poorest housing you'll encounter in Madeira.

CÂMARA DE LOBOS

WINSTON CHURCHILL IN MADEIRA

Before embarking on his political career, **Winston Churchill** worked as a reporter for the *Morning Post* during the Boer War and visited Madeira in October 1899 en route to South Africa. It must have made a big impression on him, because half a century later, following a heavy defeat in the 1945 general election and a minor stroke in 1949, he decided to return, hoping that the island would be "warm, paintable, bathable, comfortable, flowery" and the ideal place for him to write his memoirs. Churchill stayed at *Reid's* (see p.78), though the suite he was put up in was in a state of disrepair after the war years and ended up being partially furnished by donations from the island's British community. Here he wrote the fourth volume of his war memoirs, *The Hinge of Fate*.

When he wasn't writing, Churchill liked to relax by painting, and the harbour in Câmara de Lobos was one of his favourite subjects. He travelled to the village in a grey Rolls-Royce owned by the Leacocks, a wealthy family of wine merchants, who are said to have stuffed the Rolls' boot with drink to "help" him with his painting. A more famous tipple was the 1792 Madeira Churchill was served at *Reid's*, on receiving which the great man observed, "Here is a famous wine indeed, vintaged when Marie Antoinette was still alive", before placing a napkin over his arm and serving the guests at the table himself.

Churchill's visit to Madeira was cut short when Clement Attlee declared a new election date, and he returned to Southampton by flying boat in late 1949 to campaign for what proved to be another defeat. He is still remembered fondly on the island, and *Reid's Palace Hotel*'s top room remains the Churchill Suite, much improved from the time he stayed there himself.

The road ends above the harbour. From here you can turn right onto narrow Rua da Administração, which winds down to Rua Nossa Senhora da Conceição, the road linking the old town with the harbour. On your left you'll see the chapel of **Nossa Senhora da Conceição**, a fishermen's chapel said to be the second oldest on the island, which is decorated with pictures depicting scenes of shipwrecks and drownings in the life of St Nicholas, the patron saint of seafarers.

The harbour and around

Just below the chapel the road reaches the main **harbour**, the focus of the town, surrounded by colourful beached fishing boats, with new ones being constructed in boat yards at the back below a low cliff. After the day's catch, fishermen while their time away mending nets or playing animated games of cards on the upturned boats. It was this sort of scene that attracted Winston Churchill, who painted the harbour during his stay on the island in 1950 and is often credited with raising Madeira's profile as a holiday destination. If you head up the steps at the far end of the harbour along Caminho do Calhau, you'll find the spot where the British Prime Minister liked to sit – it is marked by a small plaque. Just above here is the *Churchill's Restaurant* (see p.265), which milks the Churchill connection for all it's worth, with countless pictures of the man painting in a Panama hat – there are even plans to open a Churchill museum next door.

After the harbour, the most characterful part of Câmara de Lobos is north of the Nossa Senhora da Conceição chapel: the best route is to head up Rua Nossa Senhora da Conçeição and then go left into **Rua João de Deus**, an atmospheric street full of traditional shops and bars. This leads up to the eighteenth-century **Igreja de São Sebastião**, an airy church complete with Baroque altar, overbearing chandeliers and a sky-blue ceiling painted with clouds; there are also some attractive *azulejos*. Continue past the church and you will find yourself back on Largo da República by the tourist office.

ESTREITO DE CÂMARA DE LOBOS

Map 3, B5. Rodoeste bus #7, #27 and #137 (7–12 daily).

The road from Câmara de Lobos to Cabo Girão winds up for 10km through traditionally terraced vineyards to **ESTREITO DE CÂMARA DE LOBOS**, the centre of one of Madeira's most important wine-producing areas. The village is decidedly quiet but a very attractive place to stop off, centred round a nineteenth-century **church**, with superb views over the surrounding valleys. There's also a

WINE PRODUCTION

Vines were one of the first plants brought over to Madeira by the early settlers (notably the Jesuits, who brought Sercial grapes from Germany, Vedelho from Italy, Bual from Burgundy and Malmsey from Crete), and the plants quickly thrived in the rich volcanic soil. As in northern Portugal, the vines, which can grow up to six feet in height, are supported by wooden frames, leaving space underneath for other crops to be grown.

The grape harvest on Madeira goes on for longer than anywhere else in Europe because of the differing altitudes the vines are grown at. The lower slopes are harvested for sweet grapes from the end of August, then again in October or November, when Muscatel grapes ripen. The upper slopes produce the Sercial vines, which grow up to altitudes of around 700m and are the last grapes to ripen, producing a drier wine. Autumn sees trucks laden with fruit jamming the roads on their way to the wine producers.

Until recently grapes were trod in cement tanks called *lagars* – treaders were spurred on by traditional musical accompaniment lively covered **market** (Mon–Sat), downhill from the central square, Sítio da Igreja, which is a good place to buy fresh local produce.

Estreito de Câmara de Lobos comes alive during the September Madeira Wine Festival, when the harvest is celebrated with traditional bare-foot wine treading and folk dancing.

If you continue downhill from the market past the flash *Estalagem Quinta do Estreito* (see p.227), you'll see a sign to the **Levada do Norte**, which offers some lovely walking opportunities. The *levada* runs north to the Boca da

– but today the majority are pressed mechanically. However, the foot-pressing techniques can still be enjoyed during the September Wine Festival in Estreito de Câmara de Lobos, and it continues on a less commercialized basis in some of the smaller vineyards in the north of the island.

Most of Madeira's grapes are used to produce fortified wines (see box on p.286), although some of them go into locally produced **table wines**. These are young and fruity, a bit like Portuguese *vinho verde*, such as *Canina* from Estreito de Câmara de Lobos, *Jaquet* from Seixal and Porto Moniz, and *Americana* from Porto da Cruz – this last, a drier and harsher wine, was actually banned by the EU in 1996, as it was said to be partially toxic, but it continues to appear in local bars. Little of Madeira's unfortified wine reaches the touristy restaurants, and the only wines to be produced commercially are *Atlantis Rosé* – from the Tinta Negra grapes grown largely around Estreito de Câmara de Lobos – and *Atlantis Branco Seco*, produced from Verdelho grapes mostly in the north of the island. Both of these are drinkable but not a patch on the wines from the Portuguese mainland.

Encumeada (see p.161), but the easiest walk from here is south to Quinta Grande (a 2hr 30min walk) and Campanário (a further 1hr 30min) through verdant vineyards, with beautiful views over the coast.

CABO GIRÃO

Map 3, A6. Rodoeste bus #154 stops near the cliffs (4 daily, 1 on Sat); only the 9am bus (10.30am on Sat) stops at the clifftop itself.

The road from Câmara de Lobos continues past Estreito de Câmara de Lobos roughly parallel with the Levada do Norte for some 4km, after which a sign points you to the top of **Cabo Girão**, one of the highest sea cliffs in Europe.

Cabo Girão was so named as Zarco got this far on his first exploration of Madeira's coast in 1418 before he did an about turn (*girão*) back to Funchal. There is a small and thankfully well-railed *miradouro* at the top, from which you can look straight down the 580m drop to the sea below you, with superb views across towards the distant Hotel Zone to the east. It's a lovely and tranquil spot, with the smell of pine and eucalyptus in the air. As you look down, you'll see that some of the cliff face has been terraced by farmers, who use the fertile and warm slopes to grow grapes and vegetables, though the slopes are so steep that sometimes farmers are lowered into their fields using ropes. Below the cliffs, some of the coastal strip is also divided into neat little fields.

To see the cliffs from the sea, take one of
the half-day boat tours to the waters below
Cabo Girão from Funchal (see p.55).

Opposite the *miradouro* there's a small **café** (Mon–Fri 9am–4pm), in a modern pink building, with an adjacent temporary exhibition space displaying art and photographs, usually related to the cliffs in some way.

FAJÃ DOS PADRES

Map 3, A6.

Continuing west from Cabo Girão, the road passes the sprawling hilltop town of Campanário, where there are several cafés catering to the walkers who end up here from the Levada do Norte, before bending down to rejoin the main highway linking Funchal to Ribeira Brava (see p.144).

Just before you rejoin the highway you'll see signs to **Fajã dos Padres**, a tropical fruit farm with its own beachside restaurant in a spectacular location below 300-metre-high cliffs. The farm was once part of the vast Quinta Grande estate, originally owned by Zarco's descendants but which was gradually sold to the Jesuits, who had acquired the whole estate by 1595. As well as farming the land, the Jesuits used Fajã dos Padres as a retreat, setting up a chapel, which has now been converted into an *adega* (wine lodge). The Jesuits ran the estate until 1759, when they were expelled from Portugal by the Marquês de Pombal, who was suspicious of the power they wielded. After the Jesuits left, Fajã dos Padres, which was then considered to be the most important Malvasia vineyard on Madeira, was sold to private owners and it remains in private hands.

Fajã dos Padres's sheltered position makes it ideal for growing vines, and the warmth radiating from the cliffs also helps the growth of tropical fruits, such as mangoes, bananas, papaya, avocado, passion fruit and guavas. No buses run here, though travel agents in Funchal sometimes arrange boat trips here and give guided tours of the *adega* and the tropical produce on the estate; try RR Tours, Rua Dr Pita, Funchal (map 3, D6; ☎291 764 733, ℻291 764 728), who offer half-day trips from 4600$00/€24 per person. Otherwise it is best reached by car or taxi; it is signed when you leave the main Funchal–Ribeira Brava road at the junction with the Cabo Girão road. You can park at the top of the cliff, from where you can follow steps weaving down the cliff, or you can go down the improbable and somewhat scary modern **lift** (Mon–Fri 11am–5.30pm, Sat & Sun 11am–7.30pm; 1500$00/€7.50 return per person; ticket valid for a free drink at the café), which glides down the sheer cliff face. There is a pricey **café-restaurant** just below the lift, sitting just above a stony beach where the calm waters are great for swimming. If you fancy a longer stay here, you can rent out renovated **cottages** from the old estate; for details call ☏291 944 538.

INLAND TO CURRAL DAS FREIRAS

To get an idea of the remote beauty and dramatic mountainous nature of Madeira's interior, it is well worth making the relatively easy 22km trek north of Funchal to **Curral das Freiras**, one of the most picturesque villages on the island. The easiest way to get there is by car from Funchal: head along the coast road through the Hotel Zone, following signs to the church of São Martinho along Caminho do Amparo and Caminho do Esmeraldo to **Pico dos Barcelos**, a good place to stop and admire the views back over the Hotel Zone. From here it's a straightforward journey to Curral das Freiras, though a short detour to **Eira do Serrado** will be rewarded by more stunning inland scenery high above the Curral das Freiras valley.

Pico dos Barcelos

Map 3, D6. Horários do Funchal city buses #9, #12 and #13 (every 20–30min).

High above the Hotel Zone the tree-topped *miradouro* of **PICO DOS BARCELOS** enjoys sweeping views over the coast to the south and the impressive twin-spired church of Santo António to the north. If you want to pause longer, there's a handy **café-restaurant** here, too, the *Barcelos à Noite* (see p.266).

From Pico dos Barcelos, the road passes out of Funchal's suburbs and up steeply through eucalyptus woods. As you climb higher, just as the trees give way to a Scottish-like landscape of gorse and grassland, look out for a small **cave** on the right with a natural spring, set up for barbecues.

Eira do Serrado

Map 3, C2. Autocarros da Camacha bus #81 (8–12 daily).

A little beyond the cave, a sign points to the right for the one-kilometre detour up a cobbled road to **EIRA DO SERRADO.** Here you'll find a car park and an unlikely shopping centre, restaurant and hotel complex. The **shop** sells all sorts of tourist tack, along with traditional woolly hats with earflaps and chunky knitted jumpers. The far side of the hotel marks the starting point of a stepped five-minute walk up to a **miradouro**, a spectacular and hair-raising rock ledge, overlooking Curral das Freiras in the horseshoe-shaped valley of the Ribeira dos Socorridos far below. The valley, whose three sheer sides tumble down from the serrated peaks of Madeira's highest mountains, was mistakenly believed for many years to have been a volcanic crater, but it is now known that its astonishing geographical shape was created in large part by the river itself.

Back at the car park, you will see another cobbled track, which winds steeply down towards Curral das Freiras, a manageable ninety-minute walk away. Though sometimes closed because of landslides, it offers a very beautiful approach to the village – indeed, until 1959, it was the only way to get there.

INLAND TO CURRAL DAS FREIRAS

Curral das Freiras

Map 3, B2. Autocarros da Camacha bus #81 (8–12 daily).

The precipitous road down from Eira do Serrado cuts through three tunnels and passes several stabilized rock-fall sites, before finally snaking down to the upper reaches of **CURRAL DAS FREIRAS**, one of the most traditional rural settlements on the island. The village was founded in the sixteenth century by the nuns of Funchal's Convento de Santa Clara, who had fled the capital after a vicious pirate attack in 1566, when around 1000 French pirates looted the island over a period of sixteen days, killing anyone who tried to stop them. Understandably scared for their safety, the nuns sought refuge in a remote valley almost at the centre of the island, which they had traditionally used for farming, and the village that subsequently grew up here became known as the Curral das Freiras, "the Nun's Valley".

The nuns (and their convent) are no longer around, and today's villagers survive on agriculture and, increasingly, on tourism – quite a feat considering that TV only arrived in the village in 1986. Life revolves round the cafés and bars (see p.295 for review) on the small **central square** – a superb spot, surrounded by a pretty collection of white, shuttered houses overhung with blossom, vines and orange trees.

In November Curral das Freiras holds the
Festa da Castanha, a lively chestnut fair.

Next to the town square, steps lead down to the attractive town church, **Nossa Senhora do Livramento**, built in the nineteenth century to replace the crumbling older church, which had been built by the nuns. It contains some lovely *azulejos* and – unusually for Portugal – an attractive stained-glass window. In front of the church there is a narrow cemetery neatly decorated with flowers and photos of the deceased.

To see the best of the village and its surroundings away from the square, take the path heading up the side of the *Nun's Valley Restaurante* (see p.265) for lovely views over flower-draped houses and little orange groves. A pleasant alternative is to follow the road for twenty minutes or so down the valley from the main square, meandering past more attractive houses and terraces stuffed with orchards and vegetable plots; at the bottom of the valley is a small stone **bridge** over the river, a great spot for a picnic.

INLAND TO CURRAL DAS FREIRAS

Eastern Madeira

With a wooded interior, craggy easternmost point, wild northern coast and relatively developed south, **eastern Madeira** offers some of the island's most diverse landscapes. The east is also more accessible than ever, thanks to the impressive **south-coast highway**, opened in 2000, which has reduced the journey time from Funchal to Madeira's second town, Machico, to around thirty minutes. Not surprisingly, this transport corridor has attracted development around it, including the package-holiday destinations of **Garajau**, **Caniço** and **Caniço de Baixo**, but if you carry on driving east, you'll soon find more typically Madeiran attractions. Perhaps the most unexpected of these is the charming little town of **Santa Cruz**, right by the airport, with a bustling market and its own lido complex. Just beyond the airport, **Machico**, set round a pebble and sand beach, is one of Madeira's most enjoyable and historic towns, full of lively cafés and restaurants. It is also a convenient base for visiting **Caniçal**, a former whaling centre now given over to marine conservation, and exploring the extraordinary craggy peninsula of **Ponta de São Lourenço**, which offers exhilarating clifftop walks and Madeira's best sandy beach at Prainha. Inland, it is a short hop to the mountaintop village of **Santo António da Serra**, a traditional retreat for the island's wealthy, who have established villas, a fabulous park and a superb golf course there. From Santo da Serra, you can take a spectacular drive over the mountain pass of **Portela** to the breezy fishing port of **Porto da Cruz,** one of the most picturesque villages on the dramatic north coast. From Porto da Cruz, you can now take a short cut back to Machico via the EU-funded Maroços road tunnel, opened in 2001, though a more memorable experience is to walk back along the dizzying **coastal path** via Lorano.

Reviews of accommodation, restaurants and bars in the east start on p.228, p.267 and p.296 respectively.

GARAJAU

Map 4, A7. Empresa de Automóveis do Caniço bus #155 (Mon–Sat 14 daily, Sun 9 daily); also bus #109 (Mon–Sat 4 daily, Sun 1 daily).

Perched on a rocky headland, a twenty-minute bus-ride east of Funchal, **GARAJAU** is little more than a strip of modern cafés, restaurants, shops and one giant hotel. The village gets its name from the *garajaus* – terns – that nest on the cliffs round here, and it is the cliffs that are the only reason to pay the place a visit.

From the main strip, a road forks to the right and winds down the cliff face past pristine new villas to a **statue of Christ** – a miniature version of those in Rio and Lisbon – more impressive for its location than for any artistic merit. Erected in 1927 on a rocky bluff, it offers fine views of Funchal and of passing tankers heading for the harbour. From the dusty car park in front of the statue, a small track snakes down to the right to a rocky **beach** at the foot of the cliffs. If you fancy a swim, however, you're better off heading for the **swimming pool** (with its own café) on the other side of the car park, though this is officially for guests of the hotel *Dom Pedro Garajau* at the top of the cliff.

CANIÇO

Map 4, B7. Empresa de Automóveis do Caniço bus #2, #109 and #155 (Mon–Fri 14 daily, Sun 9 daily); also Autocarros da Camacha bus #110 (Mon–Fri 7 daily, Sat & Sun 2 daily).

Set on a hillside just 10km east of Funchal along the south coast highway – and the same distance from the airport in the other direction – the thriving satellite town of **CANIÇO** originally owed its wealth to its position on the divide of Madeira's two "captaincies", or regions, and it was for a long time an important agricultural centre. Today the town's most notable feature is its handsome, tall-spired Baroque **church**, which dominates one side of the attractive central square, **Largo Padre Lomelino**. The square makes a pleasant spot to watch the world go by, with a row of green benches beneath leafy canopies and dragon trees, a kids' play area and small aviary.

There is not a lot to Caniço beyond the square and the church, though it is well stocked with **restaurants** (see p.267 for reviews). It's also worth looking round the **botanical gardens** of the *Quinta Splendida*, just south of the main square, a luxurious hotel offering sweeping views over the sea (see p.228).

CANIÇO DE BAIXO

Map 4, B7. Empresa de Automóveis do Caniço bus #155 (Mon–Sat 14 daily, Sun 9 daily).

From Caniço, a road snakes downhill to **CANIÇO DE BAIXO** (Lower Caniço), 2km away, a string of modern villas and hotel complexes built on a low cliff, all set round a rather unnecessary one-way system. Unlike Caniço and

Garajau, Caniço de Baixo has enough to keep its visitors fairly occupied without resorting to the daily buses to Funchal, including its own **Lido** and a stony beach, **Praia dos Reis Magos**, both of which are great for swimming.

However, you shouldn't expect to meet many Madeirans here: the resort is something of a German enclave, with German expats settled in the string of neat villas to the west side of town and running several of the town's facilities. The **tourist office** (Mon–Fri 9.30am–1pm & 2.30 –5.30pm, Sat 9.30am–noon; ☎291 932 919), just below the prominent *Hotel Ondamar*, can give out brochures and details of local buses.

Lido Galo Mar

Daily: June–Sept 9am–7pm; Oct–May 10am–6pm; 500$00/€2.50.

The best place to enjoy the superb sea water round Caniço de Baixo is the **Lido Galo Mar**. From the tourist office, head along the adjacent path towards the sea – or take the next road towards the sea just uphill from the tourist office – and you will reach a white tower marking the lift entrance at the top of the cliff. The lift takes you down the cliff to a series of rock and cement sun terraces by a sea-water pool and some slippery ladders that you can climb down into the superb, clear blue sea – there is a small platform to swim out to. The water off this part of the coast is part of the Reserva Natural Parcial do Garajau, an underwater park which extends from the high tide line to a depth of 50 metres. You can hire out snorkelling equipment from the **Manta Diving Centre** (May–Oct Mon–Sat 10am–5pm, Sun 10am–noon; ☎291 935 588, ⓦwww.mantadiving.com), which is based here, and if you have a diving certificate, log book and medical statement of health, you can hire scuba diving equipment from 4000$00/€20 a day; alternatively, the company offers four-

CANIÇO DE BAIXO

to five-day internationally recognized diving courses for beginners from 65,000$00/€325. They also arrange boat trips for dives off other parts of the island and night dives; if you are lucky, you'll see the giant Atlantic Manta Rays, which appear off the coast here at any time from August to October.

Praia dos Reis Magos

East of the Lido Galo Mar, an attractive seafront promenade leads past another cluster of modern hotels for around 1km down the hill to **Praia dos Reis Magos**, a traditional fishing harbour, with a stony beach and jetty; you can swim here for free and, apart from the stones, conditions are just as good as at the lido. The beach has a much more local feel than the rest of Caniço de Baixo, with most people ending up at the simple beachside **café**, *Restaurante Praia dos Reis Magos* (see p.268).

SANTA CRUZ

Map 4, D5. SAM bus #20 and #53 (Mon–Fri 5–6 daily, Sat & Sun 1 daily); also bus #78 (1 daily).

From Caniço, the south coast highway veers northwards towards the airport via the village of **SANTA CRUZ**. Despite its proximity to the highway and the runway, it's a surprisingly appealing place, with a lovely palm-lined **seafront** – well worth a detour or even an overnight stay on your first or last night on Madeira.

The town is centred round attractive, white **Igreja de Santa Cruz**, one of the oldest and least changed churches on Madeira, with its original Manueline touches dating back to the sixteenth century. From the church, Rua Conégo César de Oliveira leads down to **Praceta**, a small square where elderly men hang out on benches under leafy trees and arbours. There are several local cafés here, though you're probably better off buying a drink or picnic from the big *Supermercado Santa Cruz* (Mon–Sat 9am–8pm) and heading down to the seafront. Just east of the square you'll see the old nineteenth-century **court-house**, a lovely grey-and-white building, with hour-glass-shaped stairs leading up to one of two external balconies; it now shelters government offices and the local police headquarters.

The seafront

If you head downhill from the courthouse, you'll reach the **seafront** at the town's pleasant **lido**, Praia das Palmeiras (daily 9am–7pm; ☎291 524 248; free). There's a seawater pool and a separate kids' pool opposite the town jetty, and you can also hire sun umbrellas and loungers. Just east of the lido on a raised bluff, look out for the attractive **public gardens**, sprouting palms and dragon trees, with picnic tables offering fine views towards Ilhas Desertas.

Spreading west from the lido, the town **beach** is a long stretch of pebbles dotted with little palm shades and backed by palm trees, cafés and a big children's play area; when the sea's calm you can swim out to offshore bathing platforms. Behind the beach at the lido end, you'll also find the small covered **market** on Rua da Praia (Mon & Sun 7am–1pm, Tues–Thurs 7am–5pm, Fri 7am–7pm, Sat 7am–4pm), selling every imaginable fruit and vegetable at one end and an array of fish at the other. Continuing along the seafront from here, you'll pass the sandy village soccer pitch and, beyond it, the walls of a small ruined **fort**, which once guarded Santa Cruz.

SANTA CRUZ

MACHICO

Map 4, E3. SAM bus #113 (Mon–Fri 18 daily, Sat 12 daily, Sun 7 daily); bus #53 & #156 (5 daily); bus #20 (Mon–Fri 6 daily, Sat & Sun 1 daily); express bus #23 (Mon–Fri 3 daily); bus #78 (1 daily).

Madeira's second town, **MACHICO**, lies just ten minutes' drive east of the airport in a beautiful natural bay, surrounded by steep, terraced slopes and fronted by its own stony beach. Though little more than an overgrown village, its laid back atmosphere, good range of accommodation and restaurants and modicum of nightlife make it a great base for a holiday, or at least a night or two's stopover.

For details of getting to and from the airport, see p.48.

Legend has it that Machico's name derives from Robert Machin, an English merchant who eloped from Bristol with his wealthy lover Anne d'Arfet in 1346. Their boat was thrown off course and blown against the rocks off Machico, and although they managed to swim ashore with other members of the crew, Anne later became ill and died. The broken-hearted Machin was said to have placed a cross on her grave. Some versions of the legend say Machin also died here, others that he managed to escape from the island on a raft, before being captured by pirates and sold as a slave in Morocco. Here, Machin apparently related his woes to a Spanish slave, who, on returning to Iberia, spread Machin's tale. News of the Atlantic island eventually reached the Portuguese court, inspiring Zarco to search for Madeira. When he first landed on the island, Zarco was said to have found Anne's grave, leading him to name the place after Machin. A less romantic explanation is that Machico is named after Monchique, Zarco's home town in Portugal.

Either way, Machico was the first spot on the island to be colonized and was Madeira's capital from 1440 to 1496

MADEIRA AIRPORT

Madeirans are very proud of their **airport**, and you will find postcards of various stages in its development all over the island. Once considered one of the world's most dangerous places to land, an extension was opened in 2000 and now planes can land on a runway built on stilts over the sea – the coast road passes under the extension. It is long enough to take jumbos, though many still refer to it as the "aircraft carrier", which it resembled when it first opened in 1964.

under Tristão Vaz Teixeira, whose statue still stands in the main square. When the island was unified in 1497, the capital moved to Funchal, and Machico became a centre for sugar production and fishing. More recently, tourism has taken over, but development is decidedly low key and the town's buildings are interspersed with banana plantations and vegetable plots, with virtually the only trace of modernity being the high-rise *Hotel Dom Pedro* at the southern end of the beach.

Largo Dr António Jardim d'Oliveira and around

Though most tourist activity is focused on the seafront, the rest of Machico's life revolves around **Largo Dr António Jardim d'Oliveira**, the town's cobbled main square, where taxi drivers chat by their yellow cars in the shade of tall oak trees. The north of the square is taken up by the fifteenth-century **Igreja Matriz**, built under the orders of Tristão Vaz Teixeira's wife, Branco. Its most distinctive feature is a gracefully arched Manueline door, with three small marble columns, though the interior has an attractive painted ceiling and contains a statue of the Virgin – a gift from Manuel I, Portugal's king during the great age of the discoveries. To

MACHICO

127

the east of the church, look out for an ornate, shell-shaped **fountain**, built in the 1920s.

Machico's holiest bulding, however, is the Capela dos Milagres, a short walk to the east. From the main square, head past the town hall and its adjacent gardens, bursting with roses and sunflowers, towards the bridge over the **Ribeira de Machico**, little more than a weedy trickle in summer, but pretty lively in winter.

> If you fancy a pleasant diversion, take the little stone walkway from the bridge north along the river, over the reedy marshland behind the Igreja Matriz, to the old mill chimneys – relics of the time Machico was a major centre for the sugar trade. From here you can head back to the main square along Rua da General António Teixeira D'Aguiar, the town's main shopping street.

Over the bridge sprawls **Banda de Alén**, an area of old fishermen's houses centred round the Largo Senhor dos Milagres, a quiet square where old men play cards beneath shady trees. On the southern side of the square, you'll see the simple whitewashed **Capela dos Milagres** (Chapel of Miracles), built in 1815 to replace an earlier structure and to house one of the island's holiest remains. The original chapel – said to have been constructed on the site where Anne d'Arfet (and possibly Robert Machin) was buried – was destroyed by a flood in 1803, but miraculously a wooden crucifix survived (having been swept out to sea, it was rescued by a passing ship). The recovery of the crucifix is still celebrated every 8 October with a torchlit procession and a local public holiday on the following day. You can see the crucifix on the far wall of the chapel, though you get a better idea of its pitted appearance from the row of photos down the right-hand wall of the chapel.

The seafront

From Largo Dr António Jardim d'Oliveira, it is a short walk down Rua da General António Teixeira to the pedestrianized Praça do Dr José António d'Almada, just back from the seafront. At the end of this street you'll see the old **market building**, now a restaurant (see p.269), opposite which is the **Forte do Amparo**, a low, pale-yellow fort built in 1706 to protect the town against pirate attack. Passing pirates were a permanent menace to the local population, and Machico's forts were built so that soldiers could hole up after the women and children had retreated inland. Nowadays the fort houses the **tourist office** (Mon–Fri 9am–12.30pm & 2–5pm, Sat 9.30am–12.30pm; ☎291 962 289), but echoes of its past remain in the shape of its row of cannons, still ranged in front of the building and pointing out to sea. Below the cannons is a pretty garden containing a well-equipped **playground**, a good spot to gaze out over the beach.

One of the best times to visit Machico is during the *Festa do Santissimo Sacramento* (Festival of the Holy Sacrament) on the last Sunday of August, when a carnival-style procession culminates in a huge bonfire on Pico de Facho.

Just east of the fort lie the town **market** (daily 9am–6pm) – a modern row of booths selling fish, fruit and vegetables – and some appealing cafés (see p.297); to the west stands a small soccer **stadium**, the most prominent structure on the seafront. The dusty pitch is used by local clubs and schools in the evening (Machico's team plays in a stadium to the north of town) and as a car park during the day.

Below the stadium, spreading west, Machico's **beach**, backed by cafés, palm trees and a couple of children's swimming pools, is very much the focus of the town in summer.

MACHICO

129

DIVING OFF MACHICO

The coast off Machico is part of a marine reserve; if you are interested in diving, the Baleia Diving Center, based at *Hotel Dom Pedro Baia* (see p.231), can rent out equipment or give beginners' diving courses, starting off in the hotel pool and graduating to the bay – courses cost around 90,000$00/€450. Experienced divers are taken to explore the best local underwater sites, including a sea cave just beyond the Forte São João Baptista to the north of the bay, where at around 18 metres down, a beautiful red-tree coral can be seen at the foot of the rock known as Pedra de Fora. Further north, outside the bay, at Baixa da Cruz, there is an impressive black coral reef at a depth of some 30 metres. Baleia can also take divers to other good diving spots round the island near Funchal, Garajau and Ponta de São Lourenço, including the wreck of a sand vessel which sank in 1995 an hour from Funchal; the boat makes an excellent spot to see several native fish who have now made it their home.

At low tide the sea withdraws to reveal a narrow sandy stretch, onto which everyone descends to avoid walking on the large, steeply-banked pebbles behind; at other times – when the sea is not too rough – many people swim off or between the two jetties, located in the middle and at the southern end of the beach. The water in the bay isn't the cleanest, though its brown colour is caused by the mud seabed rather than anything more unpleasant. You can hire out beach chairs and sun umbrellas from Nautileste (℡291 962 248) in front of the fort; they also arrange water sports and fishing trips.

The west end of the beach leads on to the **Passeio Marítimo**, a palm-lined promenade offering great views, which curves round beneath the *Hotel Dom Pedro Baia* past a kiosk café and a small jetty. The promenade ends below a

MACHICO

chapel, the **Capela de São Roque**, built in 1739 in thanks for the town avoiding the plague. Inside are some beautiful eighteenth-century *azulejos* showing São Roque, a saint who dedicated his life to helping plague victims; unfortunately the chapel is normally locked.

The opposite side of the bay has a much more down-to-earth atmosphere, with a collection of boat yards and fishermen hanging out their lines along the side of the road. The lines are phenomenally long – so take care not to trip on them – as they are used to catch *espada* (scabbard fish), which only live at extreme depths. The road ends at the **Forte de São João Baptista**, another town defence, erected in 1708 and later turned into a cholera hospital; today it is a private house. Just below the fort, a jetty marks the spot at which the first ever Portuguese set foot on Madeira: a sign reads "Tristão Vaz Teixeira and João Goncalves Zarco disembarked here on 2 July, 1419".

PICO DO FACHO

Map 4, E3. SAM bus #113 (Mon–Fri 18 daily, Sat 12 daily, Sun 6 daily) passes the turning to Pico do Facho; press the bell to stop.

The eastern side of Machico's bay is dominated by **Pico do Facho**, a 320-metre-high peak named after the beacon (*facho*) that used to be lit here to warn residents of approaching pirates during the early colonial days. You can walk to the top of Facho from Machico by taking the road parallel to the river in Banda de Além and turning right (see map 4, E3), which takes around three hours return and offers superb views over the coast. Alternatively, with a car, drive out of town for around 2km towards Caniçal and turn right 200m or so after *Restaurante Típico O Túnel* (if you pass through a tunnel you have gone too far) onto a side road signed Pico do Facho. Continue up the road until the tarmac runs out and becomes a dirt track; park here and walk the remaining one kilometre up the track to the peak. The tradition of lighting a beacon is resurrected on the last Sunday of August, when a large bonfire is lit here to celebrate the *Festa do Santíssimo Sacramento* (see p.31).

CANIÇAL

Map 4, F2. SAM bus #113 (Mon–Fri 18 daily, Sat 12 daily, Sun 6 daily).

Thanks to a tunnel bored through Pico do Facho in 1956, you can easily drive from Machico to the neighbouring whaling centre of **CANIÇAL** in around ten minutes; before then it could only be reached by boat or by hiking up over the peak. Today Caniçal remains a pretty but earthy fishing village spread along a rather tatty pebbly beach. Just above the beach are the main **square**, where yellow taxis line up alongside the squat town church and the densely packed cemetery, and the interesting **Museu da Baleia**, dedicated to marine conservation.

Below the museum is a jetty alongside the scruffy and somewhat pungent pebbly **beach**, packed with swimming kids in summer who share the space with brightly painted fishing boats. At the western end of the beach is a walled-off seawater pool, in which you can swim when the waves get too big elsewhere.

The eastern end of the beach has been fenced off, marking the limits of the **Zona Franca industrial complex**. This incongruous collection of factories and modern warehouses was set up in an attempt to attract industry to locations away from Funchal, though the Madeiran government was so generous with its tax breaks that in 2000 it was castigated for unfair practices by the European Commission.

CANIÇAL

Museu da Baleia

Tues–Sun 10am–noon & 1–6pm; 250$00/€1.25.

Caniçal is best known for its tiny **Museu da Baleia**, a museum dedicated to whale conservation. Until 1981, the village still had a thriving whaling industry and it briefly achieved some sort of fame when part of John Huston's *Moby Dick* was filmed here in 1956. To research the film, Huston and American star Gregory Peck joined the local fleet on a whale hunt, witnessing the death of some twenty animals, a fair slice of the 300 whales that were killed annually off Madeiran waters. Then, in 1981, an international memorandum ended the whaling industry in these parts and the coastal area off Caniçal became a marine reserve. The museum traces the development of the whaling industry, with model boats, maps and photos – the 16.5-metre-long lower-jaw bone of a sperm whale gives some idea of their size. There is also a video explaining schemes to protect sperm, fin, humpback and blue whales that cruise past Madeiran waters, along with other threatened marine species such as dolphins and the rare monk seal.

**For details of whale- and dolphin-watching
trips from Funchal, see p.317.**

PONTA DE SÃO LOURENÇO

Map 4, F2–H3.
East of Caniçal, the road heads down the spine of **Ponta de São Lourenço**, Madeira's craggy easternmost tip. The peninsula has a very different feel to the rest of the island, at once exposed and barren, the spinning wind turbines at its southwestern end giving it a slightly eerie air. But it is well worth the short drive out here for a visit to Madeira's only

A WALK DOWN PONTA DE SÃO LOURENÇO

The three-hour walk from the Baia de Abra car park to the tip of the headland and back is one of the most dramatic on Madeira. The route follows a well-worn path, much of it over bare rock, but clearly marked with stones, cairns, white posts or green arrows when the path itself is not clear. Parts of the walk involve fairly steep scrambles over loose scree, and it can be extremely slippery when wet, so make sure you have good footwear. In winter, high winds can also make the walk hazardous, though the steepest parts of the walk have good fences for protection.

Start off heading east from the car park and you quickly pass a sign announcing entry into the Parque Natural. After five minutes, the path splits, with a faint downward fork leading steeply down to a lovely stony beach. The left-hand fork goes up to a viewpoint with great views over the north coast and huge cliffs falling into the sea. Continue on this path and after about half an hour you cross bare rock, a fairly steep route marked by stones and green arrows. The path then

truly sandy beach at **Prainha**, and for one of the island's most exhilarating walks, to the very tip of the headland around **Baia de Abra**.

Prainha

Map 4, G2.

A couple of kilometres east of Caniçal – and usually marked by a cluster of parked cars – steps lead down the cliff to **Prainha**, a small bay in which Madeira's usually hefty pebbles and stones have been replaced by wonderfully soft, dark-grey sand. The swimming off the beach is also superb, with refreshing, crystalline water. Unfortunately, all this attracts a fair few day-trippers, especially at weekends in the goes over a narrow pass with views over both sides of the headland.

Around ten minutes later, you reach the steepest section, with wire fencing on one side leading you down to a very narrow neck of the headland with sheer drops, especially to the north side. Once past here, the path crosses wide fields lined with big purple thistles and red ice plants.

After about an hour, you will reach the ranger's house, a pretty building surrounded by palm trees and more thistles. From the house, you could detour along the path which heads southwest to the coast, a ten-minute walk to a small jetty where you can swim if the sea is not too rough – this is where the ranger lands his boat.

Back at the ranger's house, the main path climbs steeply to the east for another half hour to the very tip of Ponta de São Lourenço. The grassy incline suddenly ends in a dramatic cliff; the views from here are stunning, making you realise how precipitous your walk was to get to this point. Allow another hour and a half to return the way you came.

summer, so space on the sands can be limited. However, you can always retreat to the beachside **café** (daily summer only 10am–8pm; closed when the weather is bad), which has a large terrace facing the sands, where you can get slightly pricey fish and seafood, snacks and drinks; the place also hires out sun beds and umbrellas.

The top of the steps to the beach faces the chapel of **Nossa Senhora de Piedade**, which comes to life on the third Sunday of September, when a statue of Nossa Senhora de Piedade – which some say was the work of an unnamed sixteenth-century Flemish master – is taken from the chapel to Caniçal accompanied by a procession of fishing boats; at other times, the chapel remains locked and unkempt-looking.

PONTA DE SÃO LOURENÇO

Baia de Abra

Map 4, G2–H2.

From Prainha, the road continues east past a *miradouro* at Ponta do Rosto, just above a series of spinning wind turbines. After another kilometre, the road ends at a little car park – often occupied by a van selling snacks and cold drinks. Here people stop to admire the views over the sheer cliffs – some up to 180m high – round the **Baia de Abra**, which stretches round to the offshore islets of Ilhéu da Cevada and the lighthouse-topped Ilhéu de Farol. The geography of the landscape here is more like that of Porto Santo and the Ilhas Desertas than the rest of Madeira, and the vegetation is also distinctive, consisting of cacti, thistles and the red-tipped, seaweed-like ice plants.

Just above the car park there are picnic tables with superb views towards a rock arch at the far end of the headland, though there is little shade here and you'll find yourself in lizard territory – sit still enough and the reptiles will crawl up your leg and into your picnic.

The car park also marks the starting point of a **footpath** which passes into the Parque Natural de Ponta de São Lourenço right to the tip of the headland, an exhilarating and at times vertiginous three-hour return walk (see box above).

SANTO ANTÓNIO DA SERRA

Map 4, C3. SAM bus #20/25 (Mon–Fri 6 daily, Sat & Sun 1 daily); also bus #78 (1 daily); Autocarros da Camacha bus #77 (Mon–Fri 7 daily, Sat & Sun 5 daily).

Some 6km inland from Machico – and around the same again from the airport – lies the small, unassuming hillside village of **SANTO ANTÓNIO DA SERRA**, which has become the centre for some of the island's neatest villas, one of its finest parks and its most famous golf course, the spectacularly sited **Clube de Golf Santo da Serra**, 1.5km southeast of the village on the EN207. At a height of 670m, the air is cool here, and at times clouds float between the golf course and the coast below; if you are unlucky the whole place will be swathed in low cloud. Even if you do not like golf, it is worth sneaking into the club house for a drink to admire the stunning views, encompassing the whole of the eastern tip of the island and out to Ilhas Desertas.

Once a year in February or March the Clube de Golf Santo da Serra is host to the Madeira Open, which attracts international stars. For more information about the tournament and playing the course yourself, see p.320.

Heading northwest from the golf course, the road passes a series of flash *quintas* and villas, belonging to wealthy Madeirans and expats who have built summer homes here from the eighteenth century onwards amongst the green woodland. The most striking of these is the elaborately turreted **Casa da Cha**, currently being renovated.

The village itself does not have an awful lot going for it. Buses stop in front of the **church**, a nineteenth-century structure that is said to have housed a famous Flemish work of art, nearly used by the local priest as a wedge to help a passing motorist who had got stuck in mud here in the 1930s. When, by chance, it was discovered how valuable the "board" was, the rest of Madeira was scoured for similar works of art, leading to the collection in Funchal's Museu de Arte Sacra (see p.64).

In front of the church, the wide **main square** is surrounded by a few local shops and cafés and a small children's play area; just below here, you'll find **Parque de Feiras**, a little park which at weekends and holidays is given over to stalls selling barbecued chickens; at other times it becomes the local car park.

SANTO ANTÓNIO DA SERRA

137

Parque do Santo da Serra

Santo António da Serra's main attraction is its extensive park, **Parque do Santo da Serra**, consisting largely of woodland, to the southeast side of the village, 200m or so from the church. Wooden gates mark the entrance, from where a cobbled track, lined with agapanthus, camellias and hydrangeas, leads down into the park itself. The grounds were once part of an estate owned by the Blandy family (see p.101), and you can still see the family's pink *quinta* as you go into the park on your left; it is now a government office. After a couple of hundred metres you will come to a children's play area next to deer and bird enclosures, along with tennis courts and a crazy golf course; at weekends, families gather here for picnics. Beyond here, the path winds down under pine and eucalyptus trees to a *miradouro*, where you can watch clouds scud up from the valley above Machico and the distant Ponta de São Lourenço.

PORTELA

Map 4, B2. SAM bus #78 (1 daily).

From Santo António da Serra, you can return to Funchal via Camacha (see p.104) or cut through to the Poiso pass (see p.190), but it's worth pressing on north to Ponta da Cruz via the dramatic mountain pass of **Portela**. At 622m, the pass offers dazzling views over the north coast, here dominated by the giant, cube-shaped rock of Penha de Águia (see p.184). The highest point of the pass is usually marked by stalls selling plants or souvenirs, along with a taxi or two waiting for walkers from Ribeira Frio (see p.184). You'll also find a good **restaurant** here, the *Miradouro da Portela* (see p.270 for review).

PORTO DA CRUZ

Map 4, B1. SAM bus #53 and #78 (Mon–Fri 5 daily, Sat 3 daily, Sun 1 daily).

From Portela, the road drops steeply downhill for the five kilometres to **PORTO DA CRUZ**. One of the most spectacularly sited fishing villages on the north coast, Porto da Cruz is also one of the liveliest and looks set to develop

THE COAST PATH FROM LORANO TO MACHICO

Before the road over the mountains was built, the three- to four-hour walk along the **coastal path** from Lorano to Machico was the main route for people going from Porto da Cruz to Machico and beyond. The path, which skirts the north coast's dramatic cliffs before a gentle descent to Machico, is at times precipitous and also passes through fairly dense areas of bramble, so be sure to wear trousers and sturdy walking boots.

From Porto da Cruz, it is a tough climb to **Lorano**, some 3km up the coast to the east, so it's probably best to take a taxi straight to the village. Reached off the Porto da Cruz–Portela road, Lorano consists of little more than a couple of farms on either side of a wide dirt track. Once in Lorano, continue along the track past fields dotted with sheds containing cattle until it narrows into a path, after about 20 minutes' walk. A little further on the path splits; make sure you take the upper path, which climbs steeply at first, continuing past rock myrtle, bracken and the odd house leek and Madeiran orchid. Behind you there are great views over the coast back towards Porto da Cruz.

After about an hour, you'll go round a headland, at which point you'll suddenly see Ponta da São Lourenço stretched out in front of you. For the next twenty minutes or so, the scenery changes dramatically, the dense undergrowth giving way to barren, exposed rock as you skirt the edge of a concave cliff. There are wooden fences on the seaward side, but these are often in disrepair and you have to watch your footing, especially when it is wet.

rapidly with the opening of the Maroços tunnel to Machico. The village is also a good starting point for one of the island's best **coastal paths**, which goes via Lorano across to Machico.

Porto da Cruz's most prominent building is a massive, expensively restored **church**, a ghastly structure with one

After eighty minutes, a handrail leads over a particularly steep rocky section of this cliff with a stream gushing down it. Shortly after this, you leave the cliff behind and the scenery changes again as the path plunges through a dense under-growth of bracken, brambles and broom heather – this can cover the steep edge of the path, so take care. In another ten minutes, you will see a row of tree stumps lined up like poles, where fierce gales have snapped the trunks – most of the trees on this stretch are bent over away from the prevailing wind.

After two hours, the scenery opens up again as you emerge from the dense undergrowth onto a grassy mountainside; with-in ten minutes you'll reach the pass of **Boca do Risco** (the Risky Mouth) – so-called because when gales blow, the wind funnels through the pass and crossing it can be risky indeed. Climb a small path to the right and you'll find a relatively flat grassy area, a good picnic spot.

The path continues over the pass, just beyond which you'll see a shepherd's cave. From here, you descend into a wooded valley of pines and bracken and, after around two hours and forty minutes, cross a tiny *levada*. Carry straight on and you'll shortly skirt the side of a farm building. Within five minutes of the building, you will join a small road, opposite the *Bar Boca do Risco* in the village of Ribeira Seca do Machico. Turn left down the road for 200m or so, then right onto the main road and it is just a further half an hour's walk downhill to Machico's main square (see p.127).

external wall lined with statues of saints and a modernist-tower stuck at the front. But if you take the steps below the church past the children's playground to the stone **harbour**, you'll be rewarded with stunning views of the north coast – on one side the towering rock of Penha de Águia and the other the steep cliffs and terraced slopes of Pico da Coroa.

If you ask around, you may be able to find *vinho Americano*, a locally produced table wine, which the EU tried to ban, as it is said to be toxic; it is popular with locals, however, and tastes similar to a rough *vinho verde*. The other local plonk is *aguardente*, a firewater produced from the local sugar mills.

The harbour is fronted by a **beach** made up of giant boulders and backed by a small promenade lined with cafés. Most people head to the west end of the promenade, where there's a superb large seawater **swimming pool**, complete with a special children's area and a small Astroturf sunbathing deck.

The west coast

The **west coast** of Madeira is one of the island's least spoilt and little visited regions. Although the opening of the south-coast highway in the 1990s dramatically reduced the journey time to what were previously remote villages, tourism has yet to make major inroads, and only the lively town of **Ribeira Brava** has anything approaching resort status.

Much of the west coast is rocky, backed by steep wooded slopes and valleys sheltering banana plantations, vineyards and rural settlements. The coast road links a series of small villages, each with their own stony beaches – the attractive **Ponta do Sol**, historic **Madalena do Mar** and **Calheta**, a former sugar production centre. Further west, the road climbs inland above a series of dramatic cliffs. At their foot nestle **Jardim do Mar**, one of Madeira's most attractive villages and a burgeoning surf centre; and **Paúl do Mar**, another surfers' hang-out. Above here, the wooded valleys around the village of **Prazeres** offer some superb walking country. The coast road continues to **Ponta do Pargo**, the starting point for two attractive *levada* walks. Inland lies **Rabaçal**, perhaps the most beautiful valley on the island and a base for more wonderful *levada* walks. For a complete contrast in scenery, head further east to the wild, windswept plateau of the **Paúl da Serra**.

Reviews of accommodation, restaurants and bars on the west coast start on p.233, p.272 and p.298 respectively.

RIBEIRA BRAVA

Map 6, K9 & Map 7. Rodoeste bus #7 (7–10 daily).

Just thirty minutes' drive west from Funchal lies the buzzing resort of **RIBEIRA BRAVA**. Located at the foot of a dramatic gorge and endowed with numerous shops, a variety of restaurants and an attractive seafront, the town makes a good day-trip from the capital or a pleasant overnight stop. If you are here in June, you should definitely stay over for the Festa de São Pedro (June 28–29), celebrated with music, dancing and processions. The other highlight of the calendar is the annual music festival which takes place in October.

Rodoeste Buses (☎ 291 220 148) leave from Rua Ribeira João Gomes in Funchal (map 2, H1).

Ribeira Brava's origins go back to the fifteenth century when it became an important staging post on the trade route from the north of the island to Funchal. Its sheltered position also favoured the cultivation of sugar, at that time the island's major crop. Ribeira Brava translates as the "angry river", a reference to the river which flows to the west of the town and which still comes alive after heavy rains, especially in the autumn, though at other times it is a decidedly meek affair.

Buses from Funchal pull in at the seafront, while boats moor at the jetty to the east of the bay. Located on the seafront is the **tourist office** (Mon–Fri 9am–12.30pm & 2–5pm; Sat 9.30am–noon; ☎ 291 951 675), housed in a

RIBEIRA BRAVA

small stone tower, the Forte de São Bento, originally built to protect the town from pirate attack. The office can supply town maps and brochures on local events and walks.

The Town

The main focus of the town is the fairly modern **seafront**, giving onto a wide stony beach and lined with a series of bustling esplanade cafés and restaurants. The town market, decorated with attractive modern *azulejos*, and the main shopping street, **Rua Visconde da Ribeira**, are west of the tourist office. The bottom end of Rua Visconde da Ribeira is lined with tacky tourist shops, though further up there are some more characterful traditional stores. A hundred metres or so up on the right are some small, attractive public gardens, belonging to the **town hall**, built in 1765 and originally the home of a local sugar merchant; you can still see bits of sugar-mill machinery dotted round the grounds.

Opposite the gardens on Rua dos Camachos stands the beautiful **Igreja de São Bento** (daily 7am–1pm & 3–7pm), a sixteenth-century church with some wonderful Manueline touches, including a stone font and pulpit carved with plants and animals. The characteristic chequered-tiled roof is one of the most beautiful in Madeira.

For more on Manueline architecture, see p.150.

Ethnographical Museum
Map 7, F3. 24 Rua de São Francisco. Tues–Sun 10am–12.30pm & 2–6pm; 350$00/€1.75.

Continuing north up Rua Visconde da Ribeira Brava you reach a square, Largo das Herédias, harbouring a few cafés with outdoor tables. A couple of minutes' walk north from

RIBEIRA BRAVA

here is the **Ethnographical Museum**, set in a distinctive pink sixteenth-century town house. It used to be a rum distillery and later became a water-powered sugar-cane and cereal mill. Since 1996, it has been a museum dedicated to local crafts. Although the displays aren't exactly thrilling – fishing boats, mill equipment and looms – they do give an insight into the development of the fishing and weaving trades and the importance of wine and cereals to the area.

João Carlos Abrue Collection
Map 7, E2. Tues–Sat 10am–12.30pm & 2–6pm; 150$00/€0.75.
From the Ethnographical Museum it is a short walk – turn left then right onto the main ER104 out of town – to Ribeira Brava's other museum, the **João Carlos Abrue Collection**, a wonderfully eclectic collection of model horses – toy horses, hobby horses, horses made from porcelain and glass.

Frequent boat trips run to Ribeira
Brava from Funchal (see p.55).

PONTA DO SOL

Map 6, I9. Rodoeste bus #4 (2 daily except Sat & Sun), #115 and #142 (1–2 daily).
Continuing west along the coast road, you pass the little fishing village of Lugar do Baixo, before reaching, after some ten minutes' drive, **PONTA DO SOL**, a smaller, quieter and prettier version of Ribeira Brava, with a relaxed and lively air. Ponta do Sol is reputedly the sunniest spot on the island – its name means "sunny point". The population of just 4500 is shoe-horned into the bottom of a steep valley, overhung with dense banana plantations: Ponta do Sol is in fact the island's main banana production centre, with

some 600,000 kilos of fruit going from here to Portugal annually.

The town's Baroque church, **Nossa Senhora da Luz**, on Rua Dr João Augusto Teixeira, was built in the eighteenth century on the site of an older medieval structure; it's an airy place with mock-marble wooden pulpits, a painted wooden ceiling showing biblical scenes and a stone font; its best feature, however, is its beautiful seventeenth-century decorative *azulejos*.

Opposite the church, at 35–37 Rua Dr João Augusto Teixeira, is a superb traditional shop-cum-bar, with wooden cabinets stuffed full of old bottles.

The streets beyond the church become steeper, with tarmac giving way to cobbled alleys and steps linking the ever higher shops and houses. A plaque on a house in Rua Príncipe Dom Luís I marks the birthplace of the grandparents of American novelist **John Roderigo dos Passos**, (1896–1970), likened to James Joyce and known for his novels *42nd Parallell, USA* and *Manhattan Transfer*.

The town **beach** isn't up to much, consisting of little more than a stretch of coarse grey stones. The palm-tree-lined seafront does have the perfect spot for a drink though – the balcony of the *Café Poente* (see p.274); for something more substantial, head over the road to *Poente's* **restaurant**. Jutting out beyond the restaurant is the town's jetty, built in the nineteenth century, and the only link with the outside world until just after World War II.

Madalena do Mar

Map 6, H6. Rodoeste bus #4 (2 daily except Sat & Sun).

Another ten minutes up the coast from Ponta do Sol lies **MADALENA DO MAR**, a rather rambling and characterless village spread out along a long stony beach backed by extensive banana plantations. There's not much cause to stop here, though it does have an interesting history. The village is said to have been founded by King Wladislaw II of Poland. After a disastrous defeat in battle against the Ottomans in Varna in 1414, Wladislaw disappeared and legend has it that he resurfaced in Madeira, having been offered asylum by King Dom João. He was granted vast estates by Zarco (see p.57), including the area around Madalena do Mar, and settled there after marrying a local woman. He concealed his identity and became known locally as Henrique Alemão (Henry the German – the locals mistook his accent). He was sent supplies by the court of Lisbon, and was eventually summoned to Lisbon by the king. However, his boat sank off Cabo Girão on the return journey and he went down with it, though his body was later recovered. The family was obviously fated – his son Segismundo later set off to try and discover more about his father, but he, too, died at sea. Wladislaw's body lies in the village church, the **Igreja da Santa Caterina**, parts of which date back to 1457. A painting that once hung in the church and now hangs in Funchal's Museu de Arte Sacra is thought to portray Wladislaw and his wife in the guise of Saint Arine and Saint Joaquim. The house where Wladislaw is said to have lived is just below the church – the one with a distinctive coat of arms by the door.

The Museu de Arte Sacra in Funchal (see p.64) displays a number of important Flemish works of art from Madalena do Mar's church.

THE OLD ROAD TO CALHETA

Rodoeste bus #115 and #142 (1–2 daily).

If you are in no hurry and fancy a detour inland, you could skip Madalena do Mar and take the **old road** from Ponta do Sol to Calheta, further up the coast (see p.150). It takes about forty minutes rather than the ten minutes that it would along the coast road. The route winds along mountainsides, following every contour, and takes in a few small villages, plus a couple of important religious sites.

About ten minutes out of Ponta do Sol you come to **Canhas**, which has a series of stations of the cross leading to a modern concrete monument to St Teresa, patron saint of lacemakers. A series of tortuous bends takes you further up to **Arco da Calheta** (map 6, H7), a tiny place with some great views down over the coast. As you head out of Arco da Calheta, you'll see on the left the Nossa Senhora da Loreto chapel, one of Madeira's oldest chapels boasting superb examples of Manueline architecture. The fine Manueline door architrave was commissioned by Dona Joana de Eça, one of Zarco's daughter-in-laws; the interior of the church contains further elaborate decorative twirls. Like other rural churches, the door is usually kept locked but often opens at 5pm for mass when you can nip in just before or after a service. The best time to be here is September 7–8 for the Festa da Nossa Senhora da Loreto, the annual celebration of the grape harvest, when the village is draped with flowers, and the evening comes alive with music and fireworks. Continuing west along another series of tortuous bends, you rejoin the main coast road just above Calheta.

MANUELINE ARCHITECTURE

Manueline architecture is a uniquely Portuguese style of architecture which emerged during the reign of Manuel I (1495–1521) and developed from the Gothic. The early sixteenth century was the age of Portugal's maritime discoveries and it was these that provided the inspiration for Manueline motifs, drawn from ships' masts, ropes, anchors and the exotic animal and plant life encountered abroad and which frequently adorned windows, doors and columns. It would be hard to imagine an art more directly reflecting the achievements and preoccupations of an age. Another peculiarity of Manueline buildings is the way they often adapt or encompass any number of different styles. Often there are Moorish touches, for example. Many of Madeira's earliest buildings incorporated elements of Manueline architecture, though now little survives. Some of the best examples are to be found in Funchal's Quinta das Cruzes (see p.72) and the Jardins Tropicais do Monte Palace in Monte (see p.97).

CALHETA AND AROUND

Rodoeste bus #107 (1–2 daily).

From Madalena do Mar the coast flattens out slightly, allowing a relatively straight ten-minute drive to **CALHETA** (map 6, F7), a pretty village set below a cliff. Calheta was given its town charter in 1502 and was governed by Zarco's children. It later became a customs post for sugar exports, but waned in importance with the decline of the sugar trade in the nineteenth century and remains something of a cultural backwater with an end-of-the-world feel. The attractive old town, with its neatly manicured gardens, sits on the eastern bank of a small river. Just before you enter the village you come to a pretty garden wedged beneath the cliffs containing the remains of an old rum distillery, founded in 1909.

If you're interested to find out how rum is made you can visit a working rum distillery in the village, called the **Engenho da Calheta** (Mon–Fri 8am–5pm; free). You're allowed to wander round the rather antiquated-looking collection of cogs and wheels, used to grind, press and extract the juice from raw sugar cane. You'll also see the large fermentation vats, where the juice is distilled into *aguardente* white rum. There's usually a chance to taste the end product or buy some from the souvenir shop.

Just above the distillery lies the village church, **Igreja Matriz**, which dates back to 1430, though most of it was rebuilt in 1639. Whilst its exterior is unexceptional, it is worth looking inside if you can (the church is often locked) to see a gloriously ornate and over-the-top ebony and silver tabernacle donated by Manuel I.

At the eastern end of the beach clusters the new part of town, set round a dull modern harbour sheltering a black sandy beach. This is where you'll find Calheta's only hotel, the *Hotel Calheta Beach* (see p.233).

Estreito da Calheta

Map 6, F6

From Calheta, you can either head north to Rabaçal (see p.156) and the Paúl da Serra on the EN211, or continue west along the coast road. This climbs through the dull town of **Estrela**, which has its own guesthouse but not much cause to stay here. The next place of any interest is **Estreito da Calheta**, worth a detour for its Capela dos Reis Magos (Chapel of the Three Kings), graced with some Manueline touches and a wonderfully vibrant sixteenth-century Flemish altar carving, *The Adoration of the Magi*.

CALHETA AND AROUND

JARDIM DO MAR

Map 6, E6. Rodoeste bus #115 (1 on Mon & Fri only).

From Estreito da Calheta a road winds down for around 4km to the traditional fishing village of **JARDIM DO MAR**, an instantly likeable place, consisting of a warren of traffic-free, cobbled alleys set on a low cliff and for much of the year laden with the smell of honeysuckle. You could easily while away a day or two here strolling along the beach or up into the banana plantations which line the steep slopes above the village.

Recently given a new lease of life as a surfing centre, Jardim do Mar now regularly hosts the annual leg of the World Surfing Championship in January.

The centre of the village is well cared for and is full of neat wooden street signs and carefully tended paths. From the main square, with its aviary and colourful murals, a road takes you past the ruined Quinta Piedade and *Tar Mar* restaurant (see p.272) to Portinho, a small boat jetty lined with colourful fishing boats, just below the local cemetery.

West of the main square, below the village church, narrow alleys weave past flower-covered houses to viewpoints on a cliff ledge above the rocky beach and crashing waves; to the west you can make out the village of Paúl do Mar set beneath its majestic cliffs. The jumble of houses in this lower stretch are quite run-down, with outside washboards a sign that many lack decent washing facilities.

To the west of the village above the church, a neat cobbled path leads past the local shop to a T-junction. Next to a sign pointing left here to the neighbouring village of Paúl do Mar (see p.154) is a glass case containing a *rede*, a kind of hammock. These hammocks were traditionally used as a sort of stretcher for ferrying around the sick or wealthy and would have been carried by two men known as *rodeiros*. In the nineteenth century, this particular *rede* was the favoured mode of transport for a local overweight priest who got his *rodeiros* to carry him as far as Ponto do Pargo, Calheta and even Funchal – the steepness of the cliffs round here make this seems cruel in the extreme.

At low tide it's possible to follow the coast path from Jardim do Mar to Paúl do Mar (see p.154) – a delightful three- to four-kilometre walk. You'll need to arrange transport for your return journey, though, as the beach is not exposed long enough for a two-way walk. Check locally for tide information.

PRAZERES AND THE LEVADA NOVA

Map 6, E6. Rodoeste bus #115 (1–2 daily).

From Jardim do Mar the inland road climbs through lush woodland to the village of **PRAZERES**, a small agricultural settlement clustered round a twin-spired church. It's a good place from which to start walking the nearby **Levada Nova**, which finishes at Ponta do Pargo (see p.155), taking in the village of Raposeira en route – a three- to four-hour walk in all. The Levada Nova is one of the island's most attractive *levadas*, winding through idyllic, largely wooded, countryside. For much of the way it shadows the gentle gradients of the coast road 101, indeed crosses it at several points, so if you find yourself flagging you can always jump on a #107 bus. The *levada* stops above Ponta do Pargo, and a signed track points you down to the village itself.

A WALK FROM PRAZERES TO PAÚL DO MAR

Prazeres' *Hotel Jardim Atlântico* (see p.235) marks the starting point of a spectacular ninety-minute walk down the cliffs to the seaside village of Paúl do Mar. From the top of the cliff, the boats below look like tiny specks, and there is total silence but for the sound of cicadas and birds. Clearly signed steps to the far side of the hotel car park lead down the pot-holed cliff face – if you aren't up to the whole walk you could just descend a little way to a bench and admire the views from there (10min). From here the path descends dramatically; after a while you'll see a waterfall behind you, then you cross a stone bridge for the final section. A left-hand turn will take you to the quay of Paúl do Mar (see below). To avoid climbing back up the cliff again it's best to arrange someone to collect you or to order a taxi either from Prazeres or from the restaurant *Largo-Mar* (see p.273) in Paúl do Mar; the ride will cost around 1500$00/€7.50.

PAÚL DO MAR

Map 6, D5. Rodoeste bus #107 (1 daily except Sat & Sun).

The road west from Prazeres passes a series of attractive farming villages, among them **LOMBO DOS CEDROS**, a bucolic, leafy hamlet, surrounded by neatly cultivated terraces worked on by elderly, black-clad women. A little further west, a small flower-covered junction points you to **PAÚL DO MAR**, in itself an unexceptional little fishing village, but worth a detour for its spectacular position beneath towering cliffs. Until the access road was built in the 1960s the village was only accessible by sea. Soon, it will be even easier to reach, as a tunnel linking it with neighbouring Jardim do Mar is currently under construction. For now, though, reaching the village from the

Prazeres road is all part of the fun, each loop and turn revealing heady views of the village below.

The village itself, however, is something of an anticlimax after the exciting approach. It has an ungainly modern church and there is a string of new apartments along the seafront. The beach, obscured by a hefty sea wall, consists largely of concrete sea defences. The town does have a certain gritty atmosphere though, and its position beneath the cliffs is undeniably stunning.

PONTA DO PARGO

Map 6, C3. Rodoeste bus #107 or #142 (1–2 daily).

The inland road from Paúl do Mar, crisscrossed by the Levada Nova, is lined with purple-flowering agapanthus and passes through beautiful wooded countryside. After twenty minutes or so the landscape opens up as you approach the small village of **PONTA DO PARGO** – "Dolphin-fish point", so called because Zarco caught dolphin fish (better known as sea bream) here while exploring the area. The village is surrounded by cultivated fields filled with vines and vegetables, worked on largely by hardy-looking women wrapped in headscarves and carrying huge bundles on their heads. The village is centred on an attractive church whose terrace overlooks fields and the coast below. To the left of the church there is a recently restored fountain, the Fontanaria São Pedro, built in 1899 and covered with beautiful *azulejos* showing São Pedro (Saint Peter), Santo António (Saint Anthony) and various cherubs.

Opposite the church is a decent café–restaurant, the *Solar do Pero* (see review on p.273). From here, go straight on and take the next turning on the left to Madeira's westernmost tip, marked by a stumpy, red-topped lighthouse. Alternatively, you can walk to the lighthouse from the café in about twenty minutes. Follow the signpost to Salão de

Baixo which takes you downhill past a farm and through low, twisted vines. The path joins a bigger road; turn right for the lighthouse, the last building between Madeira and America.

Just north of Ponta do Pargo you can join the Levada Nova, which runs east via Raposeira to Prazeres – see p.154 for details of the walk from the other direction.

From Ponta do Pargo the coast road twists through fairly desolate countryside to the north coast at Porto Moniz (see p.164). Alternatively, turn right a little after the small town of Achadas do Cruz to climb up to the extraordinary plateau of Paúl da Serra via Rabaçal.

THE ROAD TO RABAÇAL

From the junction off the Ponta do Pargo–Porto Moniz road, the EN204 climbs through virgin lauricious forests towards the Paúl da Serra; there is no public transport to this part of the island. The road passes a couple of *miradouro* viewpoints en route: one at Quebradas, with excellent views to the south coast towards Ribeira da Janela, the other at Fonte de Bispo, from where you can sometimes spot the lighthouse in Ponta do Pargo. From Fonte do Bispo you can cut down to the coast road at Prazeres (see p.153) or continue 7km to **RABAÇAL** (map 6, H5), one of the most beautiful valleys on the island and the location of two popular *levada* walks: one to 25 Fontes, the other to Risco Waterfall. Just above Rabaçal, a very different walk can be had across rugged moorland to a mini statue of Christ, Cristo Rei (see p.159).

A gravel *miradouro* viewpoint marks the turning to Rabaçal. A bumpy single-track road descends in a series of rather alarming hairpin bends to Rabaçal's car park – if

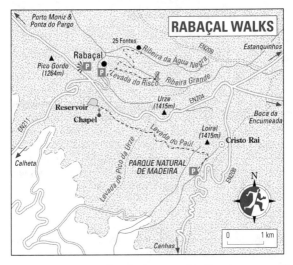

RABAÇAL WALKS

Porto Moniz &
Ponta do Pargo

25 Fontes

Ribeira da Água Negra

EN209

Estanquinhos

Rabaçal

Ribeira Grande

Pico Gordo
(1264m)

Levada do Risco

Urze
(1415m)

EN204

Reservoir

Chapel

Levada do Paúl

Loiral
(1415m)

Cristo Rai

Boca da
Encumeada

EN211

Levada do Pico da Urze

Calheta

PARQUE NATURAL
DE MADEIRA

EN208

N

Canhas

0   1 km

you meet a car coming in the opposite direction, one of
you will have to reverse either steeply up or downhill until
you reach one of the marginally wider passing spots. But
this is well worth the drive. Set in a breathtaking, densely
wooded valley, its trees draped in lichens and mosses,
Rabaçal is completely uninhabited and untouched by the
outside world, except for a small government rest house,
some public toilets and a few stone picnic tables. From the
rest house there are stunning views of the surrounding
wooded valleys and the towering peaks. The government
rest house also makes a superb place to stay, and despite
what you may be told to the contrary, it is open to the
public. However, it must be booked in advance from
Quinta Vigia in Funchal (see p.75) and Madeirans are
always given priority – as a result it gets booked up very
quickly.

A walk to Risco Waterfall

Both *levada* walks start below the car park and are signpost-ed. The easier of the two is the one to **Risco Waterfall**. Follow the steps downhill onto the mossy *levada* path. The path soon splits, the left-hand fork heading to 25 Fontes (see below). Keep to the upper, right-hand path which follows an old *levada* through tranquil woodland. The valley gradually becomes steeper and narrower, and you'll see the distant, lower *levada* to 25 Fontes coming into view to the left. Around twenty minutes from the car park you'll reach the sheer sides at the valley's end, with the narrow Risco Waterfall spilling down a high mossy cliff. You can go quite close to the falls along the *levada* wall, but as you approach, signs warn you not to proceed any further. The *levada* actu-ally passes right under the waterfall, partly through a tunnel, though if you try it you will get soaked. Do not attempt to go beyond the waterfall where the wet *levada* walls are pre-cipitous and decidedly dangerous.

A walk to 25 Fontes

For a more strenuous walk – just over an hour one-way – follow signs from the car park to **25 Fontes** (going left where the path splits to Risco). Turn right onto the *levada*; for a while it runs parallel to the *levada* to Risco but at a lower level – indeed you'll see Risco Waterfall after about half an hour. At the head of the valley at the point where you come to a small water house, you'll need to cross a river bed. The *levada* is quite narrow here, with fairly sheer drops to the left. After another thirty minutes you cross a path heading down to the left, but carry straight on for another ten minutes. You then reach a sluice where a right-hand turn takes you to 25 Fontes – literally 25 springs, an enchanting jumble of little waterfalls and rivulets – though

25 is probably an exaggeration. This is a lovely spot to have a picnic, assuming there aren't too many other walkers who have got here first.

A walk to Cristo Rei

From the *miradouro* above Rabaçal there is another interesting but very different *levada* walk, called the Levada do Paúl. It takes around eighty minutes and ends up at the **Cristo Rei**, a mini version of Rio's Christ statue, built in 1962 and also known as *Nosso Senhor do Montanha*, Our Lord of the Mountain. The walk starts at the small reservoir opposite the *miradouro* and heads off in a southeasterly direction – look for a tiny chapel marking the spot where the *levada* comes out of a channel. You pass a couple of waterfalls, but for the most part the landscape consists of lonely moorland, and you get superb views down to the south coast on a clear day. The *levada* crosses the EN208 – the road from Paúl da Serra to Canhas and Ponta do Sol – at a car park just below the Cristo Rei statue.

You will have to walk back the way you came unless you want to chance hitching a lift on the little-frequented Canhas road.

ACROSS THE PAÚL DA SERRA

East from Rabaçal the EN204 passes the barren plateau of the **Paúl da Serra**, which translates roughly as "mountain plain". On clear days it can seem delightfully empty and fresh, with spectacular views down to the coasts, though when wind or mist sweeps across the boggy ground it can be bleak in the extreme. The plateau is 1300m high and covers an expanse of moorland 17km by 6km, the flattest continuous area on the island. Little grows here except for coarse grassland and the area is subject to low clouds and harsh winds. It's prime grazing land for cattle, the only place on the island where it is safe for cows to wander freely without risk of falling down a precipice. The numbers of livestock are restricted, however, to prevent soil erosion. Hardy shepherds can be seen tending their flocks, sheltering from the elements in the concrete shelters which have replaced caves traditionally hacked into the boggy embankments. The plateau also supports a wind generating farm, which helps supply the north coast with electricity. In summer, when bilberry trees bear fruit, local youths often come up to the plateau to camp. Bird-watchers are also attracted by linnets, goldfinches and the rare Berthelot's pipit, found only here and on the Canaries.

Located on the plateau, seemingly in the middle of nowhere, is the *Estalagem Pico da Urze* at Ovil (map 6, I6), an unlikely modern complex complete with shops, restaurant and four-star accommodation. If you want to do some early morning walks, you could do worse than bed down at one of the 27 rooms (for reviews see p.234 and p.273).

Bica da Cana

Map 6, K5.

Continuing east on the EN204, you pass a series of wind generators just before **BICA DA CANA**, the impressive setting for another government rest house. The house is about ten minutes' walk from the main road up a stone track; there is a *miradouro* just above here at a height of 1620m, with fantastic views on clear days. From Bica da Cana, the road begins to descend along the edge of a dramatic, craggy mountain valley and you suddenly remember how high up you have come as the road pitches through rough road tunnels – keep your windscreen wipers at the ready as mini waterfalls often crash over the car as you enter or leave the tunnels. The EN204 then ends as the road joins the main north–south route, the EN104, at Boca da Encumeada.

BOCA DA ENCUMEADA AND SERRA DE ÁGUA

Rodoeste bus #6 (2–3 daily).

A small lay-by at the end of the EN204 marks the **Boca da Encumeada** (map 6, M5), the "mouth of altitude", a mountain pass at 1007m, marking the highest point of the road linking the north and south coasts. On a clear day you can see down to the coast at São Vicente in the north (see p.169) and Ribeira Brava in the south; at other times you look down on a sea of white clouds. Often, late afternoon sees cloud rise up from the north coast before spilling like froth over the pass and down towards the south. In early summer the pass takes on extra colour when the rocks come alive with yellow broom.

South of the pass, the road descends steeply through the picturesque wooded valley of the Ribeira Brava to the mountain village of **SERRA DE ÁGUA** (map 6, M7), a somewhat sprawling place without any clear centre. However, its position, in one of Madeira's most dramatic valleys surrounded by craggy peaks, is hard to beat and it's the site of one of the island's two *pousadas* (see p.236).

From here, the road descends dramatically for 7km past the sheer terraced slopes of the valley to the noticeably warmer air of the valley floor, marked by an out-of-town supermarket just above the main coastal highway. Here the road forks and you can either head east to Funchal (see p.45) or go straight on to Ribeira Brava (see p.144).

Northern and central Madeira

T hough the highway makes the south coast of Madeira easier to explore, a trip to the **north** of the island is a must if you want to see Madeira's beauty at its rawest and most dramatic – even if the weather tends to be less clement. In the far northwest of the island, **Porto Moniz** is a bustling little place with natural sea pools, its own campsite and a plethora of hotels and restaurants. East of here, the coast road hugs the dramatic contours and steep slopes of the mountains that spill down to the sea, with the section from the picturesque village of **Seixal** to São Vicente one of the most expensive – and scary – stretches of road in Europe. **São Vicente** is a burgeoning resort on the junction of the road over the island to Ribeira Brava – its old town is one of the prettiest and least spoilt on the island – and it lies within easy reach of the extraordinary **Grutas de São Vicente**. From here, the coast road passes the fishing port of **Ponta Delgada**, with its own modest lido, before snaking up to **Boaventura**, a mountainside village with great walking possibilities. Further east lies some of Madeira's lushest

THE ROAD FROM PORTO MONIZ TO SÃO VICENTE

The sixteen kilometres of road from Porto Moniz to São Vicente is considered to be, in real terms, the most expensive stretch of road ever built, with the last section from Seixal to São Vicente being the most dramatic. The road was started in the early twentieth century and was completed by hand at a rate of about one kilometre a year – it took sixteen years in all. The road and tunnels had to be hacked out of sheer slopes and cliffs; at times workers had to be suspended by ropes to dig out the steeper sections. Not surprisingly, the road is extremely winding and narrow, with precipitous – but well-guarded – drops on the coastal side. By the end of the twentieth century, the increased volume of traffic had turned the narrower sections of the road into dangerous bottlenecks, with cars having to reverse to marginally wider sections or squeeze past each other and risk being scraped against the rock walls. To ease the problem, new tunnels have been cut along these sections, boosting the cost of the road but making the route much less harrowing. Nevertheless, drivers should still take great care.

agricultural land, amongst which you'll find the unspoilt village of São Jorge and the larger, bustling Santana, famous for its triangular houses and its hair-raising cable car down a sheer cliff face. Santana is also the gateway to Madeira's richest inland walking country, round Queimadas, and its highest peak at Pico Ruivo. Back on the coast, the northeast of the island is dominated by the towering rock of Penha de Águia, which casts a shadow over the little mountain village of Faial. From here it is a short drive inland to more excellent walks around Ribeiro Frio and Pico do Arieiro, the start of a peak-to-peak trek to Pico Ruivo.

Reviews of accommodation, restaurants and
bars in the north and centre of Madeira start
on p.237, p.274 and p.299 respectively.

PORTO MONIZ

Map 6, G1. Rodoeste buses #80 and #139 (Mon–Fri 2 daily, Sat 3 daily, Sun 1 daily).

Despite being as far away from Funchal as it is possible to get on Madeira, **PORTO MONIZ** is the north coast's liveliest and most developed town, with a cluster of cafés, restaurants and hotels gathered round its main attraction, two sets of natural **rock pools**, at either end of the main strip. There is also a small **harbour**, used when the town was a whaling station, and a historic **old town** slightly uphill from the development, spreading across a steep terraced hillside.

The town was originally named Ponta do Tristão, after the nearby headland, which marked the dividing point between the two captaincies – the administrative areas run by Zarco and Tristão Vaz Teixeira during the early colonial days. From 1533, however, the running of the town was taken over by Francisco Moniz – who later married Zarco's granddaughter – and in 1577 it was renamed after him. Thanks to its sheltered harbour – protected from the elements by the offshore islet, Ilhéu Mole – Porto Moniz became a major whaling centre in the nineteenth century, but until tourism began to make an impact in the late twentieth century it remained a remote outpost, its residents relying on the produce of the steep terraces, which are still farmed in the traditional way. Up the slopes around the old town you will still see fields lined with drystone walls or fences made of heather broom, which shelter the vines and crops from the northerly winds.

PORTO MONIZ

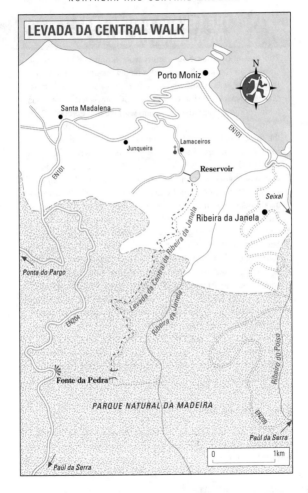

LEVADA DA CENTRAL WALK

Porto Moniz

Santa Madalena

Junqueira

Lamaceiros

Reservoir

Seixal

Ribeira da Janela

Ponta do Pargo

EN101

EN204

Levada da Central da Ribeira da Janela

Ribeira da Janela

Ribeiro do Poiso

Fonte da Pedra

EN209

PARQUE NATURAL DA MADEIRA

Paúl da Serra

Paúl da Serra

0   1km

N

THE LEVADA DA CENTRAL DA RIBEIRA DA JANELA

The two-and-a-half-hour return walk along the **Levada da Central da Ribeira da Janela** (or ninety minutes if you opt for the shorter walk) takes you up one of the north coast's most dramatic valleys and into the UNESCO-protected lauraceous forest, some of the oldest surviving woodland in Europe.

To get to the start of the walk, drive or take a taxi the 3km to the top of the hill on the the main Porto Moniz–Ponta do Pargo road. A few hundred metres after the road levels out, you'll see a side road on the left signed towards Lamaceiros, a pretty agricultural village around 1km off the main road. Alternatively, you can take bus #80 to the Lamaceiros turn-off – from where it is around fifteen minutes' walk to the start of the *levada* – though it leaves Porto Moniz at 5am (Mon–Sat). On reaching Lamaceiros, go through the village past its low church, then, beyond the village, head straight on down a track where the road doubles back on itself. You'll soon see a small reservoir on your left: leave your car here and walk down to the reservoir, to the right of which you'll pick up the start of the *levada*.

The *levada* path is well worn and easy to follow, with handy picnic tables set out at regular intervals – there are even green plastic bins alongside for rubbish. After a minute's walk, you'll come to the first picnic table below a radio mast. From here, the path passes rows of agapanthus and hydrangeas, which are dazzling in summer. After five minutes, you will pass another picnic table, just after which – as you turn a corner – you'll

The new town

Over the last decade or so, Porto Moniz's **new town** has become a popular destination for tourists tempted by the **natural sea pools** that have formed in volcanic rock here. The easterly pools, which are gathered below the *Restaurante*

hear then see the Ribeira da Janela way below you in the valley on the left.

A few hundred metres further on the path crosses a filtration plant. All along this stretch you'll see swifts swooping below you in the valley and hear the sound of scurrying lizards in the surrounding undergrowth. After fifteen minutes, you dive under the shade of dense trees for a short while until you emerge again to find a superbly positioned picnic table offering stunning views down to the sea and the village of Ribeira da Janela across the valley.

After another ten minutes or so you pass another picnic table in the shade of tall trees, not long after which the *levada* briefly disappears under the path. Just beyond where it re-emerges you reach another filtration plant and a sluice; walk along the side of the sluice – not up the path to the right – for more great views down the terraced valley. The next section of 200m or so is lined with little fruit trees, shortly beyond which is another picnic spot.

After forty minutes you turn another corner, allowing you to see the top of the valley, now closed in and a mass of dense green foliage – this is the lauraceous forest (see p.185). From here, the path narrows in sections and dives under the shade of trees, with gradually steeper drops. You can either turn back here or, if you want to walk through the lauraceous woodland itself, you can continue for another thirty minutes, gradually climbing the valley until the path ends where the *levada* disappears into a tunnel.

Cachalote (see p.275), consist of a series of interconnecting channels and shallow plunge pools, which get deliciously warm in summer, though sunbathing space on the surrounding rocks can get a bit squeezed. Just east of these pools lies the **harbour**, lined with colourful fishing boats; in summer, the jetty doubles as a diving board and overflow for the sea pool sunbathers. Just above the harbour you'll find the small **tourist office** (Mon 10am–3pm, Tues–Fri 10am–3.30pm, Sat noon–3pm; ☎291 852 594) and, on the opposite side of the road, the entrance to the **campsite** (see p.217) and the post office (Mon–Sat 9am–12.30pm & 2–5.30pm).

The road then continues west for 500m or so along the bottom of the campsite to another cluster of cafés and hotels above the second set of sea pools, most of which have been augmented with concrete. Although the pools are shallower and less good for swimming than their eastern counterparts, there is usually more space to lay your towel down.

The old town

While the seafront continues to sprout new hotels, the **old town** remains largely unaffected by tourism, its houses stacked up on the hill behind. The five-minute walk from the coast is very pleasant, especially during early evening when the air is cooler and the birds sing round the steep terraces. The village consists of low white fishermen's houses gathered round a faded yellow **church**, with a terracotta-tiled roof and a neat clock tower. Just below it, you'll find a couple of banks with ATMs and a mini-market for groceries.

There are good views over the coast from here, but if you have your own transport, it is worth driving through the village and zigzagging up the hillside, where the outlook gets more and more dramatic. There are two **miradouros** at which you can pull in, the lower one with a handy café, the upper with a small shrine.

The road also takes you up to the start of a superb **walk**, along the Levada da Central da Ribeira da Janela (see box on p.166). Beyond here, the main road continues south to Santa and on to Ponta do Pargo (p.155).

SEIXAL

Map 6, I3. Rodoeste bus #139 (Mon–Sat 2 daily, Sun 1 daily).

It is around 9km along the dramatic coast road from Porto Moniz to **SEIXAL**, the road looping past the offshore Ilhéus da Ribeira da Janela – so-called because one has a natural hole, or *janela* (window) right through it. Seixal itself is divided into two distinct parts: the fairly dull **upper town**, which spreads along the main road either side of the church, with a few shops and cafés, and the far prettier **lower town**, a tranquil cluster of traditional houses, connected by steep cobbled steps and interspersed with vegetable plots and vineyards surrounded by heather broom. All this overlooks a spectacular coastline backed by towering mountains.

To get to the lower town from the main road, follow the signs for the *cais* (quay); as you head down the hill, look out for the waterfalls pouring down the cliff and over a road tunnel further down the coast.

At the foot of the hill you reach the *cais*, a little **harbour** bobbing with fishing boats and overlooked by a handy café (see p.277). From the quay, you can take the steps down to the sea for some great swimming or, when the waves get up, you can swim in the new sea pools next door.

From Seixal, the coast road gets gradually narrower and more winding all the way to São Vicente, but a couple of kilometres beyond Seixal, you can park at a *miradouro*, signed Véu da Nova. Here, opposite the *Snack Bar O Véu da Nova*, which sells drinks and souvenirs, you get a great view of the aforementioned **waterfalls** spilling down into the sea.

SÃO VICENTE AND AROUND

Map 6, L3. Rodoeste bus #6 (2–3 daily); also bus #139 (1–2 daily).

Sitting at the junction between the north coast highway

and the pass over to Funchal, **SÃO VICENTE** has always been a popular stopping off point for Madeirans travelling from the north coast to the capital – and, more recently, its neatly spruced up **old town** has become similarly popular with tourists. Its neat cobbled streets, square and beautiful church make it one of Madeira's most attractive towns, with most of its touristic development concentrated out of the old centre along the coast road facing a coarse, rocky beach. A short walk inland, you can also go on a tour of the **Grutas** – an extraordinary complex of caves leading deep into surrounding hillsides.

The seafront

Coach parties disgorge their occupants at the car park by the bridge over the Ribeira da São Vicente near the sea, and most tourists head straight for the row of restaurants and shops facing the rocky beach in the area known as **Calhau**. The Atlantic here is usually far too thunderous to risk swimming, and copious amounts of driftwood are deposited on the stones – the wood is often burned in giant pyres on the beach. While at the seafront, take a look at the distinctive **Capela São Roque**, by the bridge – a rock pile with a cross on it and a chapel embedded in its front, dating from 1692.

Heading east over the bridge, it is a couple of minutes' walk to the village's surprisingly grand soccer **stadium**. Opposite here, in front of the *Estalagem Calamar* (see p.240), is a **lido**, the Piscina Calamar (open daily; free), with seawater pools and ladders down to the sea – though you should avoid sea swimming when it's rough. The pools get very lively at weekends in summer, with most people adjourning afterwards to the *Café Piscina Calamar*.

The old town

The **old town** of São Vicente lies half a kilometre up the Ribeira da São Vicente valley, and it remains one of Madeira's most picturesque spots. From the bridge, follow the old path just east of the river, which passes through a couple of rock arches and winds through undergrowth up the valley, until you come to an old bridge, which you cross to get to the centre of the old town – the walk takes about ten minutes, and bypasses the busier main road to the centre.

The central zone is completely pedestrianized and ridiculously pretty, its narrow streets lined with flowers and neatly tended cafés and shops, all gathered round a lovely seventeenth-century Baroque **church** with a chequered spire. Inside, you'll see a painting of São Vicente – Lisbon's patron saint – on the ceiling and beautiful *azulejos* on the lower walls. In front of the church is a cobbled **square**, surrounded by palm trees and adjacent to a carefully tended cemetery; locals while away their time here in the *Estoril Bar Pastelaria* (see p.299), which has outdoor tables.

Grutas de São Vicente

Map 6, L4. Daily: May–Oct 10am–7pm; Nov–April 10am–6.30pm; 30-minute tours every 15–20 minutes; 700$00/€3.50.

From the main Ribeira Brava–São Vicente road, a sign points northeast to the **Grutas de São Vicente**, a dramatic series of underground caves, 1km up the valley. The entrance is marked by a car park on the right of the road, from where a path leads to a small bridge and ticket office and on to the low, modern reception centre. There's a small duck pond, café and handicraft exhibition here to keep you amused while you await the next tour.

The **caves**, carved out of volcanic basalt rock, formed during Madeira's last volcanic eruption some 400,000 years

SÃO VICENTE AND AROUND

ago; they are about a kilometre long and some 40m underground at their deepest point. Water slowly filters through the porous rock to form a series of clear, cold rock pools and streams – you may notice it dripping on your head. The tour, accompanied by multilingual commentary, guides you through most of the cave tunnels, their chocolate-coloured roofs rippled like mousse. The caves have been lit and considerably modified since the Brit James Johnson stumbled upon them in 1855 – now you can comfortably walk upright accompanied by gentle piped music.

Nossa Senhora de Fátima

As you leave the caves, you'll see the distinctive church tower of **Nossa Senhora de Fátima**, completed in 1953, on the hilltop opposite, splendid in its solitude against a backdrop of green mountains. There are superb views of the chapel from a *miradouro* 5km above São Vicente. With your own car, take the main Funchal road inland and after 1.5km take the turn-off to the right signed Lanço/Gingas. Go past the *Casa do Lanço* and head uphill at any of the forks; soon you'll see signs to the *miradouro*.

PONTA DELGADA

Map 8, B1. São Roque do Faial bus #132 (1–2 daily); also Rodoeste bus #6 (2–3 daily).

From São Vicente, it is a six-kilometre drive east to **PONTA DELGADA**, a quiet, traditional fishing village, with an important **church**. Like Seixal, Ponta Delgada is split into two parts: the nondescript top half spreads along the main coast road, while the historic heart, which consists of a series of narrow lanes lined with local shops, lies downhill towards the sea. To get to the old centre from the main road, follow signs to the Piscina; the centre lies just above the Piscina to the east.

The seafront

Ponta Delgada's seafront is dominated by the **Igreja do Bom Jesus**, whose most famous relic is a charred cross, which becomes the focus of a religious festival in September, the **Festa de Senhor Jesus**. In common with other religious celebrations round the island, the festival commemorates the survival of a wooden crucifix after various mishaps. The first misadventure to befall this particular crucifix occurred in 1470, when it was washed ashore in a chest – presumably having been lost from a passing or sinking ship. Shortly afterwards the Capela do Senhor Bom Jesus was built to house it close to the spot where the crucifix was beached, but this burnt down in 1908. The crucifix, however, survived the fire and, though charred, now takes pride of place in the current church, constructed in 1919.

The church is flanked on one side by the giant modern Centro Social e Paroquial do Bom Jesus – a social centre for elderly locals – and on the other by a small chapel. Adjacent to the chapel is a tiny cemetery and the **Casa do Romeiro**, a small ochre-faced building, which sometimes hosts temporary art exhibitions, though its role is sure to diminish with the opening of a spanking new **Casa da Cultura** opposite. This attractive "house of culture" aims to promote local arts and sciences with regular temporary exhibitions, bringing modern Madeiran culture to one of its more traditional spots.

A couple of hundred metres east of the church, a track heads downhill past scrub and vegetable plots to the **Piscina**, the local lido. Here you'll find a sea pool, changing rooms and a small café (daily 9.30am–11pm) that offers drinks and can rustle up inexpensive snacks and seafood dishes; the octopus is usually a good bet.

PONTA DELGADA

BOAVENTURA

Map 8, C2. São Roque do Faial bus #132 (1–2 daily); bus #103 (Mon–Sat 4 daily, Sun 1 daily); Rodoeste bus #6 (2–3 daily).

From Ponta Delgada, the road loops inland for 3km east to **BOAVENTURA**, a small, agricultural hillside village clustered round a **church** set on a cobbled terrace offering fine views up the valley. The social centre of the village is the **café** opposite the church, the *Bar Café La Fé* (daily 8am–8pm), which also acts as the village shop and newsagent. There is a chemist and a bank on the main road alongside. Just below the café, a sign marked *miradouro* points you to the top of Boaventura's distinctive hillock, from where there are fine views of the coast and up the verdant valley behind. This scenic spot is also the site for the village **cemetery**. One of its graves belongs to a certain Miss Turner, an American who ran a tea room for British expats in Santo António da Serra in the early twentieth century. It is said that her gardener spoke so lovingly of his village, Boaventura, that although she never visited it, she asked to be buried there after her death. So in 1925, her coffin was dragged over the mountainous terrain so that she could be laid to rest in the graveyard under the palms.

EAST TOWARDS SANTANA

From Boaventura, the road twists up the verdant, precipitous valley of the Ribeira do Pôrco before plunging through a tunnel and winding back down to the coast through more lush farmland and vineyards. Despite the feeling of greater wealth, however, it is still a surprise to arrive suddenly at the fenced-off clifftop tourist resort of **Cabanas**, filled with bizarre circular white huts (see p.239). A little further on you come the more traditional **São Jorge**, an attractive village close to one of the north coast's best swimming spots at **Praia**, and **Quinta Furão**, a wine estate with its own hotel, shops and restaurant.

São Jorge

Map 8, F1. São Roque do Faial bus #103 (2–4 daily); also bus #132 (1–3 daily).

Beyond Cabanas, the road winds a couple of kilometres downhill to **SÃO JORGE**, a spruce little village made up of well-kept houses radiating out among vineyards from an eighteenth-century Baroque **church**. There's not a lot to do here beyond visiting the **café-restaurant** behind the church, the thatched-roofed *Casa de Palha* (literally "house of straw"; see p.276).

A five-minute drive or a pleasant fifteen-minute walk north of São Jorge is a **lighthouse**, which offers superb views down the coast. From the church, head downhill past a set of picnic tables and a small chapel on the right, following the road down and then up again through lush vineyards. At the top of the hill, opposite a small shop, turn right (away from the sign pointing to *Vigia*), and you'll soon pass a genuine *Casa de Palha*, used to store farm produce and equipment. Just past here you'll come to the little red-topped lighthouse on the Ponta de São Jorge to the left. From here you can just make out Ponta de São Lourenço. Heading back, you can detour to the signposted *Vigia*, a viewpoint looking over the coast.

Praia

Map 8, F1.

Back on the coast road towards Santana, a kilometre or so beyond São Jorge a sign points left to **Praia**, a small stony beach reached via a narrow road running parallel to the Ribeira de São Jorge. The road ends by a stone footbridge

THE COASTAL WALK FROM SÃO JORGE TO QUINTA FURÃO

São Jorge's church marks the starting point of an exhilarating two-hour **coastal walk** to Quinta Furão (see below), via Praia. From the church, head downhill towards the sea and take the first right at the small chapel. After around five minutes the road ends at a cemetery. Opposite the cemetery gates you will see some cobbled steps leading downhill. Go down these and cross a narrow road; you'll pick up the path slightly to the right. From here it's a steep, winding twenty-minute descent down to the ruins of an old port called Calhau. Turn right onto the coastal path and it is around five minutes to the old bridge at Praia, a great spot to cool off with a swim (see p.175). Continue over the bridge and you'll see the path in front of you, zigzagging steeply up the hill. Just over an hour from the bridge, the path rejoins civilization near the neat lawns of the Quinta Furão, where you can stop for a drink. From here it's a further 4km by road to Santana; you could get the Quinta to order a taxi or you could walk to the main road and catch bus #103 or #132 to Santana or back to São Jorge.

over the river – the halfway point of the coastal walk from São Jorge to Quinta Furão (see box above) – from which you can see the beach before you. However, the best place to swim is at the mouth of the river itself, which has been dammed to form a **natural pool**. In summer this remote pool can be surprisingly lively, with locals diving into the water off a makeshift diving board, and a seasonal **café** (summer only daily 9am–7pm), selling drinks and snacks.

Quinta Furão

Map 8, G2.

From São Jorge, the road winds east through increasingly

verdant farmland. After around 6km, a sign to the left points to **Quinta Furão**, a hotel and restaurant complex (see p.239 & p.276), set in one of Madeira's largest **vineyards**. The estate is run by the Madeiran Wine Company, and during the September harvest, tourists are encouraged to join in the traditional treading of the wine – bare footed, with men stripped to the waist. It's all totally geared to tourists, but free and fun nevertheless.

SANTANA AND AROUND

Map 8, G3. São Roque do Faial bus #103 (Mon–Sat 4 daily, Sun 1 daily); also bus #138 (2 daily).

Beyond Quinta Furão, the landscape gets gradually more built-up until you reach **SANTANA**, named after St Anne and famed for its distinctive **A-framed houses**, one of Madeira's most familiar images (see box on p.178). The village itself, spreading along the main coast road, is fairly ordinary, though its location, just above a spectacular **cable car** down dramatic cliffs and within easy access of some of Madeira's most impressive mountain scenery, makes it a handy base for a night or two.

Santana grew up in the centre of some of Madeira's most fertile farming land – it supports vines along with various fruits, including figs, mulberries, plums and kiwi fruits – so it is not surprising that it is a wealthy place. The modern centre is marked by a **town hall**, with a post office opposite and three distinctive, purpose-built Santana houses just below it; one of the houses acts as a public toilet, another as the **tourist office** (Mon–Fri 9.30am–1pm & 2.30–5.30pm, Sat 9.30am–1pm; ☏291 572 992). A more genuine Santana house is to be found further uphill along the main road opposite the turning to Pico Ruivo. The house is still lived in, though the owner is paid to keep it in mint condition, neatly painting the door and shutters in red and surrounding

SANTANA HOUSES

Known in Portuguese as *palheiros*, or haylofts, **Santana houses** are tiny thatched houses just big enough for a person to stand in. Consisting of little more than a ground-floor room with a platform wedged into the roof eaves – so very much like an "A" in cross-section – they are unique to Madeira. Their low, squat shape is ideally suited to withstand the wet and windy Atlantic weather that often lashes the north coast, the thatched roofs reaching down almost to the ground to protect the interior from the rain. The small, sheltered upper rooms form sleeping quarters, while the downstairs area is traditionally used for storage or as a living area. People cooked outside to avoid the risk of fires, and toilets were also well clear of the living area.

The houses first appeared in the early seventeenth century, but lost favour during the last century as modern building techniques – and Madeiran living standards – improved. A few Santana houses are still inhabited – mainly thanks to government incentives to attract tourists – but the majority of them (and there are hundreds scattered around the valleys around Santana) now house cattle, with corrugated iron roofs replacing the expensive thatch. In order to prevent cattle hurting themselves on the steep hillsides and to prevent damage to crops, cows are not allowed to roam wild in this part of the island and are kept constantly inside these triangular cow sheds – though all cattle are stringently monitored and well-cared for, it seems a fairly miserable existence.

it with dazzling flowers. In return, tourists can gawk at the tiny interior – when the owner is around.

Downhill from the town hall, the road winds past a series of small, neatly tended squares, around which you'll find a bandstand and a sunken children's playground. Next to the last of these squares – completely circular, with a fixed table-tennis table in the middle – you'll find the village **church**, with its little turreted clock tower, which marks Santana's historic centre. Just below the church you'll find a supermarket, while opposite and just uphill there are a couple of banks, shops and local cafés. If you're in a car, avoid the central zone, which has been made into a confusing and totally unnecessary one-way system.

The best time to visit Santana – and the only time it ever gets remotely busy – is during the February *Festa dos Compadres* and July's folk festival (see pp.30 & 31).

The Rocha do Navio Teleférico

Wed & Sat 8.30am–noon & 2–7pm, Sun 9am–noon & 2–7pm; 500$00/€2.50.

Below Santana's church, a signed road leads about a kilometre downhill through farmland to **Rocha do Navio Teleférico**, an extraordinary cable car which plummets terrifyingly down a sheer cliff to Rocha do Navio, a cultivated *fajã* on a rocky foreshore. The service, though popular with tourists, is geared towards the farmers working on the *fajã*; if you manage to pretend to be one, you only have to pay 100$00/€0.50. At the bottom of the cliff, there are fine views down the coast and a small **café** dispensing drinks; when the weather's calm you can also swim off the stony beach.

QUEIMADAS

Map 8, F4.

Inland from Santana lies one of Madeira's most enchanting and least spoilt **forest** areas (part of the UNESCO-protected lauraceous forest), which stretches round the **Queimadas** government rest house. *Queimadas* means "burning" – traditionally people brought combustible goods to burn here, safe in the knowledge that the cool, damp air would prevent fires getting out of control.

Unless you are very fit and fancy walking there and back from Santana, to get to Queimadas you'll need a car or taxi; follow the sign to Queimadas off the main EN101 around 200m south of Santana's tourist office, opposite a traditionally done up A-shaped house. Though only 5km away, it feels a lot longer, as the road is little more than a potholed track – some say the government

THE LEVADA DO CALDEIRÃO VERDE

The three- to four-hour return walk along the **Levada do Caldeirão Verde** (see map on pp.186–187) takes you through some of Madeira's most dramatic lauraceous woodland and across some extremely steep terrain – though the vegetation growing on the slopes removes the sense of vertigo you may otherwise experience. To undertake the walk, good footwear and a torch are essential and a jumper can be useful, as the air at this height is cool and most of the walk is in shade. In winter, rainfall is more than likely, so waterproofs are also a good idea.

Begin by heading northwest away from the road past the Casa das Queimadas and the picnic tables; you'll quickly pick up the *levada* on your right. Follow the path under ancient pine trees until you reach a gate, which you go through. Five minutes beyond here, a steep arrowed detour takes you down to the right round an unstable section of wall by a small waterfall, but it quickly climbs to rejoin the main *levada* path.

At times along this stretch the path narrows and you have to walk on the *levada* wall as it follows the twisting contours of the valley. After twenty minutes or so, you turn a corner and superb views of the densely wooded mountains come into has deliberately kept it this way to deter too many visitors.

The track climbs slowly through cultivated fields dotted with unmodernized Santana houses, most with corrugated roofs and many used to house livestock. After twenty minutes or so you will reach the **Casa das Queimadas**, an idyllic-looking thatched government rest house (see p.218), used by forestry workers and overhung with dazzling red-flowered camellia trees. The inside of the place is pretty basic, but you can use its toilets if needed. In front of the house there are wooden picnic tables under tall trees draped with Angle Hair moss and lichens, next to bubbling streams.

view. Look behind and you can see right down the valley of the Ribeira dos Arcos to São Jorge on the north coast.

After about an hour the *levada* passes through four tunnels which get progressively longer and lower. The first two are short. In the third tunnel, keep to the side of the path to avoid deep puddles which collect against the tunnel walls. In the fourth tunnel watch your head, too, as the roof juts down low in sections.

For the last half an hour or so, you'll be walking on a *levada* wall that is just 40cm wide with fairly steep drops below you. The woods here are a mixture of heather trees, lauricious forest and lily-of-the-valley trees – at one stage you pass a huge stump of a lily-of-the-valley tree thought to be over 800 years old. Finally, after around ninety minutes, you will reach a green amphitheatre of moss-covered rock, the **Caldeirão Verde**. A small path leads up to the bottom of a waterfall trickling into a small lake, a pleasant spot for a picnic. The *levada* path continues from here to Caldeirão do Inferno (Cauldron of Hell), an even more impressive waterfall about an hour further on, but it is a tough, tricky stretch, and unless you are an experienced walker it is best to turn back at Caldeirão Verde.

QUEIMADAS

Many people also come up here to walk the **Levada do Caldeirão Verde**, rated one of the best *levada* walks on the island (see box on p.180) — a great spot for a picnic or an afternoon chilling out, as many locals do at weekends. If you fancy a shorter walk (about thirty minutes each way), look for the sign by the road next to the Casa das Queimadas, which directs you onto a gentle wooded path leading to **Pico das Pedras**, a picnic spot on the road linking Santana with Achada do Teixeira and Pico Ruivo (see map on pp.186–187).

INLAND TO PICO RUIVO

Map 8, D6.

At 1862m, **Pico Ruivo** (Redhead Peak) is Madeira's highest point, offering the most spectacular views over the island. Despite its height, the peak is relatively accessible by car on the narrow EN101-5 road (clearly signposted off the main EN101 coast road) from Santana to Achada do Teixeira. Around 10km from Santana, the road passes **Pico das Pedras**, an attractive wooded picnic spot and a good base for some local walks (see map on pp.186–187). The road then climbs onto the barer lower slopes of Pico Ruivo until it ends some 15km beyond Pico das Pedras at a car park next to the somewhat ungainly **Achada do Teixeira** government rest house. If you take a look behind the house you will see an impressive series of natural basalt columns known as **Homem em Pé**, the "standing man". The grassy surrounds make a good picnic spot and on a clear day you can see right down to the north coast from here.

Back at the car park, you will see the start of a paved path to the **summit** of Pico Ruivo, a relatively easy walk along a flat ridge; allow around an hour and a half to two hours return. After around forty minutes you'll see Pico Ruivo's government rest house, a small white building. Just before here a path heads off steeply to the left; this leads on to Pico do Ariero (see box on p.188).

From the government rest house, it is a steep but short climb to a viewing platform at the summit. It's a wonderful spot: wisps of cloud and smoke-like mist drift below you or creep up from the valleys, and there is complete silence apart from the sound of the wind and the odd hardy bird. To the southwest, the valley sides tumble down to the tiny red rooftops of Curral das Freiras (see p.118), while across a wide valley to the west is the astonishing sight of the distant wind turbines spinning on Pául da Serra, almost at the same height. Southeast lie the huge craggy peaks of Pico das Torres and Pico do Ariero.

FAIAL AND PENHA DE ÁGUIA

Map 8, H4. São Roque do Faial bus #103 and #138 (2–4 daily); SAM bus #53 and #78 (1–5 daily).

Back on the coast, if you head east from Santana, you soon leave behind the sprawl of buildings along the road and pass into lush, green and undeveloped countryside once more. After around 4.5km, the road turns a bend to reveal stunning views down the coast towards Ponta de São Lourenço and the Ilhas Desertas; 200m or so further and you can pull over at a small roadside shrine. Two kilometres beyond the shrine, just off the main EN101, lies the quiet, agricultural hillside village of **FAIAL**, which takes its name from an evergreen shrub, the wax myrtle (*faia* in Portuguese), which grows in the area. The village is dominated by its **church**, with a distinctive, tall white belltower; inside, giant chandeliers dangle from the high, arched ceiling and *azulejos* adorn the lower half of the walls. From in front of the church, a cobbled **square** centred round a substantial oak tree offers great views over Penha de Águia, which looms over the village to the southeast.

From Faial, the road passes over the deep valley of the Ribeira Sêca. You'll see the old **bridge** below the modern structure, which was built after floods threatened the original crossing. In summer, the flat river bed buzzes to the sound of a go-cart track the other side of the arches.

Just beyond here, the road splits. You can either take the right hand fork to Funchal via Ribeiro Frio or continue east to Porto da Cruz and the eastern spur of Madeira (see p.139). This stretch of the coast is dominated by the sheer-sided rocky cube known as **Penha de Águia** (Eagle Rock), a 590-metre-high chunk, its lower half terraced into fields, the upper half a wilderness where ospreys nest. A small road skirts the lower slopes of the rock and there are extremely tough footpaths up to its summit – about an hour and a half's climb, and only suitable for the very fit.

RIBEIRO FRIO

Map 8, F7. São Roque do Faial bus #103 (Mon–Sat 4 daily, Sun 2 daily); also bus #138 (Mon–Fri 2 daily, Sun 1 daily).

Roughly halfway back to Funchal from Santana is the tiny village of **RIBEIRO FRIO**, named after the cold river that runs through it – cold because of its high and secluded position in a wooded valley which gets little sun. But the cool air does not stop the flora from thriving: Pride of Madeira, hydrangeas and orchids give colour to the well-tended village gardens. Its main site, however, is a government-run **trout farm**, set in more attractive gardens dotted with impressive topiary. Fed by several local springs, the fresh water pools are a teeming mass of swirling fish, some of which end up on the menu of the local **restaurant**, *Victor's Bar* (see p.276).

RIBEIRO FRIO

184

The woodland around Ribeiro Frio is part of the lauraceous forest native to Madeira and forms the backdrop for some great *levada* walks, the most popular being the gentle thirty- to forty-minute return walk to **Balcões**, a series of wooden balconies (*balcões*), which offer sweeping views over the island's highest peaks; the walk is clearly signposted to the west of the village (see map on pp.186–187). A tougher walk is signposted off to the east to **Portela** (see p.138), a twelve-kilometre hike taking three to four hours.

PICO DO ARIEIRO

Map 8, E7.

It is a short drive south from Ribeiro Frio to the turning to Madeira's most accessible mountain summit at **Pico do Arieiro**. Despite being the third highest point on Madeira at 1818m – so high that the mountain top is often well above the cloud line – Pico do Arieiro sits at the end of a road which ferries an endless stream of cars and coaches to a messy car park and *pousada* right next to the summit. This does not detract from the spectacular views, but unless you get there very early or very late, don't expect this to be a quiet experience.

As the road climbs up the increasingly barren slopes, a small sign to the left points out the **Poço de Neves** (snow well), an igloo-shaped hut built in 1800. Before electric refrigeration, ice was stored here before being carried down to local hospitals; it was also used to supply gin and tonics at *Reid's Palace Hotel*. A little beyond here is the car park, usually lined with mini buses and tour coaches. Most people head straight to the *pousada* **café** which sells over-priced sandwiches, drinks and snacks. Despite its views, the café has all the charm of a motorway service station, though the *pousada* itself (see p.237) is a good place to spend the night if you fancy an early start on the summit when it is free of crowds.

PICO DO ARIEIRO

185

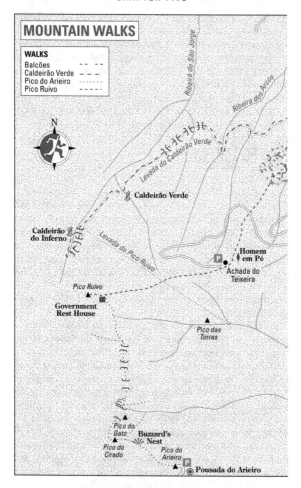

MOUNTAIN WALKS

WALKS

Balcões	– – – –
Caldeirão Verde	– – –
Pico do Arieiro	....
Pico Ruivo	– – – – –

N

Ribeira de São Jorge

Ribeira dos Arcos

Levada do Caldeirão Verde

Caldeirão Verde

Caldeirão do Inferno

Levada do Pico Ruivo

Homem em Pé

Achada do Teixeira

Pico Ruivo

Government Rest House

Pico das Torres

Pico do Gato

Buzzard's Nest

Pico do Cirado

Pico do Arieiro

Pousada do Arieiro

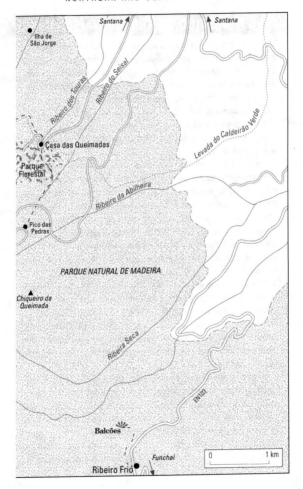

WALK FROM PICO DO ARIEIRO TO PICO RUIVO

The walk from Pico do Arieiro to Pico Ruivo (see map on pp.186–187) is the most spectacular walk on Madeira – and consequently one of the most popular. Despite going between the island's highest peaks on a path with some pretty scary drops at times, the walk is easily manageable if you take sensible precautions, wear good boots, take a torch and do not suffer vertigo – and especially if you have someone to pick you up from the other end at Achada do Teixeira, around three hours' walk away.

From around 10am, the car park at Pico do Arieiro fills with minibuses taking people on organized walks (see p.309 for more details), which are recommended to avoid the tricky return. If you are not with a group and would like the security of other people around you, just tag on to one of the groups – but don't expect to get a free lift at the other end. On the other hand if you want to avoid the walking groups, start as early as possible, when you're also more likely to get clear views.

The clearly signed path heads off from the car park along a narrow spine of rock with drops to either side, though any steep parts are fenced off and there is little danger as long as you stick to the path. During this first stretch of walk, the path passes through and above a startling volcanic landscape, with basalt columns and sills rising like bones through the soft, reddish ferrous soil.

After around 40 minutes the path splits, with the right fork passing round Pico dos Torres. Stick to the left fork (the right-hand path is unstable), which descends some steps before passing through a series of short tunnels, the first of which goes under Pico do Gato. Once through the tunnel, a gated path leads right, but continue straight on. The next section, a fifteen-minute walk until the second tunnel, is the scariest, as the narrow path crosses a very steep drop with just a rather wobbly wire fence to protect you from the precipice. But there are plenty of mountain plants to take your mind off the drop, especially in May or June when they are in flower, including tiny pink geraniums, Pride of Madeira and the weird interlocking, disk-like leaves of the horse leeks which stick out at odd angles on the cliff face. You will also smell wild herbs such as thyme and oregano.

Shortly after the second tunnel the path goes through a third, slightly longer, tunnel, soon followed by two shorter tunnels (after the fifth tunnel another path joins from the right, but continue straight on), before winding past a section of ancient, 200-year-old heather trees. At the side of the path, you'll also see some caves, which shepherds use for shelter, along with their animals. The path then climbs quite steeply; here the contorted, bleached white branches of the heather trees are intertwined along the edge of the path to stabilize the soil against rock falls.

Two hours into the walk, you come to the Pico Ruivo government rest house (see p.182), a lovely spot with trees all around (and a public toilet), where most tour groups rest for lunch. The summit of Pico Ruivo is a tantalizing climb above: the path is steep, but it only takes ten minutes to reach a viewing platform at the summit, with stunning views (see p.183).

At 1862m, this point has even more spectacular views than Pico Arieiro (which you can see in the distance). From the summit, either return the way you came to Pico Arieiro (taking great care to follow the route in reverse and not to stray from the main path) or, if you have transport to collect you, head back down to the government rest house, from where the path continues for around 45 minutes northeast across a relatively flat ridge to the car park at Achada do Teixeira (see p.182).

PICO DO ARIEIRO

From the *pousada* it's a short walk to a plaque which marks the actual **summit** of Pico do Arieiro. On a clear day the views are astounding, with both coasts of the island clearly visible, though, more often than not, at least one of the coasts will be submerged beneath fluffy clouds, itself an impressive sight. If you're unlucky, the summit itself will be shrouded in cold mist.

The car park marks the start of one of the most spectacular **walks** on the island, across to Pico Ruivo (see box on p.188). Unless you have arranged for someone to meet you at the other end, you'll need to allow around five to six hours for a tough return trip. Alternatively, consider taking one of the numerous organized walks (see p.310 for addresses), which include pick-ups at Pico Ruivo.

Another alternative is to walk just the first section of the route to Pico Ruivo, as far as the **Buzzard's Nest**, clearly signposted off the main path. This is a relatively easy fifty-minute return walk to a dizzy *miradouro* with fantastic views down to the south coast, with the distant shape of an HEP station way below and the Pico do Gato (Cat's Peak) – a craggy pinnacle with a tunnel through it – to the west. Remember, however, that the return journey is uphill.

From Pico do Arieiro, you can take the EN202 east as an alternative route to Santo da Serra and Machico (see p.136 & p.126), or head back to Funchal via Camacha (see p.104). Alternatively, you can reach Funchal on the Poiso road via Terreiro da Luta and Monte (see pp.98 & 94).

POISO AND THE PARQUE ECOLÓGICO DO FUNCHAL

Map 3, F2. São Roque do Faial bus #103 (Mon–Sat 4 daily, Sun 2 daily); also bus #138 (Mon–Fri 2 daily, Sun 1 daily).

The EN103 across the island begins its descent to Funchal at **Poiso**, a 1400-metre mountain pass. Poiso means "resting place", as this was the traditional spot for travellers to stop when heading from coast to coast. There's not a lot to the place, but many drivers still pause at the excellent *Casa de Abrigo*, a bar-restaurant serving mountain food.

The steep slopes to the west of Poiso form part of the **Parque Ecológico do Funchal**, a protected area used as an outdoor "education centre" for students. You'll see tracks signed into the park off the main Poiso–Funchal road. Once in the park, there are further marked paths, picnic tables and barbecue spots. There's also a **campsite** at Montado do Baireiro, near Poiso (see p.216), though access and use of the campsite is strictly limited to those with official permits issued by the Department of Agriculture.

The park's springs have traditionally been Funchal's main source of water. The park covers ten square kilometres of land known as the Montado do Barreiro, which stretches from the edges of Funchal to a height of 1800m, close to Pico do Arieiro. The steep slopes, fed by deep bedded water courses, create microclimates that are ideal for a variety of flora and bird life to thrive.

Since 1918, Funchal Council has been buying up private land in a bid to try to reverse soil erosion caused by overgrazing, tree felling, forest fires and the damage created by the planting of non-indigenous eucalyptus and acacia trees. The area remains home to several indigenous plants including Til trees and giant species of laurel such as Loureiro, Vinhático and Barbusano. Other slopes shelter heathers, bilberry and the rare sorveira, one of the island's most threatened native plants. It's also a great area for birds: species include the Manx shearwater, sparrowhawk, buzzard, kestrel, red-legged partridge, woodcock, rock and laurel pigeon, barn owl, Madeiran robin, blackcap, firecrest, canary and linnet.

POISO AND THE PARQUE ECOLÓGICO DO FUNCHAL

Porto Santo

The small island of **Porto Santo**, just 11km long and 6km wide, lies around 75km northeast of Madeira. Relatively flat, arid and undeveloped, with a long swathe of pristine sandy beach, the island couldn't be more different from Madeira. Porto Santo's beach is definitely its main attraction, and in summer Madeirans go over in their droves for day-trips and weekends. It's little visited, however, by foreigners and the island is still one of Europe's least discovered beach destinations.

Vila Baleira is the island's capital and the only place of any size on the island, though even this is little more than a village. Despite a population of less than three thousand, it is a surprisingly lively place graced with traditional Portuguese architecture and full of semi-tropical trees and flowers. Its main sights can easily be covered in a few hours, but a good range of shops, restaurants and hotels, all a short distance from the beach, make it a great place to stay for a few days. If you're after complete peace and quiet, you should head west to the village of **Campo de Baixo**, or to the small resort of **Cabeço da Ponta**, where the beach is wider and emptier. Between here and the furthest point, **Ponta da Calheta**, there is virtually no development. The rest of the island consists of an unforgiving landscape of eroded slopes and barren soil, but there are a few places worth heading for if you want a change from the beach. There are superb viewpoints at either end of the beach, at **Miradouro das Flores** and **Portela** respectively, and a lovely picnic spot at **Morenos**, in the west of the island. In the east, the peaks of **Pico do Castelo**, **Pico do Facho** and **Pico Branco** offer some rewarding walking possibilities.

Reviews of accommodation, restaurants and bars on
Porto Santo start on p.241, p.278 and p.300 respectively.

Some history

Porto Santo was discovered by the Portuguese explorers Zarco and Teixeira in 1418. They docked in its sheltered waters before setting off to explore the more forbidding-looking island of Madeira, its cloud-shrouded hulk clearly visible on the horizon from the west coast. Portuguese colonizers – mainly farmers and fishermen from the Algarve and Alentejo regions – settled on Porto Santo from 1420. They planted the island with vines and sugar cane and exploited the native dragon trees for their sap which could be made into dye. The island's first governor was Bartolomeu Perestrelo, of Genoese ancestry, a friend of fellow Genoese, **Christopher Columbus**, who frequently visited Madeira and Porto Santo in the late 1470s.

Unlike its sister island, Porto Santo never really prospered. The dragon trees were quickly felled, while many of the crops were decimated by rabbits introduced by the colonizers. The low-lying, broad coastline was also extremely vulnerable to **pirate attack**, and between the fifteenth and the eighteenth centuries, Moorish, French and English pirates looted more or less at will.

Madeirans often refer to the people of Porto Santo as "profetas" after a cult which grew up in 1533 under one Fernando Nunes and his niece. The pair claimed they were

PÓTO SANTO

in direct contact with God – they supposedly proved this by being able to list people's sins – and started a religious movement that was so popular that the Madeiran church felt threatened and had them arrested, putting a stop to the cult.

Porto Santo remained a backwater for much of the twentieth century; electricity did not arrive on the island until 1954. The opening of the **airport**, partly as a NATO base, in 1960, was a major boost to the economy – visitors to Madeira landed here before continuing by ferry until Madeira's airport opened in 1964. Though the opening of Madeira's own airport took this trade away, the airport still functions as a NATO base today. The island continued to rely largely on agriculture until a severe drought in the late 1960s. Years of deforestation were probably to blame and rainfall has been very low since, driving farmers out of business and all but destroying the island's wine trade. The local government has embarked on a long-term **reforestation** programme, but it will be decades before the problem is reversed.

Today's population of just over three thousand is mainly employed in public services, but an increasing number are moving into construction and tourism. The tourist trade is still pretty low-key but steadily expanding. Plans are afoot to construct a golf course, a hypermarket and marina and to double the island's visitor capacity with a new hotel near Cabeço da Ponta.

Getting there

The Porto Santo Ferry Line (☎291 982 543) runs a daily **ferry** from Funchal harbour to **Porto de Abrigo** (map 9, G5) on the south coast (Sat–Thurs 8am, Fri 6pm; ☎291

210 300; 10,000$00/€50 return). The journey time is around three hours. You should arrive at the ferry terminal at least thirty minutes before departure time. Large items of luggage can be left on the numbered palettes next to the ferry entrance; you'll need to remember the number and retrieve the luggage yourself at the other end. The boat has plenty of seating inside and out and also has a bar, self-service café, TV lounge and children's play area. A new ferry is due to enter into service in 2003 and will cut the journey time to two and a half hours. **Buses** meet the ferry at Porto de Abrigo and take you to Vila Baleira in five minutes (200$00/€1). Taxis are also available and cost around 800$00/€4. You can also hire *carriolas* (see p.196), traditional horse and traps, but as the road between the harbour and Vila Baleira is hardly the most picturesque stretch of the island, you're best off saving this for elsewhere.

Regular TAP Air Portugal **flights** from Funchal airport operate every one to two hours throughout the day (☎291 239 252/3; 15,000$00/€75 return) and take around fifteen minutes. The airport is a ten-minute drive north of Vila Baleira. There are no buses from the airport, but plenty of taxis: reckon on paying 1000$00/€5 for a trip into town.

Getting around

Six **bus** routes, operated by Horários de Transportes, run round the island serving most sights of interest – details are given in the text – but they are geared up to the needs of local people rather than tourists, so you may have to hang around for return buses. **Taxis** are relatively inexpensive; a ride from one end of the island to the other costs no more than 3000$00/€15, except during weekends and at night

GETTING AROUND

ISLAND TOURS AND WALKS

Two companies operate sightseeing **tours** on the island. An open-top bus, run by Moinho (℡291 982 780), does a daily four-hour circuit of the island all year-round, leaving at 2pm from the petrol station outside the Pingo Doce in Vila Baleira (minimum of five people; 1000$00/€5 per person). The other company, Lazer Mar (℡965 011 390), offers two- to three-hour tours on request with a pick-up from your hotel, usually at around 2.30pm (3000$00/€15 per person). They can can also organize summer jeep safaris and **walks**, usually to the western peaks, from around 500$00/€12.50 per person.

when tariffs double. The main taxi rank in Vila Baleira is on Rua Dr Nuno Silvestre Teixeira (℡291 982 334). You can phone the rank to order a taxi, or ask any hotel or café to do this for you, though some may charge up to 250$00/€1.25 for this service.

You can also rent a **car** or **scooter** – worth considering if you want to do one of the inland walks detailed in this chapter. Car rental is available at the airport from Budget (℡291 983 008), or from Moinho, on Rua Levada do Canho 2, in Vila Baleira (℡291 982 780, ℻291 982 403). You can rent scooters from Moser, Rua João Gonçalves Zarco 5, Vila Baleira (℡291 982 162, ℻291 982 163).

Another option is to rent a **bike**, a good way of getting up and down the flat coast road; bicycles are rented out to non-residents by all the large hotels (see p.241). Prices start at around 500$00/€2.50 an hour, 3000$00/€15 a day.

A slower but more traditional form of transport is the covered **carriolas**, colourful pony and traps that can be hired from the harbour or on the junction of Avenida Dr Manuel Gregório Pestana Júnior and Avenida Infante Dom Henrique in Vila Baleira. Tell the driver where you'd like to go and, within reason, he'll take you pretty much anywhere

within an hour of the capital. Half-hour rides start from
4000$00/€20 or 6000$00/€30 for an hour.

Information and services

The **tourist office** is in Vila Baleira on Avenida Henrique
Vieira de Castro 5 (Mon–Fri 9.30am–1.30pm &
2.30–5.30pm, Sat 10am–12.30pm; ☎291 982 361), just off
the main square. The helpful staff can give out details of
local events and rooms in private houses round the island.

The main **post office** is opposite the tourist office, which
contains **telephone** booths, useful for international calls.
There are **banks** with ATMs at the bottom end of Avenida
Henrique Vieira de Castro 5 on the corner with the main
south-coast highway. There are two places in Vila Baleira
where you can access the **Internet**: the gym club in the basement of *Hotel Torre Praia* (daily 8am–noon & 4–10pm at
800$00/€4 per hour ☎291 985 292; ✉cluvi@hotmail.com);
and Insulamatica, Rua João Goncalves Zarco 15 (Mon–Fri
2–6.30pm; ☎291 982 037, ✉insulamatica@insulamatica.pt).

Eastern Porto Santo

The east is the hillier half of the island, and includes the
picturesque main settlement, **Vila Baleira**. Apart from the
village of **Camacha**, the area inland from Vila Baleira is
sparsely populated, dominated by three conical peaks, Pico

do Castelo, Pico do Facho and Pico Branco, relatively green oases that offer good **walking** possibilities in an otherwise barren landscape.

VILA BALEIRA

Map 9, E5.

With its largely sixteenth- and seventeenth-century architecture, red terracotta roofs, cobbled streets and exotic plants, **Vila Baleira** is as picturesque and lively a village as any on Madeira. Buses from Porto de Abrigo stop by the Pingo Doce supermarket on the main through road, Avenida Dr Manuel Gregório Pestana, from where it is just a minute's walk west to Avenida Infante Dom Henrique, the palm-lined avenue leading to the main square, the highly attractive **Largo do Pelourinho**. This is the historic core of Vila Baleira, containing the village's liveliest café, *Bar Gel Burger* (see p.301), whose tables spill out under the palms next to the distinctive squat, two-tiered building of the **Câmara Municipal** (town hall), flanked by sentry-like dragon trees. Adjacent is the attractive seventeenth-century **Igeja de Nossa Senhora da Piedade**, built on the site of Vila Baleira's original church which was destroyed by pirates in 1667. A large decorative *azulejos* panel adorns the exterior, and there are further *azulejos* inside.

Next to the church, Rua José S. Moura Caldeira
climbs steeply above the town offering superb
views of the town and the sea.

Casa Museu Cristóvão Colombo

Tues–Fri 10am–6pm, Sat & Sun 10am–1pm; free.

An arrow to one side of the Igeja de Nossa Senhora da

CHRISTOPHER COLUMBUS ON PORTO SANTO

Christopher Columbus's links with Porto Santo began in 1478 when he visited the island while working for a Genoese sugar merchant based in Lisbon. He may have been visiting fellow Genoese Bartolomeu Perestrelo, Porto Santo's first governor, or exploring the possibilities of exporting sap from the island's dragon trees. He was soon to return, for in 1479 he married Filipa Moniz, Bartolomeu Perestrelo's daughter, whom he met after a church service in Machico in Madeira. It is thought that they lived on Porto Santo until 1484, possibly in the house which is now Vila Baleira's Columbus Museum. In 1484, they moved to Funchal, where not long afterwards Filipa died giving birth to their son.

During his time on Porto Santo, it is said that Columbus was inspired to set off for America after seeing seeds and wood washed up on Porto Santo's beach, making him wonder if there was land further west. He asked the court in Lisbon to sponsor his explorations, but was refused any help. In 1485, Spain agreed to back his journey, and in 1492 he set off from Palos, landing on the American continent three months later, though at the time he was convinced he had discovered a western sea route to India.

The house thought to have been Columbus's home on Porto Santo was turned into the Casa Museu Cristóvão Colombo in 1992 on the five hundredth anniversary of his discovery of America. Keen to exploit the Columbus connection further for its tourist potential, the island's administration inaugurated the first **Christopher Columbus Week** in September 2000, which is set to be an annual event (check the exact dates with the tourist office). The five-day festival consists of re-enactments of Columbus's landing on Porto Santo in a replica boat, a mock wedding ceremony of the kind that Columbus and Filipa Moniz would have gone through, period musical performances, flag ceremonies (parades in which flags are juggled and thrown in the air) and a medieval market.

VILA BALEIRA

Piedade points up to Rua Cristóvão Colombo, a narrow
alley housing the island's most famous building, the **Casa
Museu Cristóvão Colombo**, said to have once been
the home of Christopher Columbus (see box). Now
heavily restored, the building comprises an attractive
series of rooms displaying artefacts either connected with
Columbus or related to the history of the island. There
are various portraits of the great man and scenes from his
adventures, together with maps of his journeys and mod-
els of the boats he sailed in. There is also an eclectic array
of historic household implements donated by various
islanders. The final room, just off the central courtyard,
contains two sunken grain stores along with treasures
retrieved from the *Carrock*, a Dutch boat owned by the
East India Company which sank off the north coast of
Porto Santo in 1724 en route to Jakarta. The ship went
down with most of its crew, boxes of silver ingots,
Spanish and Dutch coins and valuable ceramics. Some of
the cargo was recovered by Englishman John Letbridge in
1726, but it was not until 1974 that the rest was salvaged
and donated to the museum by the Madeiran government.

The seafront

Leafy Avenida Infante Dom Henrique takes you from Largo
do Pelourinho down to the beach and jetty. Lined with
benches and offering superb views up and down the beach,
the jetty is a popular spot for evening walks and young
lovers. Just by the entrance to the jetty is a restored wind-
mill with white-cloth sails, housing a souvenir shop.
Windmills once played an important part in Porto Santo's
economy, and many, mostly in ruins, can still be seen dotted
around the island.

BOAT TRIPS

Boat trips from Vila Baleira to Ilhéu de Ferro (see p.208) and back are run by Moser, Rua João Gonçalves Zarco 5, Vila Baleira (Ⓣ 291 982 162, Ⓕ 291 982 163). The three-hour tours, calling at Ilhéu de Baixo and Ilhéu de Ferro and including swimming stops and free drinks, are a great half-day out and the best way of seeing the island from the sea. Trips operate on Wednesdays and Saturdays from May to October (minimum six people; 4800$00/€24 per person).

The soft sand on Porto Santo is said to have healing properties, ideal for those with eczema and varicose veins, and elderly folk can often be seen lying buried up to their neck.

From the jetty there are steps down to the blue flag **beach**, though the town stretch inevitably is the busiest on the island, and is also partially stony. The widest and sandiest bit of town beach is to the west of the jetty, backed by a couple of decent cafés (see p.301). There's also a diving platform that you can swim to offshore from the Balneários Municipal, municipal bathing facilities, which consists of a row of changing huts and is where you can rent out pedaloes. Just beyond here is the modern *Hotel Torre Praia* (see p.243).

INLAND FROM VILA BALEIRA

Inland from Vila Baleira the road heads north past the airport. This stretch of the island is quite built up. It is traditional for families to build a house as a dowry for their sons' weddings, and the amount of construction going on suggests that more than a few romances are blossoming,

INLAND FROM VILA BALEIRA

though beyond the village of **Camacha** – known for its fine restaurants – the population thins dramatically round the island's three main **peaks**. Of these, **Pico do Castelo** is the most accessible, with a road leading to a superb *miradouro* near the summit. Further east lies **Pico do Facho**, the island's highest peak which commands stunning views over the island. A third peak, **Pico Branco**, can be reached on another great walking route from the main north-coast road. South of the peaks lies the island's most barren landscape – around the remote hamlets of **Serra de Dentro** and **Serra de Fora**. The south coast becomes visible from **Portela**, a *miradouro* offering views of the whole length of the beach.

Camacha and Fonte da Areia

Map 9, F2. Bus #1 from Vila Baleira (2–3 daily).

Camacha is the main settlement in the north, consisting of a sprawl of white houses set on a barren slope overlooking the rocky north coast. Much of the local population works at the prominent Portuguese Navy radio station compound nearby, which helps to support two popular **restaurants** (see p.278), the main reason to visit an otherwise uninteresting village.

A road from Camacha heads downhill to the coast and **Fonte da Areia**, the "spring of the sands", once Camacha's main water supply. In 1843, the spring was channelled through a tap set in a stone shelter. The water is said to have healing powers, and for a time it was bottled and sold to Madeira and mainland Portugal, but the process became uneconomic. A series of stone huts providing shelter has grown up round the spring in a little oasis of palm trees, a tranquil spot for a picnic. A marked trail winds steeply down a cliff to a wave-battered sandy beach – a pleasant, if tiring, thirty-minute return walk.

Pico do Castelo

Map 9, F3.

Camacha is also the starting point of a rough, cobbled track up to **Pico do Castelo**, the wooded peak that towers over the village. The track peters out at a cacti-lined *miradouro* offering great views of the airport and both north and south coasts. A rusting cannon is the only one that remains of twelve that once circled the mountain, part of the seventeenth-century fortifications installed to keep the Spanish at bay during their occupation of Portugal from 1581 to 1640. From the *miradouro* a path continues right to the summit of the mountain, at 437m the fourth highest on the island; from here, the path continues all the way to **Pedragal**, an abandoned farm, on the main north-coast road. However, if you fancy walking the entire route – it takes around two hours – it's best to do it in reverse to avoid ending your walk in the middle of nowhere. You could easily get a taxi to Pedragal, for example, and after your walk take a bus or taxi from Camacha back to your hotel. Pedragal is a strip of barren wasteland practically devoid of any vegetation, though the relics of abandoned terraces testify to the fact that this land was once quite fertile. From Pedragal the walk to Pico do Castelo is clearly signposted, though it is a tough climb, circling the cedar-topped peaks of Pico da Gandaia and Pico do Facho en route. From Pico do Castelo, however, it is a relatively easy descent to Camacha.

Pico Branco and Terra Chã

A couple of kilometres further east of Pedragal lies the start of another signed mountain walk to the lookout point of **Terra Chã** (map 9, I3) via **Pico Branco** (map 9, H3). It's a four-kilometre return trek and takes two to three hours.

Perhaps the best walk on the island, it's relatively easy and takes in a diverse landscape, from desert-like scrub to woodland, with excellent views all the way. The path takes you up the steep, barren slopes of Pico Branco. As you approach the top of the 450-metre-high mountain the scenery becomes greener and wooded. The mountain is a refuge to a rare species of giant snail that was once common on the island, quite likely to be the only form of non-bird or insect life you'll encounter. From here the path continues to **Terra Chã**, the northeastern tip of the island, from where there are superb views of Ilhéu das Cenouras to the east.

For more information and advice on walking in Madeira and Porto Santo see p.309.

South to Portela

Bus #3 from Vila Baleira to Portela and Serra de Fora (4–5 daily).
From the start of the Pico Branco path the road swings south through the deep Serra de Dentro valley, perhaps the most depressing scenery on the island. Once, this was prime agricultural land, but over the years, owing to drought, this has given way to row upon row of deserted, terraced slopes. The tiny village of **Serra de Dentro** (map 9, H3) itself has become a ghost town of eerily decaying houses and farm buildings – the only remaining inhabitants are two elderly German ladies. The only other signs of life in the arid landscape are hardy birds, including kestrels, falcons and the crested hoopoes.

The scenery becomes a little greener beyond **Serra de Fora** (map 9, G4), a small village whose best-known resident sells traditional palm-leaf hats; she often displays them for sale by the roadside.

A kilometre south, the road swings round to the *miradouro* at **Portela** (map 9, G5), a superb viewpoint, affording sweeping views of the beach and harbour below.

Capela de Nossa Senhora da Graça

Map 9, F4.
Beyond the Portela viewpoint, past a line of deserted windmills on a blowy ridge, you'll see the hilltop **Capela de Nossa Senhora da Graça**, parts of which date back to the fifteenth century, making it one of the oldest churches on the island. The original church was built on a spring and said to have miraculous healing powers, though the spring has long since dried up. The church lay in ruins from 1812 to 1949, when it was rebuilt in its current form.

Western Porto Santo

The western part of Porto Santo is flatter than the eastern half, but the interior is similarly arid, relieved only by two green oases: the botanical gardens of **Quinta das Palmeiras** and the attractive picnic spot of **Morenos**. The prime attraction, however, is the south coast, a delicious swathe of golden sands barely touched by development. The beach gets gradually wider and more spectacular around the small resorts of **Campo de Baixo** and **Cabeço da Ponta**, before the sands end at **Ponta da Calheta**, a rocky headland below the **Miradouro das Flores** viewpoint.

Campo de Baixo and around

Map 9, D5. Buses #3 and #4 from Vila Baleira (7–8 daily).

Around 4km west of Vila Baleira lies the tiny village of
Campo de Baixo. It boasts a beautiful church, the ele-
gantly fading pink-fronted eighteenth-century Capela do
Espírito Santo, built when the village was an important
farming community – Campo de Baixo means "lower
field". Today the village relies on a handful of shops, cafés
and hotels that have grown up a short walk from the superb
wide stretch of soft sandy beach.

A dirt track just west of the church heads up to a viewpoint halfway up the wind-eroded slopes of **Pico de Ana
Ferreira** (283m). The same track splits to the west to the
Capela de São Pedro, an exposed, whitewashed
eighteenth-century church. There are good views from its
steps, but the church only opens on the Festa de São Pedro
(St Peter's Day) on 29 June.

Cabeço da Ponta

Map 9, C6. Bus #4 from Vila Baleira (6–7 daily).

Three kilometres west of Campo de Baixa lies **Cabeço da
Ponta**, consisting of a small cluster of apartments, restaurants and two large hotels just back from the island's widest,
most exhilarating part of the beach. It makes a great spot
for a beach holiday away from it all, though after dark your
options for eating and entertainment are somewhat limited.
This may change before long, though, as the stretch
between Campo de Baixo and Cabeço da Ponta is ear-
marked for several tourist developments, but for the time
being the only nightlife consists of the giant moths that
flutter round the hotel lights.

You can walk along the dune-backed beach from
Cabeço da Ponta to Ponta da Calheta in about forty
minutes; and if you eat at the *Pôr do Sol* (see p.278)
they'll give you a free lift back to your hotel.

Ponta da Calheta

Map 9, B6. Bus #4 from Vila Baleira via Campo de Baixo and
Cabeço da Ponta (6–7 daily).

West of Cabeço da Ponta, the beach, backed by steep
dunes, gets quieter and more rugged. At **Ponta da
Calheta**, the westernmost tip of the beach, the sand gives
way to a beach broken up by volcanic rock sculpted by the
elements into wonderfully shaped arches and potholes.
Some way off the coast loom the cliffs of Ilhéu de Baixo, a
craggy offshore island with an alluring sandy cove. The
only building in Ponta da Calheta is the *Pôr do Sol* restaurant (see p.278), the "sunset restaurant". Stick around until
dusk and you'll see where it got its name, the sun disappearing on the horizon beside the distant outline of
Madeira.

Boat trips from Vila Baleira visit Ilhéu de Baixo and
Ilho de Ferro to the north on Wednesdays and Saturdays
throughout the summer; see box on p.201.

Inland to Ponta da Canaveira

To explore inland you'll need to backtrack along the road
to Cabeço da Ponta and turn off along a rough track,
signed Centro Hipico (riding centre), though the riding
centre is now closed. A left turn takes you to **Miradouro**

das Flores (map 9, B6), a viewpoint right above Ponta da Calheta offering the island's most spectacular views: you can see right along the length of the beach one way and the island of Madeira the other. The dusty viewpoint is marked by a statue of deaf Portuguese painter Francisco Maya, a twentieth-century eccentric who loved to paint Porto Santo and asked to be buried at sea between this point and the offshore islet of Ilhéu de Ferro.

The dirt road continues north to **Morenos** (map 9, B5), a hilltop picnic spot neatly laid out with wooden tables, barbecue grills and freshwater taps and surrounded by cacti, aloe vera plants and dragon trees. There are great views towards Madeira and, apart from weekends in summer when locals descend in droves, the place is usually deserted.

Beyond Morenos the road descends to **Ponta da Canaveira**, a craggy clifftop above boiling seas opposite the small lighthouse on Ilhéu de Ferro.

East to Campo de Cima

Bus #3 from Vila Baleira to Campo de Cima (4–5 daily).

Heading back south, you come to a fork in the road shortly before it rejoins the coast road. A left turn takes you past the concrete **Adega das Levadas** (daily 10am–10pm; free) at Sítio das Levadas, a wine lodge where you can taste some of the local produce, though Porto Santo wine is an acquired taste, extremely sweet and strong at 14–18° proof. The lodge also serves inexpensive grilled meats and fish.

The road then skirts the base of Pico de Ana Ferreira (see p.206) towards Porto Santo's flat central plain, dotted with wind turbines, before you reach the tarred road at the village of **Campo de Cima**, a sprawling village which gives access to the charming Quinta das Palmeiras.

Funchal

Azulejos, Funchal

Risco Waterfall, Rabaçal

Levada da Central

Porto Moniz

Sáo Vicente

Quinta das Palmeiras

Map 9, C4. Daily 10am–1pm & 3–6pm; free but minimum consumption of 200$00/€1 at the bar.

Just north of Campo de Cima, up a series of ever rougher dirt tracks, you reach an extraordinary little oasis of greenery at **Quinta das Palmeiras,** a mini botanical gardens. Plonked in the middle of one of the most barren parts of the island, the *quinta* consists of a series of fruit trees, vines and exotic plants. The privately run gardens are superb, and the imaginatively landscaped paths run past cages of peacocks, turkeys, toucans, parrots and finches to a duck pond complete with swans just below a café. The only problem is getting there – it's a bleak thirty-minute walk from Campo de Cima and a confusing series of turns by car; it is probably best to splash out on a taxi from your hotel.

THE LISTINGS

7 Accommodation 213

8 Eating 245

9 Drinking and nightlife 281

10 Shopping 302

11 Sports and outdoor activities 308

12 Madeira for kids 322

13 Directory 326

Accommodation

Most people visiting Madeira have their **accommodation** included as part of a package holiday, but if you are travelling independently, you will find a good range of options, from hotels and guesthouses to rural *quintas*, or manor houses. Self-catering is also widely available at many of the bigger hotels, many of which have rooms with kitchenettes or apartments within the hotel grounds, although villas are relatively scarce, and those that are available tend to be block-booked through travel agents (see pp.5, 11 and 15 for details). There are just two campsites on Madeira – one with restricted access – and a third on Porto Santo. There is no youth hostel on either island.

Prices in Madeira are slightly higher than mainland Portugal, especially in the peak seasons of Christmas, New Year and July and August, when it is best to book well in advance. At these times, nightly rates for a standard double in a top-range hotel start at over 30,000$00/€150, and even the cheapest double room costs around 600-900$00/€30–45. During the rest of the year, most of the larger places reduce their rates to around sixty percent of their peak season rates, sometimes by even more, and you should have no problem finding the room of your choice. Smaller establishments have less dramatic discounts, but

213

ACCOMMODATION PRICE CODES

All the accommodation listed below has been price-coded according to the following scale. The prices quoted are for the **cheapest available double room in high season**. Note that prices over New Year can rise by around thirty percent above the rates given below; in low season, however, prices can be up to forty percent lower than those given. Unless stated, price includes breakfast.

① under 5000$00/€25
② 5000–8000$00/€25–40
③ 8000–11,000$00/€40–55
④ 11,000–15,000$00/€55–75
⑤ 15,000–20,000$00/€75–100
⑥ 20,000–25,000$00/€100–125
⑦ 25,000–35,000$00/€125–175
⑧ 35,000–45,000$00/€175–225
⑨ over 45,000$00/over €225

during quiet periods it should be possible to negotiate a lower price with the proprietor. Most hotels offer a fifty percent reduction for children aged 2–12, and under 2s are usually free. All room tariffs are officially fixed by the tourist authority, depending on the number of stars, and should be displayed in the reception area and usually on the back of hotel-room doors.

Around ninety percent of Madeira's accommodation is in **Funchal**, undoubtedly the most lively place to stay on the island, and with accommodation to suit all budgets. Most of it is concentrated in the **Hotel Zone**, to the west of the centre. Despite the area's popularity with package companies, there are enough hotels for independent travellers to turn up and find a room without a reservation for most of the year, though in high season it is best to book well in advance. Most of the hotels in this area have extremely good facilities, such as swimming pools and gyms, but some are quite far out from the centre and the walk along the dull Estrada Monumental quickly loses its novelty value.

The most desirable place to stay is in the relatively peaceful, atmospheric **Zona Velha**, though options are limited to a couple of budget places and one smart hotel. Failing this you could try the **centre**, which has a growing number of comfortable options, though some suffer from noise. The main drawback of hotels in both areas is that the range of facilities may not be so extensive as in the Hotel Zone. A fourth option is to stay **east** of the centre, especially in the triangle between the two rivers. This area is a little quieter than the centre but is still only a short walk from most of the central sights. Facilities are good, with most of the hotels featuring rooftop pools. Finally, west of the centre, there are a couple of places at **Praia Formosa**, Funchal's nearest stretch of beach – good options if you want to be right on the sands, though a bit removed from the capital's main attractions.

There is a far smaller but reasonable range of options in resorts such as **Porto Moniz**, **São Vicente** and **Machico** and on the island of **Porto Santo**, but elsewhere accommodation is much more limited, with many places having just one or two hotels or guesthouses. There are also some spectacular places in the middle of the countryside for those wanting to get away from it all.

HOTELS, *QUINTAS* AND INNS

Ever since *Reid's Palace Hotel* opened towards the end of the nineteenth century, Madeira has had a reputation for top-quality accommodation, and it still boasts no end of extremely comfortable **hotels**. Even simpler one- and two-star establishments usually have en-suite bathrooms and a TV, while most three-star hotels have swimming pools, restaurants and live entertainment. Four- and five-star hotels have page-long lists of facilities, offering everything from gyms to baby-sitting and aromatherapy to

CAMPING

Camping has a limited following in Madeira, with just two basic affairs at Porto Moniz and on Porto Santo and an additional restricted campsite in the Parque Ecológico do Funchal north of the capital. Camping outside these official sites is prohibited, though there is nothing to stop you sleeping under the stars on the beach on Porto Santo (see p.192). If you haven't brought your own, you can **hire** tents and sleeping bags through Amigos do Alto, Estrada Monumental, Hotel Baía Azul Loja 5, Funchal (map 3, D7; ☏ 291 776 726, ⓕ 291 762 003). It's not particularly cheap, with prices starting at 10,000$00/€50 per day for a tent and sleeping bags for two people, but the service is nevertheless extremely popular and it's advisable to book well ahead in high season.

Parque de Campismo Montado do Baireiro
Map 3, F2. Parque Ecológico do Funchal; reservations through the Department of Agriculture
☏ 291 204 200
Located in the environmentally sensitive Parque Ecológico do Funchal, this is a beautifully positioned, if very basic, free campsite. There are showers and barbecue facilities but little else. As numbers are restricted, reservations are essential, and priority is given to local students on research trips.

saunas; in addition, many rooms have their own kitchenette facilities, so you have the choice of eating in if you wish.

Before *Reid's* became Funchal's first purpose-built hotel, visitors to the island were put up at wealthy landowners' country manors, known as **quintas**. Nowadays many of these *quintas* have been adapted to offer characterful, hotel-style accommodation once more, sometimes in the original

Parque de Campismo Porto Moniz
Map 6, G1.
☎ 291 853 447

Madeira's only public campsite is a fairly basic affair where you can pitch your tent on a strip of coarse grass just over the road from the sea, between the two sets of sea pools. There are loos and cold running water, but hot showers are restricted. Prices are 180$00/€0.90 per person per night, with tents starting from 170$00/€0.85 per night.

Parque de Campismo Porto Santo
Map 9, E5. Rua Goulart Madeiros, Vila Baleira
☎ 291 982 361

Porto Santo's only campsite sits in a spacious sandy enclosure between the *Hotel Torre Praia* (see p.243) and the main south-coast highway. Basic facilities include a children's play area, cold showers and limited shade in the form of a few trees and bushes. The campsite is due to move to a new site to the east of town in 2003, when the current area will be turned into a park. The office is open daily 10am–12.30pm & 2–7pm; fees are 100$00/€0.50 per person per night for under 25s, 200$00/€1 per night for others, with tents starting at 180$00/€0.90 per night.

buildings or in modern extensions. Again, amenities tend to be first rate, with many having pools, lush grounds and self-catering facilities. Away from Funchal and the main towns you can also find quality accommodation in rural areas in **estalagems** – literally "inns", sometimes called **albergarias** – which have similar facilities to *quintas*. They also usually have decent restaurants attached.

GUESTHOUSES, PRIVATE ROOMS AND GOVERNMENT REST HOUSES

Despite its upmarket reputation, Madeira has a good range of budget accommodation. **Pensões** (singular *pensão*) and **residenciais** (singular *residencial*) are guesthouses, which can be found in most of the main resorts. They are officially graded from one to three stars; those at the top of the scale are much the same as one- or two-star hotels and often have TVs and en-suite facilities – otherwise expect basic comforts and communal bathrooms. Breakfast is usually included in the price. In rural areas, similar inexpensive accommodation can be found at a **Turismo no Espaço Rural** or **casa rural**; most offer meals and some also have self-catering facilities.

In many of Madeira's smaller towns you will see signs advertising **quartos** or **dormidas** – private rooms in people's houses, which can also be good value and offer the chance to stay somewhere more local, though most do not offer breakfast. Try asking at the local café if you want to find *quartos* in a particular place.

Another cheap option is to stay at the **government rest houses** which are dotted around some of the island's most dramatic mountain locations – where useful, these are listed in the *Guide*. Originally built to cater for forest rangers, the houses, most which have two double rooms, must be booked in advance and cost around 3000$00/€15 a night. Booking can be tricky, as priority is given to local students, but if you persevere, you can stay in extreme simplicity in idyllic locations – though you may need to take your own food and you should not expect hot water or central heating. Applications must be made in writing to the Secretaria de Agricultura, Florestas e Pescadores, Quinta Vigia, 9000 Funchal.

VILLAS AND APARTMENTS

Villas are in short supply in Madeira, though an increasing number of travel companies offer villa accommodation, usually in remote rural areas (see pp.5, 11 and 15 for details), with prices working out similar to a mid-range hotel. Most are well equipped, but as they are usually in the countryside, you'll almost certainly need a car. Villas that you can book directly include the bungalow complex near Prazeres (see p.234) or, for something more unusual, the series of mock-African circular huts in Cabanas (see p.239).

Self-catering **apartments** are more widely available, often set in the grounds of major hotels. These usually sleep two to three people and are fine if you want to save money on eating out. However, the term "apartment" usually means a room only slightly larger than a standard hotel double room, with a tiny kitchenette wedged into a corner. Apartments usually cost around 4000$00/€20 per night more than a double room of similar quality.

FUNCHAL

THE CITY CENTRE

Hotel Madeira
Map 2, C4. Rua Ivens 21
T 291 230 071, F 291 229 071
A white, modern building with red-faced, angled balconies in an attractive position opposite the Scottish kirk and near the Jardim de São Francisco. Facilities include satellite TV, a billiard lounge and a small rooftop pool. Pretty good value for so central a position. **3**.

Pensão Astória
Map 2, E3. Rua de João Gago 10, 4°
T 291 223 820, F 291 227 229
One of Funchal's most central options, with clean, though spartan, rooms, on the upper

floors of an old building
facing the Sé. Rooms come
with sinks but bathrooms are
communal. Price includes
breakfast. ❶.

Residencial Chafariz
**Map 2, E3. Rua do Estanco
Velho 3–5**
☎ 291 232 260, Ⓕ 291 232 250
Central and relatively quiet
option on a narrow
pedestrianized street
opposite the Sé. Rooms are
small but come complete
with cable TV and en-suite
bathrooms. There's a
downstairs bar and price
includes breakfast. ❸.

Residencial Colombo
Map 2, C3. Rua do Carreira 182
☎ 291 225 231/2, Ⓕ 291 222 170
Modern, ungainly-looking
guesthouse at the west end of
Rua do Carreira, but rooms
are good value, with phones,
TV, private bathroom and
there's also a sunny roof
terrace. The upper-floor
rooms have views over the
sea. There are also some basic
rooms in an older annexe
round the corner on Rua da
Mouraria. ❷.

Residencial Gordon
**Map 2, B3. Rua do Quebra
Costas 34**
☎ 291 742 366, Ⓕ 291 743 948
Attractive, cool, stone town
house with traditional decor
on a steep cobbled side street
just above the English
Church. There's a downstairs
breakfast room and bar, a
small back patio and pleasant,
spacious rooms with TVs and
en-suite facilities. ❷.

Residencial Zarco
**Map 2, E4. Rua da Alfândega
113**
☎ & Ⓕ 291 223 716
A large, rambling *residencial*
with slightly shabby rooms,
each with its own shower and
TV. Rooms at the front can
be noisy, but the position on
the edge of Largo dos
Varadouros just by the
seafront can't be faulted.
Price includes breakfast. ❷.

EAST OF THE CENTRE

Hotel do Centro
**Map 2, F3. Rua do Carmo
20–22**

Ⓣ 291 200 510, Ⓕ 291 233 915
Certainly lives up to its name, but on a busy road. Rooms are decently sized compared with others in this part of the city and there's also cable TV and a hotel bar. ❹.

Hotel Santa Maria
Map 2, F2. Rua João de Deus 26
Ⓣ 291 225 271, Ⓕ 291 221 542
Largish but inconspicuous three-star hotel a short walk east of the centre, close to IBTAM and the market. Rooms are reasonably sized, some with balconies, and all come with TVs and bathrooms. There's a restaurant with live entertainment twice weekly, a games room and a small rooftop pool with views of the harbour in the distance. ❹.

Hotel Windsor
Map 2, F2. Rua das Hortas 4C
Ⓣ 291 233 081, Ⓕ 291 233 080
A neo-Art Deco block with unevenly shaped rooms, none of which are particularly big, but it has a friendly atmosphere and a small café and restaurant

downstairs. There's also a rooftop pool with attractive views. ❹.

Quinta Mãe dos Homens
Map 3, F6. Rua Mãe dos Homens 39
Ⓣ 291 204 410, Ⓕ 291 204 419, Ⓦ www.qmdh.com
A small complex of spotless, roomy self-catering studios and apartments set behind an old *quinta* amidst a mini banana plantation in the attractive residential suburb of Rochinha close to the botanical gardens. Most rooms have superb views over the harbour from balconies or terraces. There's a pool, a morning courtesy bus into the city (but not back), honesty bar and weekly barbecue evenings. The only drawback is it's a steep fifteen-minute climb uphill from the centre. ❼.

Residencial Mónaco
Map 2, F2. Rua das Hortas 14
Ⓣ 291 230 191, Ⓕ 291 233 080
Small rooms with tiny bathrooms, but a clean, reasonably comfortable budget option in a central

FUNCHAL

221

position between the two rivers, some five minutes' walk from Praça do Município. **❶**.

ZONA VELHA

Quinta Bela São Tiago
Map 2, I4. Rua Bela São Tiago 70

ⓣ291 204 500, ⓕ291 204 510, ⓔhotel.qta.bela.s.tiago@mail.telepac.pt

Built in 1894, this stunning *quinta* has been tastefully extended with two modern wings just a stone's throw from the Zona Velha. Most rooms have balconies with superb views over the spires of the old town and the sea. There's also a pool, terrace and small garden, along with a gym, sauna, jacuzzi, restaurant and bar. The only thing that spoils it is a slightly cheesy live entertainment programme most evenings. **❾**.

Residencial Mira Sol
Map 2, H4. Rua Bela de Santiago 67

ⓣ291 201 740, ⓕ291 201 741

An attractive white town house with shutters and wrought-iron balconies just north of the Zona Velha, offering simple, clean rooms with TV and bathroom. It's on a busy road and rooms at the front can be noisy. The best rooms are at the top with their own balconies and sea views. **❷**.

Vitorina Augusta Becker Côrte
Map 2, H4. Rua de Santa Maria 279

ⓣ291 220 249

Unsigned, extremely characterful family house in the Zona Velha just before the Barreirinha Lido. Rooms come in an array of sizes but all are clean, airy and simply furnished, with electric coffee-makers the only touch of sophistication. There's an apartment with a kitchenette on the ground floor, but the upper rooms are most appealing, especially those with sea views. The best room is the "tower" room jutting out from the roof, with its own shower and small covered terrace facing the sea. Recommended. **❷**.

HOTEL ZONE

- - - - - - - - - - - - - - - - - -

Carlton Park Hotel

Map 2, A5. Rua Imperatriz
Dona Amélia
ⓣ291 209 100, ⓕ291 232 076,
ⓦwww.pestana.org
Formerly the *Casino Park
Hotel*, this is a vast structure
resembling the bridge of the
Starship Enterprise on stilts,
with a lobby full of over-the-
top lights and glitter.
Nevertheless, the position
can't be faulted, especially if
you fork out extra for sea
views. Rooms come with all
mod cons. Popular with
visiting soccer stars from Porto,
Sporting and Benfica. ⑧.

Cliff Bay Hotel

Map 3, D7. Estrada
Monumental 147
ⓣ291 707 700, ⓕ291 762 524,
ⓔinfo@cliffbay.com
Extremely stylish, high-tech
hotel moulded into a series of
terraces spilling down the
cliffs. Rooms are plush with
large balconies. Facilities
include indoor and outdoor
pools, gym, kindergarten,
four restaurants and two bars.

Tennis, windsurfing, massages
and fishing trips can be
arranged. Disabled access. ⑧.

Crowne Plaza Resort

Map 3, D7. Estrada
Monumental 175–177
ⓣ291 717 700, ⓕ291 717 701,
ⓔcrowne-plaza.md@mail
.telepac.pt
Opened in 2000, this colossal,
twin-winged glass-fronted
building sits right on the edge
of a cliff, boasting 300 rooms,
all with sea-facing balconies.
The lifts in the modern, art-
decked interior whisk you
down the cliff to seaside
pools. There's also hydro-
massage, thalassotherapy (sea
therapy), two outdoor pools,
a kids' pool, games room,
tennis and squash,
windsurfing, four restaurants,
shops and an Irish pub, as well
as disabled access. ⑨.

Estalagem Monte Verde

Map 3, D7. Azinhaga Casa
Branca 8
ⓣ291 774 072
Attached to the *Residencial
Melba* (see below), this is a
good-value, low-rise inn in a
quiet part of town, five

FUNCHAL

minutes' walk above the Hotel Zone. The spacious rooms all have balconies, some facing the sea, and there's a small pool at the side. ❷.

Estalagem Quinta da Casa Branca

Map 3, D7. Rua da Casa Branca 7

Ⓣ 291 700 770, Ⓕ 291 765 070, Ⓔ estalagem@quintacasabranca .pt

Stylish modern glass-fronted inn designed by local architect João Favila, situated a short walk uphill from the the city centre in a tranquil part of town and set in substantial grounds behind a historic family *quinta* (which is still privately occupied). Each well-equipped ground floor room opens onto its own lawnside terrace. There's also a separate restaurant building and a large pool. ❼.

Hotel Girassol

Map 3, D7. Estrada Monumental 256

Ⓣ 291 764 051, Ⓕ 291 765 441

An unpromising L-shaped concrete block on the wrong side of the Estrada Monumental, with its sea views partially obscured by the *Crowne Plaza* opposite. Nevertheless, the good-sized rooms and suites can't be faulted, and there are two pools, a bar, restaurant, cable TV, babysitting, a games room, sauna and gym. ❻.

Hotel Savoy

Map 2, A5. Avda do Infante

Ⓣ 291 222 031, Ⓕ 291 223 103, Ⓔ savoy@mail.telepac.pt

Probably Funchal's top hotel after *Reid's*, a short walk from the centre and the Parque Santa Catarina. No rooms come cheap here, even the unexceptional ones with "mountain view" – actually a view over the hotel car park and a busy part of the city, though trees help to muffle the noise. Sea views will set you back substantially more. But the tariffs do cover a vast range of facilities including inside and outside pools, bars, three restaurants (see p.261) and a garden with golf-driving nets, a giant chess set and a playground. There's also a gym and beauty treatment room. From late

2001, a new extension is due to open right on the seafront, complete with more pools. Disabled access. ❽.

Palms Hotel Ocean Resort

Map 3, D7. Rua do Gorgulho 17
ⓣ 291 766 100, ⓕ 291 766 247
Also known as *Carlton Palms*, this is set in the lovely grounds of an old *quinta* which spread along the eastern edge of Rua do Gorgulho a stone's throw from the lido. The *quinta* is now a library, with most of the hotel rooms in a stylish modern circular block on a clifftop. Plush rooms have kitchenettes and balconies with fantastic sea views. There's also a restaurant, healthclub, an outdoor pool by the sea and private access to the sea. ❼.

Quinta do Sol

Map 3, D7. Rua do Dr Pita 6
ⓣ 291 764 151, ⓕ 291 766 287,
ⓦ www.madinfo.pt./hotel/quintasol
There's no longer a *quinta* here, just six floors of concrete faced with zig-zagged green shutters. The four-star facilities mean large rooms, most with balconies, plus a restaurant, cocktail bar, live entertainment, barbecue nights and a small garden with pool. Upper floors are best for sea views and are further from the adjacent busy road junction. Back rooms don't have balconies, but face the tranquil gardens of Quinta Magnolia (see p.78). ❺.

Quinta Perestrello

Map 3, D7. Rua do Dr Pita 3
ⓣ 291 763 720, ⓕ 291 763 777
Lovely 150-year-old *quinta* set in small grounds with its own pool and terrace café opposite the *Quinta do Sol*. Rooms are airy and wood-floored, with those in the modern extension having their own terraces. The only disadvantage is its position wedged in by a busy road junction and next to a new hotel development. ❻.

Reid's Palace Hotel

Map 3, D7. Estrada Monumental 139
ⓣ 291 717 171, ⓕ 291 717 177,
ⓦ www.orient-expresshotels.com

FUNCHAL

225

Madeira's first and most famous hotel (see p.78) and rated one of the best hotels in the world. Much of its appeal lies in its size which seems to absorb any number of visitors without ever seeming full. Its array of facilities include three restaurants, pools and sea access, a poolside café (see p.293), sweeping views over Funchal, tranquil gardens and entertainments programme, including special "Fun at *Reid's*" days for children, timed to coincide with British school holidays. Rooms are sumptuous and spacious, though nothing beats the Churchill Suite, bigger than some people's houses and complete with pop-up TV at the end of the bed. Some people come here every year, though others claim that its ongoing renovation programme and the steady development of the coast around it has taken away some of its traditional exclusivity. **❾**.

Residencial Melba

Map 3, D7. Azinhaga Casa Branca 8

Ⓣ 291 774 072

Probably the best-value place in Funchal, sharing the facilities of the *Estalagem Monte Verde* (see above) for about half the price. Rooms are simple but clean, and it's in a tranquil location five minutes' walk up from the Hotel Zone. All it lacks is a sea view. **❶**.

Vila Rosa

Map 3, D7. Estrada Monumental 159

Ⓣ 291 766 884, Ⓕ 291 766 881

Decent self-catering apartments for two with balconies in a pleasant low-rise building close to the coast. Unfortunately its sea views are all but obliterated by the *Cliff Bay Hotel* which completely dwarfs the older building. **❺**.

PRAIA FORMOSA

Atlantic Bay

Map 3, C7.

Ⓣ 291 701 900, Ⓕ 291 761 694, Ⓦ www.pestana.com

Newer of the two blocks on Praia Formosa. The hotel has

an impersonal, international feel with the usual range of facilities, including a pool, sports room, jacuzzi and health club. Bedrooms are spacious and come with kitchenettes, though the advertised views of Cabo Girão are disappointing. You'll need to rely on courtesy buses or public transport to Funchal, a good ten minutes' drive away. The hotel can arrange diving trips. ❻.

AROUND FUNCHAL

CAMACHA

Estalagem Relógio
Map 3, H4. Achada
Ⓣ 291 922 114, Ⓕ 291 922 415
Good-value four-star inn tacked on to one side of the O Relógio complex. From reception, the lift goes four floors downwards, with most rooms having balconies with great views over the valley. The spacious, spotless rooms all come with satellite TV, bath and the odd bit of wicker

Atlantic Gardens
Map 3, C7.
Ⓣ 291 700 120, Ⓕ 291 766 733,
Ⓦ www.pestana.com
Older, more tired-looking of the two blocks on Praia Formosa. Inside, however, it has a more local and friendly feel, with a small terrace and pool at the back. Lacks many other facilites, but rooms are pleasant enough and not bad value if you can face the long trek into Funchal. Price does not include breakfast. ❹.

furniture. Breakfast in the next door restaurant is included. ❹.

ESTREITO DE CÂMARA DE LOBOS

Estalagem Quinta do Estreito
Map 3, B5. Rua José Joaquim da Costa
Ⓣ 291 910 530, Ⓕ 291 910 549,
Ⓦ www.charminghotelsmadeira .com
Flash, tastefully converted five-star *quinta* set in its own sumptuous grounds. Rooms

FUNCHAL

come with cable TV, all mod cons, verandas and great views over the valleys around. There's also an outdoor pool, sun terrace and sauna. .

QUINTA DO PALHEIRO FERREIRO

Casa Velha do Palheiro
Map 3, G6. São Gonçalo

ⓣ 291 794 901, ⓕ 291 794 925, ⓔ casa.velha@mail.EUnet.pt

Exclusive, slightly stuffy hotel, catering to the wealthy golfing set come to play at the adjacent course – Madeira's finest (see p.321). As well as free access to the golf club, it offers such luxuries as a heated outdoor pool, sauna, games room, tennis courts and a restaurant. .

EASTERN MADEIRA

CANIÇAL

Quinta do Lorde
Map 4, F2. Sítio da Piedade
ⓣ 291 960 200, ⓕ 291 960 202

This flash complex sits on an isolated clifftop a couple of kilometres east of Caniçal on the way to Ponta de São Lourenço. Large rooms – complete with lurid colour schemes – all come with roomy sun terraces lined with green Astroturf. There's a pool and access to the sea, along with satellite TV, a couple of bars, a restaurant, sauna and a children's entertainment programme. A good spot for those seeking comfort and seclusion. , or with a sea view.

CANIÇO

Quinta Splendida
Map 4, B7. Estrada da Ponta da Oliveira
ⓣ 291 930 400, ⓕ 291 930 401, ⓔ quintasplendida@mail.telepac.pt

If you are after a bit of pampering, this could be the place for you: an impressive hotel complex of rooms and apartments – each with kitchenette and balcony – set round beautifully landscaped botanical gardens, and most with views over the sea to boot (though you pay extra for this). There are two restaurants (see p.267), two bars (one by the pool), a nightly entertainment programme, a fitness centre, Turkish bath and outdoor swimming pool. **⑤**, or **⑦** for double apartments.

Residencial A Lareira
Map 4, B7. Largo Padre Lomelino ⓣ 291 934 284
The budget option in Caniço, with decent rooms, most with balconies facing the main square – or the cemetery. Breakfast is served downstairs in a lurid room guaranteed to wake you up in the morning. **③**.

CANIÇO DE BAIXO

Hotel Inn & Art
Map 4, B7. Rua Robert Baden Powell 61–62
ⓣ 291 938 200, ⓕ 291 938 219, ⓦ www.inn-art.com
German-run restaurant and hotel offering a mixed bag of rooms, some of which are in a separate annexe up the hill with a small plunge pool. Front rooms have great sea views – for which you pay around 2000$00/€10 extra – but it's all rather expensive for what you get. **⑥**.

Hotel Oasis Atlantic
Map 4, B7. Reis Magos
ⓣ 291 930 100, ⓕ 291 930 109, ⓔ oasis.atlantic@mail.telepac.pt
Located some five minutes' walk east of the centre, next to Praia dos Reis Magos, this terracotta-tile-roofed modern hotel is well designed in that virtually all rooms have sea views of some sort (though you may have to crane your neck in some). A cavernous lobby leads onto landscaped gardens with a pool and a children's play area. There's also an indoor pool, jacuzzi, sauna, restaurant and cocktail bar. The hotel rents out bikes and jeeps, too. **⑤**, or **⑥** with a sea view.

Hotel Ondamar
Map 4, B7. Apartado 12
ⓣ 291 930 930, ⓕ 291 934 555,

Ⓦ www.galoresort.com

Popular with German package tours, this huge hotel consists of a series of four-star rooms and apartments set in attractive grounds either side of the road above the tourist office. Rooms come with small kitchenettes, en-suite bathrooms and balconies. Price includes a large buffet breakfast which you can eat by the hotel pool. Residents also get free access to the Lido Galo Mar and a local gym. ❺.

Hotel Rocamar

Map 4, B7. Caminho Cais da Oliveira

Ⓣ 291 934 334, Ⓕ 291 934 044, Ⓔ rocamar@mail.telepac.pt

A big, modern hotel stacked on a cliff, with 100 rooms, its own lido complex and access to the sea. Front rooms have great views, and all have bath, TV and balcony. There's also a restaurant, two bars, a billiards room and a courtesy bus (Mon–Sat) to Funchal. ❹.

Vila Ventura

Map 4, B7. Caminho Cais da Oliveira

Ⓣ 291 934 611, Ⓕ 291 934 680,

Ⓦ www.villa-ventura.com

A relatively small hotel by Caniço de Baixo standards, with 22 spacious rooms, each with TV, bath and balcony – though any sea views are partially blocked by the *Tropical Hotel* opposite. It also has a younger feel than most round here, with its own bar. It can rent out mountain bikes and arrange sailing or diving trips. Breakfast is 900$00/€4.50 extra. ❸.

GARAJAU

Dom Pedro Garajau

Map 4, A7. Sítio Quinta Garajau

Ⓣ 291 930 800, Ⓕ 291 930 801

A giant, but rather anonymous, three-star hotel, with some 400 rooms divided into four blocks, that takes up one entire side of the road into Garajau from Funchal. If you get rooms at the top of block one or two you're likely to get the best views over the sea. There are studios with tiny kitchenettes for those into self-catering, though standard double rooms are slightly larger.

Facilities include a small covered pool, table tennis and restaurant, along with access to a pool and tennis courts by the Cristo Rei. A nightly entertainment programme includes pianists, video nights and folk evenings. **④**.

MACHICO

Alujamento Familia
Map 5, B8. Sítio Pé-da-Ladeira
ⓣ 291 969 440, ⓕ 291 969 447
Right opposite the *Hotel Dom Pedro Baia* (see below), this small, family-run guesthouse offers bright, airy rooms, all of which have a shower room and toilet and satellite TV. Get one at the front and you'll have a balcony with a sea view – though you'll pay around 2000$00/€10 more for it. Price includes breakfast in the decent downstairs restaurant with its own patio. **②**.

Hotel Dom Pedro Baia
Map 5, B8. Estrada de São Roque
ⓣ 291 969 500, ⓕ 291 966 889,
ⓔ dp.baia@mail.telepac.pt
Machico's only high-rise

building dominates the west side of the beach and is fairly soulless. The main block has reasonably sized rooms with good views over the bay but bizarrely these lack balconies – though those in the low-rise annexe nextdoor do have them. Four-star facilities include a pool in the small grounds, tennis, in-house restaurant and access to watersports facilities and diving (see box on p.315). Price includes a large buffet breakfast. **⑤**.

Residencial Amparo
Map 5, D7. Rua da Amargura
ⓣ 291 968 120, ⓕ 291 966 050
A modern, pristine *residencial* built in traditional style behind the *Mercado Velho* restaurant (see p.269). Its twelve rooms are not huge but they are spotless and come with en-suite bathrooms and cable TV. **②**.

Residencial Parisienne
Map 5, D7. Praceta 25 de Abril
ⓣ 291 965 330, ⓕ 291 965 563
Not terribly *Parisienne*, but certainly good value, with modern, clean rooms all

EASTERN MADEIRA

231

featuring bathrooms, cable TV, balconies and fridges. The owner swears that all rooms are sound-proofed against the disco *La Barca* downstairs (see p.297), and no one has complained yet – according to the owner. ❷.

PORTO DA CRUZ

Albergaria Penedo
Map 4, B1. Casais Próximas
ⓣ 291 563 011, ⓕ 291 563 012
Overlooking the harbour and right above the restaurant of the same name (see p.271), this inn is the best place to stay in Porto da Cruz, especially if you get a room with a sea view (which costs 2000$00/€10 extra) and a balcony. All rooms come complete with TVs and bathrooms. ❸.

Quinta da Capela
Map 4, B2. Sítio do Folhado, off Porto da Cruz–Portela road
ⓣ 291 562 491
This is serious get-away-from-it-all stuff, on a blowy hillside some 3.5km above Porto da Cruz (signposted off the road to Portela). Set in a beautiful seventeenth-century manor house reached by steep steps up from the road, the *quinta* has five spacious and traditionally furnished rooms and its own gardens, full of agapanthus, offering great views over the coast. But unless you have the legs of a donkey, a car is essential. ❹.

SANTA CRUZ

Hotel Santa Catarina
Map 4, D5. Rua do Bom Jesus 7 ⓣ 291 520 000, ⓕ 291 520 001
Built on the site of the village's former sugar mill, this four-star hotel is just north of the church and right below a flyover – which rather detracts from an otherwise decent enough place with biggish rooms, each with a balcony. There's a billiards room, a small pool, a restaurant and disabled access. ❹.

Residencial Santo António
Map 4, D5. Rua Cónego César de Oliveira

EASTERN MADEIRA

Ⓣ 291 524 198, Ⓕ 291 524 264
Attractive guesthouse on the
main drag to the beach from
the church. *Azulejos*-lined
corridors lead to large, clean
rooms, each with their own
bathroom, TV and either a
balcony or terrace. ❷.

SANTO ANTÓNIO DA SERRA

Estalagem A Quinta
Map 4, C3. Casais Próximas
Ⓣ 291 550 030, Ⓕ 291 550 049
Just below town on the
Funchal–Portela road, this
place offers decent modern
rooms with private
bathrooms, TV and a small

communal garden. There's
also a small pool and a
moderately priced restaurant
(daily noon–11pm), offering
the usual range of meat and
fish dishes inside or on a
small covered terrace. ❹.

Estalagem do Santo
Map 4, C3. Sítio dos Casais
Próximos
Ⓣ 291 552 611, Ⓕ 291 552 596
Four-star splendour just south
of the park on the way to the
golf course – golfers make up
a fair share of its clients.
Spacious rooms all come with
satellite TV and most open
onto sumptuous lawns. There's
also an indoor pool, tennis
courts and a restaurant. ❺.

THE WEST COAST

CALHETA

Hotel Calheta Beach
Map 6, F7.
Ⓣ 291 820 300, Ⓕ 291 820 301,
Ⓦ www.calheta-beach.com.
A four-star hotel block with
its own pool, terraces, gym,
satellite TV and restaurant; it

can also arrange watersports
and makes a good retreat if
you just want an extremely
quiet spot by the sea. ❼.

JARDIM DO MAR

Hotel Jardim do Mar
Map 6, E6.

Ⓣ 291 823 616, Ⓕ 291 823 617
Right on the main square, this is a surprisingly plush place with decent-sized rooms offering exhilarating sea views, though the plastic animal heads stuck to the corridor walls are off-putting. The hotel has its own bar and reasonable restaurant (daily noon–3.30pm & 7–11pm), with a superb sea-facing terrace. The hotel can also arrange windsurfing. ❸.

Moradia Turistica Cecilia
Map 6, E6.
Ⓣ 291 822 642
This characterful guesthouse with its own sea-facing garden is at the west end of town – follow the signs – and offers simple, clean rooms. It's a popular spot with local surfers. ❷.

PAÚL DA SERRA
- -

Estalagem Pico da Urze
Map 6, I6. Ovil
Ⓣ 291 820 150, Ⓕ 291 820 159
Located on the remote Paúl da Serra plateau, this is a

modern complex, consisting of a four-star hotel, shops and restaurant. All the rooms have balconies affording sweeping views over the moors. Bike rental available. ❹.

PAÚL DO MAR
- -

Casal São João at Sítio do Macapez
Map 6, D5. Faja da Ovelha
Ⓣ 291 872 660, Ⓕ 291 741 040
An attractive house, part of the *Turismo no Espaço Rural* scheme (see p.218) and located on a side road off to the right as you descend to Paul do Mar. It's wedged on a terrace halfway up the cliff – so not for vertigo sufferers. Accommodation consists of reasonable double rooms and larger rooms with kitchens, each with a shower. There is also a basic gym and a pool, though the latter isn't always open. ❷.

PRAZERES
- -

Estalagem Casa de Chá
Map 6, E6. Sítio da Estacada

ⓣ 291 823 070/1, ⓕ 291 823 072
Located just before the
church right in the centre of
Prazeres, this modern low-
rise place is tastefully
decorated in traditional style
with an attractive lawned
garden at the back. All rooms
come with satellite TV and a
terrace. There's also a
restaurant and bar, though
they're somewhat pricey. ❹.

Hotel Jardim Atlântico
Map 6, E6. Lombo Da Rocha
ⓣ 291 822 200/523,
ⓕ 291 822 522
For location this four-star
development, five minutes'
drive from Prazeres
(continue on the road past
the Estalagem Casa de Chá),
is hard to beat. A series of
apartments, bungalows and
hotel rooms are stacked on
the lip of a 400-metre-high
clifftop affording stunning
views over the coast below.
The main building contains
studios (with their own
balconies and kitchenettes),
with apartments and
bungalows (for two or three
people) arranged on terraces
below. The complex has its

own restaurant, gym, pool,
tennis courts, sauna,
whirlpools, games rooms
and live entertainment.
There's even a hotel
supermarket, while local
walks and bike rental can
also be arranged. ❺.

Vista Prazeres
Map 6, E6. Lombo da Rocha
ⓣ 291 822 150
Located just above the *Hotel
Jardim Atlântico* and run by a
South African family, the
Vista Prazeres offers small,
rather dark apartments for
rent and a couple of clean
double rooms with shared
bathroom facilities. The
upstairs restaurant (daily
9.30am–10pm) offers decent,
inexpensive Madeiran food
with good views from the
terrace. ❶.

RIBEIRA BRAVA
- -

Hotel Brava Mar
Map 7, D8. Rua Comandante
Camacho de Freitas
ⓣ 291 952 220, ⓕ 291 951 122
A modern seafront hotel at
the eastern edge of town on a

busy road junction. Three-star comforts include its own pool and restaurant. Most rooms have a sea view. There are also suites and apartments for longer stays. ❹.

Residencial São Bento

Map 7, C6. Rua 1° Dezembro ⓣ 291 952 220, ⓕ 291 951 122 The best place to stay in town, with giant, well-furnished rooms, some with sea views, in a modern but attractive building above a shopping centre. Sun terrace on the roof. ❷.

SERRA DE ÁGUA

Pousada dos Vinháticos

Map 6, M6. ⓣ 291 952 344, ⓕ 291 952 540, ⓔ info@dorisol.pt/www.dorisol.pt A couple of hundred metres below *Residencial Encumeada* on the right lies one of Madeira's two *pousadas*. Set in a stone building with a modern wooden annex, this has a friendly, Alpine feel with cosy, small rooms, leafy gardens and a highly rated restaurant. There is also a basement bar, a good place to hole up on cool evenings. Non-residents can use another bar just below the *pousada* (open daily 2–6pm). Best of all are the views from the *pousada* of the dramatically rising peaks all around and the terraced valleys below. ❷.

Residencial Encumeada

Map 6, M6. ⓣ 291 951 282, ⓕ 291 951 281 A couple of minutes south of the Boca da Encumeada pass, on the EN104, the *Residencial Encumeada* was built in 1999 but has a traditional feel with tasteful wooden decor. Rooms are large and comfortable, each with a bath, TV and stunning mountain views from their balconies. The spacious downstairs bar–restaurant often fills with passing tour groups but offers reasonably priced grills and Madeiran staples. ❸.

NORTHERN AND CENTRAL MADEIRA

BOAVENTURA

- - - - - - - - - - - - - - - - - - - -

Solar de Boaventura
Map 8, C2. Serrão Boaventura
ⓣ 291 860 888, ⓕ 291 863 877
Very plush and imaginatively designed hotel set in a huge lawned area in a valley below the church off the road to Santana. The original *solar* (manor house) dates from 1776 and served as a school and medical centre before its current reincarnation as the hotel reception and pricey restaurant (daily 1–3pm & 7–10pm). The *solar* has been lavishly enlarged with a series of modern extensions, comprising atriums, bedrooms and communal areas. All rooms have bathrooms and TVs. ❸.

PICO DO ARIEIRO

- - - - - - - - - - - - - - - - - - - -

Pousada do Arieiro
Map 8, E7.
ⓣ 291 231 011
Built in 1998, right next to the summit of one of Madeira's highest mountains, this *pousada* offers incredibly dramatic views – when the clouds aren't swirling round the windows. The 18 rooms are snug and warm (the air outside is permanently fresh this high up) and the restaurant does pretty good food. ❸.

PONTA DELGADA

- - - - - - - - - - - - - - - - - - - -

Casa de Capelinha
Map 8, B1. Terreiro
ⓣ 291 862 127,
ⓔ casacapelinha@aeiou.pt
Attractive guesthouse in the old centre with four rooms complete with TV and kitchenettes with their own fridge, microwaves and coffee machines (breakfast is not included in the price). The traditional house sits in its own lawned garden surrounded by vineyards. The *casa* takes its name from the rather sorry-looking eighteenth-century *capelinha*

– small chapel – which sits next door. ❸.

PORTO MONIZ

Alojamento Rodrigues
Map 6, G1.
☏ 291 853 233
One block back from the *Restaurante Cachalote* (see p.275) and the sea pools, this traditional-style guesthouse has the best budget rooms in town – so it quickly gets booked up. There are small but clean rooms, some with sea-facing balconies and wooden shutters. Price includes breakfast. ❷.

Orca Residencial
Map 6, G1. Sítio das Poças
☏ 291 853 359, ⓕ 291 853 320
Slightly shabby but wonderfully positioned *residencial* right opposite the western sea pools. Large rooms come with ancient TVs, bathrooms and giant sun terraces. The best rooms are the front ones overlooking the sea pools – room 12 has the largest terrace. Price includes breakfast. ❸.

Residencial Atlântico
Map 6, G1.
☏ 291 852 500, ⓕ 291 852 504
Friendly, modern *residencial* done out in traditional style opposite the tourist office. Rooms are spotless – some face the sea, and all come with private bathrooms and satellite TV. ❸.

Residencial Calhau
Map 6, G1. Sítio das Poças
☏ 291 853 104, ⓕ 291 853 443
This imaginatively designed place, next to the *Orca Residencial* (see above), has decent, airy rooms with private bathrooms and small balconies overlooking the sea pools. There's a sunny breakfast room and an upstairs games and TV room with sweeping views. Good value and popular with students. ❷.

SANTANA

Estalagem O Escondidinho das Canas
Map 8, G3. Pico António Fernandes
☏ 291 572 319
Just uphill from the post

office, this guesthouse consists of two traditional Santana house façades above a small restaurant facing the main road. The houses, which have small shower rooms, sleep up to three people. There are also a couple of tiny additional double rooms squeezed into a conventional neighbouring building with communal bathrooms. ❷.

Quinta Furão
Map 8, F2. Achada do Gramacho
ⓣ 291 570 100, ⓕ 291 573 560
This large, modern three-storey hotel is spectacularly positioned in one of Madeira's largest vineyards (see p.176) on a clifftop some 4km west of Santana. The third-floor rooms have balconies with great views over the cliffs. There's also a pool and gym, and a restaurant, bar and shop in a separate building 50m down the hill (see p.276). ❺.

Residencial O Colmo
Map 8, G3.
ⓣ 291 572 478, ⓕ 291 574 312
On the main road just up

from the post office, this place offers standard, plain rooms with small shower rooms above a restaurant (see p.276). There is a communal lounge area and a small outdoor terrace, but it all feels a bit shabby. It will shortly be eclipsed by a brand new four-star extension taking shape behind it. ❷.

SÃO JORGE

Cabanas
Map 8, E1.
ⓣ 291 576 291
Tourist complex, located 2km west of São Jorge and reached by São Roque do Faial bus #138 (2 daily), consisting of 25 circular bungalows, each of which sleeps up to two adults and a child and contains bathrooms and a TV. Some of them lie close to the clifftop, with great views down the coast, though most of them are set back in an area of lawns and gardens. The complex contains its own mid-price restaurant, a

NORTHERN AND CENTRAL MADEIRA

239

tiny swimming pool, a craft shop and a bar, along with two recreated Santana houses next to the restaurant. The location is certainly impressive, but the huts – said to have been inspired by Zulu huts after the founder's stay in Africa – are too densely packed and gimmicky for a stay of more than one night. ❸.

SÃO VICENTE

Casa da Piedade
Map 6, L4. Sítio do Laranjal
Ⓣ 291 846 042, Ⓕ 291 846 044
About a kilometre uphill beyond the *grutas*, and set in its own lawned grounds just below the chapel of Nossa Senhora de Fátima, this idyllic white, terracotta-tiled eighteenth-century manor house makes for a great rural retreat. There are just six rooms, all filled with antiques, though they also boast modern comforts such as satellite TV and central heating in winter. Guests can use the kitchen and the communal lounge,

with a log fire for cool evenings. ❹.

Estalagem Calamar
Map 6, L3. Juncos-Fajã da Areia
Ⓣ 291 842 218, Ⓕ 291 842 250
Overlooking the lido, this place feels like it has its own pool – making the spacious rooms with TVs and private bathrooms good value. Most rooms have sea-facing balconies and there's an excellent restaurant downstairs (see p.277). ❷.

Estalagem do Mar
Map 6, L3. Juncos-Fajã da Areia
Ⓣ 291 840 010, Ⓕ 291 840 019,
Ⓔ estalagem.mar@mail.telepac.pt
Just west of the bridge on the seafront, this fairly unattractive but well-equipped low-rise modern block constitutes the most comfortable hotel around São Vicente. The decently sized – and decently priced – rooms all come with bath and TV and have either sea-facing balconies or open onto a lawned area near the hotel's outdoor pool, which

is surrounded by gardens neatly landscaped above a rocky foreshore. Facilities also include an indoor pool, sauna, gym, jacuzzi and tennis courts. There is also an in-house restaurant facing the pool serving expensive traditional Madeiran dishes and seafood (daily 12.30–3pm & 7–9.30pm). **4**.

Estalagem Praia Mar
Map 6, L3. Calhau
T 291 842 383, F 291 842 749
This big, prominent but traditional-style building with green shutters sits at the west end of the row of restaurants facing the sea. All the rooms are large and airy, though the front, upper ones – some with balconies – have the best outlook. Price includes breakfast. **3**.

SEIXAL

Casa Santo Antão
Map 6, I3. T 291 854 21, F 291 854 212
Halfway down the hill to Cais, this is a lovely traditional house divided up into neat apartments, sleeping up to three people. Each one has a small kitchenette and bedroom-cum-living area. Most rooms face the sea, and price includes breakfast. **4**.

Estalagem Brisa Mar
Map 6, I2. T 291 854 476, F 291 854 477
Decent if simple rooms with private bathrooms above a restaurant on the harbour front. There are great sea views from the front rooms, though they lack balconies. Price includes breakfast. **2**.

PORTO SANTO

CABEÇO DA PONTA

Hotel Dom Pedro Porto Santo

Map 9, C6.
Sítio do Cabeço da Ponta
T 291 980 800, F 291 980 801,
E dp.portosanto@dompedro -hotels.com

Opened in 2000, this pink high-rise hotel has 256 rooms and a separate annexe with 56 apartments. Both blocks are set back from the sea on the wrong side of the coastal highway and bizarrely skewed so that none of the large, functional rooms directly face the Atlantic. Facilities are first rate, with an in-house restaurant, indoor pool, shops, games room, children's room and bar, but it all feels international and lacking in any atmosphere. A tunnel under the road leads to a thelassotherapy centre (open to non-residents), along with an open-air pool, children's play area and a restaurant (daily 11am–3.30pm) for barbecued sardines, chicken and pizzas. The hotel also lays on live entertainment and can arrange watersports, car and scooter hire. Double rooms ⑦, apartments ⑥.

Luamar Suite Aparthotel
Map 9, C6.
ⓣ 291 984 121, ⓕ 291 983 100,
ⓔ luamar.suite.hotel@netc.pt
This low-rise hotel, set on a wide, sandy beach, is ideal for families and self-caterers; the compact, well-designed apartments, which sleep up to four people, come with living room, bathroom and kitchenette. It is worth paying extra to have an apartment facing the sea rather than the main road, and all rooms come with balconies or – for those on the ground floor – terraces opening up onto lawned areas. There's a large outdoor pool – which seems unnecessary with the beach right in front of you – and a lunch-time café offering barbecues and buffet lunches. Facilities also include a mini-market, a sauna, gym, a daytime courtesy bus to Vila Baleira and bike hire. ⑥, or ⑦ with a sea view.

CAMPO DE BAIXO

Hotel Porto Santo
Map 9, D5. Ribeiro Cochino
ⓣ 291 980 140, ⓕ 291 980 149,
ⓦ www.qbvista.pt
The island's most sophisticated hotel, with antiques adding a formal air to a discreet, low-

rise four-star set in its own palm-tree-studded lawns just back from the beach. The modestly sized rooms all have cable TV, air conditioning and balconies facing the lawned areas or fields at the side. There's a restaurant and terrace facing the outdoor pool with a separate children's pool. Other facilities include a crazy golf course, tennis courts and playground; the hotel can also arrange water sports, horse riding and bike hire. The beachside café does grills, omelettes and baguettes. **❼**.

Residencial Virgilio
Map 9, D5.
Sítio do Espírito Santo
☎ 291 980 112, ⓕ 291 980 115
Large, three-storeyed modern *residencial* on the main south-coast highway, some five minutes' walk from the beach. Its well-sized rooms are spotless and come with balconies and private bathrooms; you pay a little more for those facing away from the road. The complex includes a dull restaurant downstairs (daily noon–3pm & 7–10pm),

offering moderately priced Madeiran staples, a decent modern café (daily 10am–10pm) and a shop (daily 10am–2pm & 5–9pm), selling touristy handicrafts and wine. **❹**.

VILA BALEIRA
- - - - - - - - - - - - - - - - - - -

Hotel Torre Praia
Map 9, E5. Rua Goulart Madeiros
☎ 291 985 292, ⓕ 291 982 487,
ⓔ torrepraia@mail.telepac.pt
A large, modern four-star hotel right on the beach in the west of town, imaginatively constructed round the stone tower (*torre*) of an old cement factory which dominates reception. The best rooms are those on the upper floors with sea views; lower ones overlook lawned areas to the side. There's a small pool, restaurant, squash court, gym, sauna, jacuzzi and direct access to the beach. The distinctive raised panoramic bar (daily from 9pm) jutting from the top of the building offers superb views. **❼**.

Pensão Palmeira

Map 9, E5. Avda Vieira de Castro 6

ⓣ 291 982 112

This big, rambling pension wins on character even if not on modern comforts, and its position, right on the main square, could not be better. Along with rooms in the main building – which have communal bathrooms – there are several set back across an interior courtyard with small patios offering sea views. As in the main building, these simple rooms have seen better days but come with a small shower room. Price includes breakfast in the restaurant, which also does decent budget lunches. ❷.

Residencial Central

Map 9, E5. Rua C. Magno Vasconcelos

ⓣ 291 982 226, ⓕ 291 983 460

Modern white, low-rise *residencial* on a hill five minutes' walk from the centre – the best-value budget option in town. Rooms are spotless and include en-suite bathrooms and TVs. There are sweeping sea views from the upper rooms and the small, leafy terrace, though only the more expensive suites have balconies. Facilities include a bar and large breakfast room. ❷, or ❸ for room with balcony.

Eating

Madeira has a good range of **places to eat** in all price ranges, from upmarket restaurants facing the sea to tiny backstreet cafés. Restaurants geared to tourists – in particular, hotel restaurants – tend to serve expensive, high-quality Madeiran and international cuisine. You'll find better value and more authentic Madeiran cuisine at smaller restaurants and cafés, especially outside Funchal – good places to try are *marisqueiras*, restaurants specializing in seafood, and *churrascarias*, which specialize in grills. If you fancy a change from Madeiran cuisine, you'll also find a number of restaurants serving specifically **international** food, especially in Funchal. Italian food is popular and inexpensive, there are the usual collection of reasonable Chinese and Indian restaurants, while French food is predictably good but pricey.

Though often lacking in character, hotel restaurants can be a good option for a quality evening meal; particularly good ones are listed below.

As with hotels, the vast majority of Madeira's restaurants are in Funchal. Most of the top establishments lie in the **Hotel Zone**, but as you would expect, these places are very touristy, with a three-course meal costing around

COMMON FOOD TERMS

Starters and side dishes

Azeitonas – olives

Batatas fritas – chips

Batatas cozidas – boiled
 potatoes

Canja – chicken broth

Manteiga – butter

Ovo cozido – boiled egg

Pão – bread

Pão com alho – garlic bread

Presunto – smoked ham

Queijo – cheese

Salada – salad

Sopa – soup

Sopa de peixe – fish soup

Meat

Borrego – lamb

Carne de porco – pork

Carne de vaca – beef

Costeletas de porco – pork
 chops

Dobrada/Tripas – tripe

Febras – pork steaks

Fígado – liver

Frango – young chicken

Galinha – chicken

Vitela – veal

Fish and seafood

Atum – tuna

Bodião – parrot fish

Camarões – shrimps

Caranguejo – crab

Carapau – mackerel

Chocos – cuttle fish

Espada – scabbard

Espadarte – swordfish

4600\$00/€23 a head. For atmosphere, you're better off eating in the **Zona Velha** or around the **marina**, where the food may be less sophisticated but is more than compensated for by the location. Restaurants in the Zona Velha are cheaper and vie with each other to offer two- or three-course tourist menus (usually featuring a combination of Madeiran and international cuisine) at bargain prices (around 3000\$00/€15 per head), while restaurants around the marina tend to specialize in simple grilled fish dishes. The majority of Madeirans, however, head for the cafés and

Gambas – prawns	*Pescada* – hake
Lagosta – lobster	*Polvo* – octopus
Lapas – limpets	*Salmão* – salmon
Linguada – sole	*Salmonete* – red mullet
Lulas – squid	*Sardinhas* – sardines
Pargo – sea bream	*Truta* – trout

Desserts (Sobremesa)

Gelado – ice cream	*Pudim flan* – crème caramel
Melão – melon	*Salada da fruta* – fruit salad
Morangos – strawberries	*Uvas* – grapes

Other useful terms

Aberto – open	*Jantar* – dinner
Almoço – lunch	*Mesa* – table
Cadeira – chair	*Pequeno almoco* – break-
Colher – spoon	fast
Conta – the bill	*Pimenta* – pepper
Copo – glass	*Quanto é?* – How much is
Ementa – menu	it?
Faca – knife	*Quarto de banho* – toilet
Fechado – closed	*Queria...* – I'd like...
Garfo – fork	*Sal* – salt

restaurants in the **centre** – especially at lunch time – where you will find some of the least expensive local cuisine. Here, a three-course set menu (an *ementa turística*) costs around 1800–2500\$00/€9–12.50; stick to just a main course or the dish of the day (*prato do dia*) and it will be even cheaper.

Outside the capital there is much less choice, but the simplicity and freshness of the food often more than compensates, with restaurants and cafés generally more reliant on local produce – especially fresh fish – than imports.

COMMON FOOD TERMS ●

Hotel restaurant prices are pretty similar all over the island, but prices at other cafés and restaurants outside the capital tend to be comparable to the cheaper establishments in Funchal.

Menus generally appear in Portuguese with an English translation. All restaurants have **opening times** posted on or just inside their doors, though these are not rigidly adhered to. Most restaurants open for lunch from around noon until 3pm and offer dinner from around 7pm to 11pm. Some close for one day during the week. However, you can get a reasonable snack in a café at any time of the day, and, in Funchal, most restaurants are open every day, usually from 11am to 11pm, though they may not have their grills lit for all this time.

Madeiran **portions** tend to be a lot smaller than the giant helpings served in mainland Portugal, but they are quite adequate for a full meal. Many places also offer *mini pratos* (half portions) which make good light lunch-time snacks.

MEALS AND SNACKS

Breakfast is not a big meal for the Portuguese: it usually consists of a croissant or pastry, though larger hotels and cafés will serve more substantial continental breakfasts, with everything from bread and jam to scrambled eggs with cold meats, fruit and cereal.

The Portuguese make up for not eating breakfast with a steady intake of **snacks**, ranging from sandwiches to cakes and pastries. As a result, cafés and *pastelarias* (patisseries) are bustling from mid-morning to late-afternoon, with people tucking into something to help their coffee go down. As well as the local specialities listed in the box on p.250, *sandes* (sandwiches) – usually with *queijo* (cheese) or *fiambre* (ham) – *tostas* (toasted ham or cheese sandwiches) and *prego* (garlic beef in a roll) can be bought pretty much at any time of the day in cafés and some bars and make a decent light meal on their own.

Cafés that serve particularly good food are listed below; those which are best for a drink and a snack are listed in Chapter 9 (see p.281)

Lunch is served from around noon to 2.30pm, and it is customary for most Madeirans to eat out in a café or restaurant during their work lunchbreak. Head for a place catering for local workers and you'll find exceptionally good-value set lunch menus, with a three-course meal costing in the region of 1800–2500$00/€9–12.50.

Dinner is usually served any time after 7.30pm, though most locals eat later, at around 9pm. Starters usually consist of garlic bread, though more expensive restaurants offer northern European starters such as shrimp cocktail or melon. Outside Funchal, restaurants tend to be more similar to the Portuguese mainland, offering olives, bread and sometimes plates of seafood. You will be charged for anything you eat; tell the waiter if you do not want these starters (and check that they are not on your bill if you do not eat them). In tourist districts – which means most of Funchal – main courses are often presented with bland sauces which drown out the natural flavours, along with overboiled vegetables such as broccoli, carrots and sprouts, in a misguided attempt to appeal to northern European tastes. Your best bet is either to go for one of the traditional local dishes described in the box on p.250, or stay on safe ground with grilled or barbecued meat and fish, which is usually accompanied by *batatas* (potatoes, usually chips) and *salada* (salad). If you have room for desserts, do not expect a great variety. Some places try their luck at international favourites such as cheesecakes and crumbles, but the results can be hit or miss, so again it's best to stick to fruit or local dishes.

MEALS AND SNACKS

MADEIRAN CUISINE

Madeiran cuisine is typically Portuguese, making the most of local ingredients (especially fish), which are simply cooked – usually with garlic, olive oil and herbs such as coriander – without elaborate sauces and embellishments.

Nearly every restaurant on Madeira can rustle up a decent grilled fish. The most common fish is the unattractive looking *espada* (scabbard fish), a long, eel-like, white-fleshed fish that only lives in deep waters round Madeira and Japan. It is fairly ubiquitous, commonly fried *com banana* (with bananas) or *com vinho e alhos* (in wine and garlic), though it often tastes best when barbecued on its own. The delicate, white-fleshed *bodião* (parrot fish) is another local speciality, while more familiar fish such as *atum* (tuna), *salmonete* (red mullet), *pargo* (bream) and *espadarte* (swordfish, not to be confused with *espada*) are also common. A typical Portuguese dish to look out for is *bacalhau* (salted cod): there are reputedly 365 different versions of the dish, some of which are an acquired taste, but at its best – such as the creamy *bacalhau a bras* (with eggs fried with strips of potato) – it can be delicious. Also worth trying is *caldeirada*, a fish stew made with assorted fish and vegetables.

For **seafood** fans, *gambas* (prawns), *lagostas* (lobsters) and *arroz de marisco* (rice and seafood stew) can be excellent but are usually expensive as seafood is all imported. Less expensive are the *lapas* – limpets – which are found locally, traditionally served in garlic butter or with rice. In restaurants, seafood is often accompanied by *açorda*, a local bread and garlic sauce traditionally prepared by shepherds, who mixed stale bread with water and anything they could find around them, such as birds' eggs and mountain herbs, before heating the mixture over a fire.

Most Madeiran grilled or barbecued **meat dishes** are similar to those served on the Portuguese mainland: *porco/febras* (pork), *frango na churrasca* (barbecue-grilled chicken), *cabrito* (kid) and *bife* (beef) tend to be the best bet. However, it's worth trying the *espetada* (kebab), another Madeiran speciality, not to be confused with *espada* (or *espadarte*!). Traditionally cooked by farmers, who impaled cubes of beef on laurel branches before cooking them over the ashes of a fire, the best kebabs are made with meat rolled in garlic, then grilled with chunks of onions, peppers and tomatoes. These dishes are usually accompanied by *batatas* (potatoes, usually chips) and *salada* (salad). Unlike mainland Portugal, however, *milho frito* – tasty cubes of fried cornmeal – is sometimes served instead of potatoes. Meat stews can also be good and extremely filling: *feijoada* is a meat and bean casserole, while *feijão guisado* is bacon and haricot beans stewed in tomato sauce.

Desserts aren't deemed to be particularly important in Madeira. The most popular Portuguese desserts are *arroz doce* (rice pudding) and *pudim flan* (crème caramel) and, in season, *maça assada* (baked apple). The best local produce is ice cream (*gelado*) and the locally grown tropical fruits, many of which flavour the ice creams. Sometimes these are combined in fruit salads, though likely as not some of the fruit will be tinned.

As in Portugal, savoury snacks (*petiscos*) are popular, and most cafés feature *rissois de camarão* (fried shrimp puffs), *pastéis de bacalhau* (salted cod rissoles) and *empadas* (pies, usually stuffed with chicken). Most visitors to Madeira also quickly become fans of the sweet cakes (*bolos*). Madeira cake itself is a purely British invention rarely found in Madeiran cafés. Much better is *bolo de mel* – literally "honey cake" – a Madeiran speciality, actually made of dried fruits, spices and molasses, a natural by-product of the island's sugar industry. A popular pastry is *pastéis de nata* (custard-cream tarts). Less common but worth trying if you get the chance are sweets called *rebucados de funcho*, which are made of puréed fennel and syrup dried into strips.

Vegetarians are not particularly well catered for in Madeira and, despite the superb vegetables available from shops and markets, most of those that make the restaurants are overcooked and unappetising. Soups, such as *sopa de legumes* (vegetable) and *sopa de tomate* (tomato, cooked with onions and an egg) are good bets, but even *caldo verde* – a popular green soup made with cabbage and potatoes – often has a chunk of ham thrown in for extra flavour. Most restaurants can rustle up a large *salada mista* (mixed salad), though sometimes these have rolls of ham. Otherwise you may find omelettes the best option.

See opposite for details of the island's only
specifically vegetarian restaurant, *Bio-Logos*.

FUNCHAL

THE CITY CENTRE

Adega A Cuba
Map 2, E3. Rua do Bispo 28
Daily 8am–10pm. Inexpensive
Barn-like *adega* (wine cellar) with upstairs balcony and vast wooden barrels serving as tables. Popular all day, with decent croissants for breakfast, good sandwiches and Portuguese dishes, plus a lively bar (see p.288), serving superb cold sangria.

A Pipa
Map 2, E3. Rua da Queimada de Cima 13
Daily noon–4pm & 6–midnight. Inexpensive
An attractive restaurant, popular with locals, with an arched-ceilinged interior and a few tables out the front on the pedestrianized street. Serves very reasonable soups, salads and pasta and usually superb *pratos do dia* (dishes of the day).

RESTAURANT PRICES

The restaurants below have been divided into three categories: Inexpensive (less than 2500$00/€12.50); Moderate (2500–4500$00/€12.50–22.50); and Expensive (above 4500$00/€22.50). These prices refer to the **cost of a two-course meal including wine**, but excluding tips. All the places listed accept major credit cards unless stated otherwise. Telephone numbers are given when bookings are recommended.

Apolo
Map 2, E4. Rua Dr J. António Almeida 21
Daily 8am–11pm. Moderate
High-profile restaurant and café on a sloped pedestrianized street linking the Sé with the seafront. The extensive menu is surprisingly reasonable with a long list of starters and good fish and meat main courses. The house salads make an excellent light lunch. It's a popular stopping-off point for locals on their way home from work, though most sit in the rather dull Art Deco interior leaving the attractive outdoor tables for tourists to sit and watch the world go by.

Bio-Logos
Map 2, C3. Rua Nova de São

Pedro 34
Mon–Fri noon–3pm & 2–pm, until 7pm for drinks and snacks. Inexpensive
This slightly worthy, old-fashioned canteen is the only vegetarian restaurant in Funchal. Made mostly from organic produce, dishes include baked tofu, vegetable pies, sandwiches, pizzas, quiches and appetizing desserts. The set meal is particularly good value at 800$00/€4. It also does freshly squeezed fruit and vegetable juice.

Golden Gate
Map 2, D4. Avda Arriaga 21
Sun–Wed 8am–midnight, Thurs–Sat 8am–2am. Moderate
The first-floor restaurant of the *Golden Gate* hotel, opened

FUNCHAL

●

253

in 1814, was a fashionable meeting place and remains the city's most atmospheric place for a meal or drink. It was renovated in 1998 by architect Diogo Lima de Mayer who gave the traditional decor a modern twist: there are spinning ceiling fans, wicker chairs, green shutters and mirrors. Pasta, sandwiches, salads, pastries and homemade ice cream are served inside or on the first-floor balcony, overlooking Avenida Arriaga and the Palácio de São Lourenço.

Jardim da Carreira
Map 2, C3. Rua da Carreira 118
Daily 10am–11pm. Moderate
Popular largely with tourists thanks to a superb, tranquil back courtyard full of flowers and trees. It serves Madeiran staples, such as tomato and onion soup with egg, and *espadarte* (scabbard fish) with banana, as well as good-value set lunches.

Londres
Map 2, D3. Rua da Carreira 64a
Mon–Sat 8am–midnight.
Moderate
A traditional restaurant with uninspiring decor but serving a very good menu, including *bacalhau* and other fish dishes (usually sea bream, salmon and trout), along with steaks.

Mezanino
Map 2, D4. Galerias São Lourenço, Loja 35
 291 236 300
Mon–Thurs 12.30–3pm, Fri & Sat 12.30–3pm & 8–11pm.
Moderate
A surprisingly lively, fashionable place inside a shopping centre between Avenida Arriaga and the seafront. The split-level restaurant has a good reputation for well-cooked and interesting dishes such as risotto, fish with noodles and imaginative meat dishes. Great desserts include cheesecake, crumbles and crepes. Evening bookings recommended.

Minas Gerais
Map 2, C4. Avda do Infante 2
Daily 9am–10pm. Inexpensive
Claiming to be Funchal's

oldest, this characterful restaurant opposite Parque Santa Catarina is big and airy with high ceilings, old blue-faced cupboards and cabinets full of bottles and soccer trophies. The menu is limited, but it makes a good light lunch spot.

O Lampião
Map 2, E3. Rua do Bispo 30a
Mon–Sat 7.30am–10.30pm.
Inexpensive
Join the row of workers at the bar for a bargain lunch-time menu. There's also a TV at the back and a couple of outdoor tables in front on the pedestrianized street.

Pátio
Map 2, D3. Rua da Carreira 43
Mon–Sat 8am–10pm. Moderate
Set in the superb courtyard of the currently closed photographic museum (see p.66), with an attractive indoor area and further seating at the back, this popular local restaurant serves Portuguese dishes and snacks such as *croques monsieurs*.

THE SEAFRONT

Apolo Mar
Map 2, D5. Marina de Funchal
Daily 7am–1am. Inexpensive
Small café–restaurant at the eastern end of the marina serving grilled fish and meat dishes. There's a TV above the bar and lots of outdoor tables facing the bobbing boats in the marina.

A Princesa
Map 2, D5. Marina de Funchal
Daily 10am–midnight. Moderate
Avoids the hard sell of the other restaurants along this stretch, perhaps because it can rely on the knowledge that its food will pull punters back; there's decent seafood and deliciously char-grilled fresh fish. The wine list includes a surprisingly good wine called BSE.

Caravela
Map 2, E4. Avda do Mar 15
Mon–Sat 11am–11pm.
Moderate–expensive
Set on the third floor of a modern block overlooking the busy seaside drag, this

FUNCHAL

restaurant serves unexceptional Madeiran and Portuguese dishes. However, service is attentive and you do get attractive views over the ocean – a good spot when it's not warm enough to dine outside.

Cervejaria Beerhouse
Map 2, C5. Porto de Funchal
Daily 10am–11pm. Expensive
Just above the marina with a distinctive, tent-like roof, this offers superb views of Funchal, with seating inside or out. The long menu offers decent soups, salads and specials such as seafood with *açorda* (bread sauce), lobster and chicken curry, best washed down with the home-brewed unfiltered beer.

Ducouver
Map 2, D5. Marina de Funchal
Daily 10am–1am. Moderate
The restaurant's terrace affords great views over the marina, though the aggressive marketeering to lure you in can be offputting. The food and service is good, however, with decent pasta, pizza and superb fresh fish such as

bodião (parrot fish). Other specialities include *arroz com camarão* (shrimp rice) and *peixe assado no sal* (fish baked in salt).

Restaurante Marina Terra
Map 2, D5. Marina de Funchal
Daily 10am–11pm. Inexpensive
With lots of tables on a semi-covered terrace at the west end of the marina, this is probably the best value of the larger restaurants in this area. Simple and effective dishes such as chicken and beef kebabs, tuna cooked in wine and garlic and enormous *arroz de mariscos*, plus inexpensive house wine.

The Vagrant
Map 2, D4. Avda do Mar
Daily 11am–11pm. Moderate
Also known as the Beatles Boat (see p.54), although it's hard to know what John, Paul and Co would make of the yacht's current reincarnation as an unashamedly touristy restaurant–café–bar. The tables out on deck overlooking the beach are the

FUNCHAL

best, though you can also sit in one of numerous mini boats set in shallow water and "enjoy eating with the sensation of navigating" as the publicity promises. The food itself – Portuguese dishes as well as pizza, pasta, pastries and ice cream – is adequate. The night-time lights add to the impression that this place is so kitsch it is amost cool.

EAST OF THE CENTRE

Arco Velho
Map 2, G4. Rua Dom Carlos I 42
Daily 8am–midnight.
Inexpensive
This café-restaurant (see also p.291) offers very good-value Madeiran dishes with an outdoor terrace from where you can watch the blue capsules pass overhead on the Funchal–Monte cable car.

Arsénio's
Map 2, H4. Rua da Santa Maria 169
☏ 291 224 007
Daily 7pm–midnight. Expensive

Highly rated for its fish and meat dishes, with an outdoor grill wafting mouth-watering smells to the outdoor tables under the covered porch. Most people head here for the nightly fado sessions in the traditional, *azulejos*-lined interior, which bumps up the prices, but at least the fado is more authentic than the cheesy warm-up musicians on electric keyboards. Despite the fact it takes itself a little too seriously, this is one of the old town's most popular dining spots so get there early or book ahead.

Bar Bau Botânico
Map 3, F5. Caminho das Voltas 2b
Mon 8am–5pm, Tues–Sun 8am–9pm. Inexpensive
Simple bar and restaurant just above the entrance to the botanical gardens and offering a better range of meals than the café in the gardens, including decent omelettes and salads. It's significantly cheaper, too, though your views are limited to the tour buses parked outside.

FUNCHAL

257

Marisa

Map 2, H4. Rua de Santa Maria 162

℡ 291 226 189

Daily noon–midnight. Moderate

Very attractive family-run restaurant with traditional decor and upstairs seating on a small interior wooden balcony. Specialities include *paella, arroz de marisco* (seafood rice) and prawns with chilli. It's pretty tiny, so booking is advisable.

Marisqueira Tropicana

Map 2, G4. Rua Dom Carlos I 43

Daily 10am–1pm. Inexpensive

More reasonably priced than many of the restaurants on this unpedestrianized stretch of Rua Dom Carlos, with good-value tuna, fish and Portuguese dishes. There's also a pleasant street-facing terrace.

O Almirante

Map 2, F4. Largo do Poço 1–2

℡ 291 224 252

Daily 7am–midnight. Expensive

The beautiful traditional first-floor dining room features wood beams, chandeliers and high-backed chairs – it's a lovely spot to enjoy fish, lobster, squid, kebabs and dishes such as *Fidago ao Madeira* (Madeiran liver). There's also a small covered terrace next to an old fountain at the front, though this faces a rather traffic-laden corner just south of the main market.

O Jango

Map 2, H4. Rua de Santa Maria 164–166

℡ 291 221 840

Daily 11am–11pm. Moderate

Small split-level restaurant crammed into a former fisherman's house with a reputation for excellent-value food. Stick to the simple grilled fish dishes and the reputation is justified; other dishes tend to be smothered in rich sauces and served with over-boiled vegetables. Clam *cataplana, gambas a Indiana* (Indian-style prawns) and the house wine are also good.

O Tapassol

Map 2, G4. Rua Dom Carlos I 62

℡ 291 225 023

Daily 11am–11pm. Expensive

Very good quality Portuguese

staples. Its other attraction is an upstairs terrace offering sea views. Gets booked up so booking ahead advised or turn up early.

Portão
Map 2, H4. Rua do Portão de São Tiago
Fri–Wed noon–midnight.
Inexpensive–moderate
Just behind the church with outdoor tables on a pedestrianized stretch near the castle, this restaurant also has an attractive interior, decorated with mock wood beams and *azulejos*. Service is friendly and unpretentious and the fish, meat and the *bacalhau* dishes are pretty good value.

Tartaruga
Map 2, H4. Largo do Corpo Santo 4–6
Daily 10am–midnight.
Inexpensive
A tiny place facing the Carmo church with a couple of tables wedged inside and more spreading onto the attractive square. The owner's father used to sell turtle shells here – *tartaruga* means "turtle" – but the son now

runs a very inexpensive restaurant with his Scottish wife, serving a hybrid of Portuguese and Scottish dishes to a non-local clientele. The place to go if you hanker for sausages, beans, eggs and the like, though the Portuguese-oriented set meals are perhaps the best value, including good soups, grilled sardines and tuna steaks.

Xarambinha
Map 2, H4. Largo do Corpo Santo 29
Daily noon–11pm. Moderate
Attractively positioned pizzeria with outdoor tables right by the Carmo church on a square. There are 31 types of chunky pizza to choose from, along with pasta and lasagne.

HOTEL ZONE

Bamboo Inn
Map 3, D7. Estrada Monumental 318
Tues 6.30–10.30pm, Wed–Sun 1–3pm & 6.30–10.30pm.
Inexpensive

FUNCHAL

With its entrance on Rampa do Lido just northwest of the lido, this bills itself as a vegetarian and Chinese restaurant. Though set behind a dull shopping centre, the interior is tastefully decorated in traditional Chinese style with koi fish tanks and Chinese lanterns. There is also an outside courtyard with a swimming pool which anyone can use for a small fee. Chinese dishes are excellent and vegetarian options include tofu dishes, vegetable noodles and vegetable chop suey.

Barra Azul

Map 3, C7. Praia Formosa
Daily 10am–2am. Moderate
Little more than a wooden shack on the promenade of Praia Formosa, with a stand-up bar, restaurant and appealing outdoor tables on the esplanade. It's very much a local, especially at weekends when the *Funchalense* descend for lunch. Offers excellent local fish, spicy "devil's squid", squid kebabs, garlic prawns and very salty *bacalhau* sandwiches.

Bernini

Map 2, A6. Rua Imperatriz D. Amélia 70
Daily 9am–3pm & 6–11pm.
Inexpensive
Unpretentious, glass-fronted Italian restaurant just below the casino complex with a long list of homemade pasta dishes, pizza, salads and Portuguese staples. Popular with families.

Brisa Mar

Map 3, E7. *Reid's Palace Hotel*, Estrada Monumental 139
℡291 763 001
Tues–Sat 7–9.30pm June–Sept only. Expensive
Reid's summer restaurant offers the chance to live it up with the wealthy, tucking into very pricey international cuisine; smart dress required and booking essential.

Casa Velha

Map 2, A6. Rua Imperatriz D. Amélia 69
℡291 205 600
Daily 12.30–3pm & 7–11pm.
Expensive
Set in a nineteenth-century villa, this has a semi-tropical, colonial feel with spinning

ceiling fans, old prints on the walls and lush vegetation in the garden. It's usually bustling and not too formal, with fish, meat and superb desserts, including crepes and banana flambés. Certainly the most atmospheric of the restaurants in a little triangle of traditional buildings behind the casino complex.

Casal da Penha
Map 2, A6. Rua Penha de França
Daily 11am–midnight. Moderate
The usual meat, fish and seafood including *Lulas a Diabo* (spicy squid), *Frango piri piri* (chilli chicken) and crepes, with a long list of starters and desserts. The best bit is the appealing outside terrace overlooking a quiet side street.

Cúpula
Map 2, A5. *Savoy Hotel*, Avda do Infante
☎291 222 031
Daily 7–10pm.
Moderate–expensive
Most relaxed of the *Savoy's* restaurants, with reasonably priced international cuisine served in a huge domed dining room next to the hotel gardens and pool.

Granny's House
Map 3, D7. Estrada Monumental 218
Daily 11am–midnight. Moderate
Off-puttingly named place but title reflects the olde-worlde decor of a traditional town house offering authentic Madeiran cuisine. There's an appealing outdoor terrace and you can also have afternoon teas.

Kon-Tiki
Map 3, E7. Rua do Favila 9
Daily 12.30–11pm. Moderate
An old *quinta* turned restaurant just northwest of the casino complex, with a small back patio. The walls are covered in the colourful paintings of the Norwegian artist who founded the restaurant in 1969. Now it is Madeiran-run with specialities including *bife na pedra* – steak cooked on a hot stone – and grilled meat; there are also some varied salads, though the food is often less colourful than the art.

FUNCHAL

261

Les Faunes

Map 3, D7. *Reid's Palace Hotel*, Estrada Monumental 139
☎ 291 763 001
Tues–Sat 7–9.30pm Oct–May only. Expensive

The ultimate in French *haute cuisine* – with a few oriental and Madeiran influences – in a plush restaurant tucked into a corner of *Reid's Hotel*. Original Picassos on the wall vie with the harbour views for your attention. You may find yourself rubbing shoulders with visiting celebs, and you'll need to check your bank balance carefully before you pay. Dress is smart.

Moby Dick

Map 3, D7. Estrada Monumental 187
Fri–Wed noon–4pm & 6–11pm. Moderate

Unpromisingly set back on the coastal side of the main road in a dull forecourt of a modern block between *Reid's* and the lido – and often pretty dead at lunch time – this is actually a very good place to head for. The interior is pleasantly traditional while the specialities include excellent seafood dishes such as *gambas piri piri* (spicy prawns), a few vegetarian options and what some people consider to be the best fresh fish in Funchal. The owner will pick up clients from their hotel in his mini bus (minimum of four people if you are not staying nearby).

Reid's Palace Hotel Main Dining Room

Map 3, D7. *Reid's Palace Hotel*, Estrada Monumental 139
☎ 291 763 001
Daily 7–9.30pm. Expensive

The most formal of *Reid's*' in-house restaurants, this vast, high-ceilinged hall is known as the House of Lords – partly because of the resemblance and partly because of the number of British peers who have dined here. Serves top-notch but traditional international cuisine.

Restaurante Dona Amélia

Map 2, A6. Rua Imperatriz D. Amélia 83
☎ 291 225 784
Daily 12.30–3pm & 7–11pm. Moderate

Attractive, traditional building lined with hanging plants and *azulejos* on two floors; there is also a basement bar. Sadly the waiters are over-stuffy and the clientele is largely of the over 50s-in-suits variety. The fish, meat, seafood and pasta is reasonably priced, however, as are the speciality flambées. Desserts include *kebab de frutos tropicais*.

Restaurante Lido Mar

Map 3, D7. Rua do Gorgulho-Lido
Daily noon–3pm & 6–11pm. Expensive
The lido restaurant, which you can eat in even if you're not using the Lido facilities, is surprisingly good, set in an attractive spot overlooking the sea and the pools below. The long menu offers a wide range of dishes including *arroz de tamboril* (monkfish rice), seafood *feijoada* (with bean stew) and chicken and lobster ragout.

Restaurante O Molhe

Map 2, B7. Estrada da Pontinha, Forte de Nossa Senhora da Conceiçao

☏ 291 203 804
Tues–Fri noon–3pm & 7pm–midnight, Sat 7pm–midnight. Expensive
Spectacularly positioned restaurant right on top of the rocky fort on Loo Rock jutting out of the city harbour walls (see p.77), reached by a lift. You dine in a glass structure on the fort roof offering 360-degree views over the sea, the harbour walls, the city and the mountains beyond. Offers all the usual Portuguese fish, meat and seafood and, though not cheap, it is not as expensive as you'd think. Reservation advised at weekends.

Restaurante O Portuário

Map 2, A7. Porto do Funchal
Mon–Fri 7am–10pm, Sat 7am–5pm. Inexpensive
Set in the harbour walls just below the hotel *Quinta da Penha Franca Mar*, this is very much a local used by the dock workers; no-nonsense, inexpensive Portuguese food, no windows and a TV in one corner, but stacks of atmosphere.

FUNCHAL

263

Summertime Restaurante

Map 3, D7. Estrada Monumental 219

Daily 11am–midnight. Moderate

Just west of the Lido complex, this offers decent Portuguese dishes with an attractive sea-facing terrace. This wins the tackiest name competition along with The Granny's House next door, but at least it retains the character of a traditional town house.

Trattoria Villa Cliff

Map 3, D7. Estrada Monumental 139

Daily 7pm–9.30pm. Moderate-expensive

Just above – and run by – *Reid's Palace Hotel*, this is Funchal's top Italian restaurant, offering superb cuisine and sweeping views over the city.

AROUND FUNCHAL

CAMACHA

- -

Casa de Pasto Boleu

Map 3, H4. ER102 towards Santo da Serra, opposite the old church

Daily noon–3pm & 7–11pm. Inexpensive

This place has a big outdoor barbecue and specializes in grilled meat dishes and *frango no churrasco* (barbecue-grilled chicken). There are tables inside and out and a list of daily specials.

Restaurante O Relógio

Map 3, H4. Achada

Daily noon–4pm & 7–11pm. Moderate

Despite the tourist trappings, this is the best place to eat in Camacha, mainly thanks to its unbroken views over the south coast and the Ilhas Desertas. It can seem quiet when the tour parties aren't filling up its ample spaces, but the food and service is top notch. Moderately priced dishes include omelettes, spaghetti, steaks and a mean range of desserts, including chocolate mousse and ice cream with chocolate sauce. On Fridays and Saturdays at 9.15pm, the Grupo Foclorico da Casa do Povo da Camacha, considered Madeira's best folk music group, distract your attention from the views.

CÂMARA DE LOBOS

Churchill's Restaurant
Map 3, B6. Rua João Goncalves 39
Daily 11am–11pm. Moderate–expensive
Located just above the spot where Churchill liked to paint – you'll notice black and white prints of the man all over the place – this place serves decent if slightly pricey Madeiran food, including flambés and seafood platters. Most people head to the terrace for pricey drinks overlooking the harbour; you can eat out here or in the cosy wood-lined interior.

Coral
Map 3, B6. Largo da República
ⓣ 291 942 469

Daily 11am–11pm. Moderate
Modern café-restaurant on the east side of the main square, with a superb upstairs terrace offering views over the sea and Cabo Girão. It offers a range of grilled meats and fish.

Ribar-ar
Map 3, B6. Largo da República
Daily 11am–11pm. Moderate
Small restaurant with red-chequered tablecloths inside, though most people head for the outdoor tables on the square or the roof terrace. The usual grilled meats are on offer, along with *picado* (slices of beef) and fresh local fish such as *bodião* (parrot fish) and *espada*.

CURRAL DAS FREIRAS

Nun's Valley Restaurante
Map 3, B2.
Daily 9am–8.30pm. Moderate
This is the most touristy place in the village but superbly positioned with a terrace offering sweeping views down the valley. The

AROUND FUNCHAL

usual Madeiran menu includes local produce such as chestnut soup, banana cake, chestnut cake and liqueurs made from walnuts and chestnuts.

ESTREITO DE CÂMARA DE LOBOS

A Capoeira

Map 3, B5. Sítio da Igreja

Tues–Sun noon–3.30pm & 6–11pm. Moderate

Right on the main square with an upstairs room offering unbeatable views across the precipitous valleys below. Vast slabs of meat and kebabs are grilled on metal skewers over a huge fire at the back, along with other Madeiran dishes.

As Vides

Map 3, B5. Rua da Achada

Daily noon–midnight. Moderate

Just behind the main market building in an upstairs room, this place is famed for its grilled meats; it's also a good spot to sample the local wines.

MONTE

Restaurante Belomonte

Map 3, F5. Caminho das Tílias

Daily 8am–11pm. Moderate

Just above the start of the toboggan run, the top-floor restaurant here is one of the best bets for a cooked meal in Monte, offering reasonably priced Portuguese dishes. The first-floor café is a popular if smoky retreat for the toboggan operators.

PICO DOS BARCELOS

Barcelos à Noite

Map 3, D6.

Daily 9am–midnight

Good-quality café-restaurant, with outdoor tables and a traditional-style interior for coffee or a full meal of moderately priced grilled meat or fish. On Friday nights there are fado sessions from 10pm.

EASTERN MADEIRA

CANIÇAL

Restaurante Bar Amarelo
Map 4, F2. Junto à Lota
Daily except Wed
noon–10.30pm. Moderate
The friendly "yellow
restaurant bar" sits on the
seafront just below the Museu
da Baleia; the separate
restaurant does reliably tasty
fish and seafood.

Snack Bar Pescador
Map 4, F2.
Daily 7am–10pm. Inexpensive
Just above the Museu da
Baleia and the best place for a
cheap and cheerful meal,
with inexpensive meat and
fish dishes and a few tables
and chairs out front.

CANIÇO

Café-Restaurante A Lareira
Map 4, B7. Largo Padre
Lomelino
Café daily 8am–10pm,
restaurant noon–10pm.
Moderate
The restaurant offers the
usual Madeiran staples, along
with omelettes, beef dishes
and even curry, while the
café is the best spot to enjoy a
coffee or drink in town, with
outdoor tables facing the
main square.

La Perla
Map 4, B7. *Quinta Splendida*,
Estrada da Ponta da Oliveira
☎ 291 930 400
Daily noon–2pm & 7–10pm.
Expensive
Quinta Splendida's gourmet
restaurant is set in the old
quinta building with a
modern glass extension faced
by lawns and shady outdoor
tables. Dishes include king
prawns with champagne
sauce, veal in cognac sauce
and steaks, from around
6000$00/€30 per person.

Restaurante Central
Map 4, B7. Sítio da Vargem
☎ 291 934 344

Daily noon–10pm. Moderate
Go past the cheesy front room to the lovely leafy terrace at the back for a combination of Madeiran and unusual international dishes including crepes, New England clam chowder, lobster, mussels and spaghetti dishes.

La Terraça
Map 4, B7. Sítio da Vargem
Daily noon–3pm & 6–11pm. Moderate

Head uphill past the church and bag a seat on the terrace, which has great views over the coast and the Ilhas Desertas. The menu is quite meaty with a few fish dishes.

CANIÇO DE BAIXO

Inn and Art
Map 4, B7. Rua Robert Baden Powell 61/62
Daily noon–4pm & 6–10pm. Moderate–expensive

A vaguely arty restaurant just west of the tourist office, with modern paintings on the walls, though most people head for the sea-facing terrace on a clifftop. The menu features light lunches and full evening meals with dishes including fish, risotto and "chicken stew sweet and sour". There is usually a nightly live music programme, which ranges from fado to Brazilian.

Restaurante Lido Galo Mar
Map 4, B7. Lido Galo Mar
Daily 11am–10pm. Moderate–expensive.

The lido restaurant is set on a terrace overlooking the sea and pool. Top service and good-quality fish and seafood such as *cataplana de tamboril* (monkfish stew), salmon and sole and mussels with garlic.

Restaurante Praia dos Reis Magos
Map 4, C7. Praia dos Reis Magos
Daily noon–9pm. Inexpensive

This simple beachside restaurant has a limited menu of five or six fish dishes and starters such as fish soup or *lapas* – grilled limpets. The best bets are the *peixe do dia* – the day's fresh catch – *castanhetos* (little grilled fish) or octopus stew, best eaten on the terrace surrounded by cats and families fresh from the beach.

GARAJAU

La Carbonara
Map 4, B7. Centro Commercial Infante 220
Daily noon–midnight.
Inexpensive
This cheap and cheerful place has outside tables on the esplanade of a shopping centre opposite the *Dom Pedro Garajau* (see p.230). It offers 17 types of pizza along with salads and pasta dishes.

Vista Mar
Map 4, B7.
Daily 10am–11pm. Moderate
Just out of Garajau on the clifftop road to Caniço, this place indeed has a sea view (*vista mar*) from its tiny dining room, which offers the usual range of meat, fish dishes, salads and omelettes.

MACHICO

Mercado Velho
Map 5, D7. Rua do Mercado
☎ 291 965 926
Daily noon–10.30pm. Moderate
The former small covered market building opposite the tourist office has been well converted into an attractive restaurant offering the usual Madeiran favourites, omelettes, salads and a few pasta dishes. The food is nothing special, but the setting – with seats outside on a cobbled terrace complete with a fountain and a few *azulejos* – is a cut above the rest.

Praia de Machico
Map 5, C8. Praia de Machico
☎ 291 963 025
Daily noon–11.30pm.
Inexpensive
Right on the beach, this restaurant, cafe and pizzeria has superbly positioned outdoor tables and attracts a steady flow of customers for everything from coffees and snacks to full meals; it's also the perfect place for a sunset

EASTERN MADEIRA

beer and a dish of *tremeços* (pickled beans).

Restaurante O Casco
Map 5, C7. Rua do Ribeirinho
Daily 11am–11pm; bar open until 2am. Moderate
A vaguely tropical bar-restaurant with palm-frond sun-umbrellas and an outdoor patio where you can enjoy drinks or fish and seafood.

Restaurante Típico O Túnel
Map 4, E3. Estrada do Caniçal
☎ 291 962 459
Daily 11am–10pm. Inexpensive
Just before the tunnel to Caniçal, a couple of kilometres out of Machico, this is a reasonably priced place – as long as you avoid the lobster or grilled prawns – with outdoor tables offering great views down over the Machico valley. The zebra-like interior brickwork is less appealing, but the grills are reliably tasty.

Snack Bar Praça de Machico
Map 5, D7. Mercado Municipal

Daily 8am–midnight. Inexpensive
Next to the town market, this little café does cheap dishes of the day and has appealing outdoor tables facing the sea.

PORTELA

Miradouro da Portela
Map 4, B2.
Daily 8am–midnight. Moderate
Bar-restaurant with two popular wood-panelled front rooms, warmed by log fires. If these are full, there's a spacious back room – without any views – with hooks in the ceiling from which to hang the house speciality: succulent meat kebabs skewered on long metal poles. The menu also features salads.

PORTO DA CRUZ

Praça Velha
Map 4, B1. Casas Próximas
Daily 8am–midnight.
Inexpensive
This lively bar and restaurant

has a superb sea-facing terrace along with a glassed-in veranda and a few indoor tables. The food is decent if unexceptional, with the usual range of meat, fish and salads.

Restaurante Penedo
Map 4, B1. Casas Próximas
Daily 9am–10pm. Moderate
The most upmarket place to eat round here, with an impressive upstairs dining room offering superb views over the sea – there are also outdoor tables on the beachside promenade. As you'd expect, fish is the best bet, but soups, salads, omelettes and meat also feature on the menu.

SANTA CRUZ

Restaurante Boca de Panela
Map 4, D5. Calhau de São Fernando
Daily noon–7pm. Moderate
Along the seafront west of the soccer pitch, this small beachside place does dishes such as *feijoada de marisco*

(seafood and bean stew), *arroz de marisco* (seafood rice) and crab.

Restaurante Praia das Palmeiras
Map 4, D5. Praia das Palmeiras
ⓣ 291 524 248
Daily 9am–10pm, bar open until 11pm. Moderate
The lido restaurant has a great sea-facing terrace. The house speciality is steak, though other dishes include a long list of meat, fish and seafood with salads. There is usually live music on Friday and Saturday nights.

SANTO ANTÓNIO DA SERRA

Nossa Aldeia Restaurante
Map 4, C3.
Tues–Sun noon–midnight. Inexpensive
The best bet in town for unglamorous but inexpensive Madeiran fare, with a local feel. It is situated at the bottom end

EASTERN MADEIRA

of town, just below the kids' play area: follow the sign to the right for "Parque de Feiras".

THE WEST COAST

CALHETA

Marisqueira do Camarão
Map 6, F7.
☎ 291 824 379
Daily noon–3pm & 7–11pm. Moderate
Located five minutes' walk beyond the *Hotel Calheta Beach* towards Madalena do Mar. Decent lobster, seafood and fresh fish, served on a sea-facing terrace.

Restaurante Praça Velha
Map 6, F7.
Daily 8am–midnight. Inexpensive
Just below the town hall, a big space with fish tanks on one wall and a good range of drinks, superb garlic-bread sandwiches and reasonably priced Madeiran food, best enjoyed on the outdoor terrace facing the sea.

JARDIM DO MAR

Tar Mar
Map 6, E6.
Daily 10am–11pm. Moderate
On the cobbled lane to Portinho, this restaurant offers snacks as well as fresh grilled fish and seafood inside or on a bougainvillaea-covered terrace.

MADALENA DO MAR

A Poita
Map 6, H8.
Daily noon–11pm. Inexpensive
A short walk west of the church: turn right onto the new road heading inland and it is on the right next to an old bridge. It's a simple place but does decent, inexpensive fish dishes and *caldeirada*.

PAÚL DA SERRA

Jungle Rain
Map 6, I6. Ovil

Daily noon–10.30pm. Moderate

Part of the *Estalagem Pico da Urze* complex (see p.160), this is a rather incongruous Disneyesque jungle-themed restaurant filled with mock flora and plastic jungle animals, complete with animal noises and a mini waterfall. If you're here with kids it will seem like a godsend – there's even a special kids' menu – while for adults there is an adventurous menu of game dishes, including wild goat and rabbit, as well as some vegetarian dishes.

PAÚL DO MAR

Largo-Mar
Map 6, D5.

Daily 9am–9pm. Inexpensive

At the northern end of the beachfront, this is a good place for drinks or meals. Serves local fish, including *lapas* (limpets), *bodião* (parrot fish), octopus and swordfish; there are outdoor tables too.

Restaurante O Precipício
Map 6, D5.

Daily 9am–9pm. Inexpensive

A rather aptly named restaurant on the road from Prazeres down to Paúl do Mar. It really does feel like it's on a precipice, especially when you're on the terrace. Specializes in grills, but also does a good range of drinks and snacks.

PONTA DO PARGO

Solar do Pero
Map 6, C3. Sítio Salão de Cima 4

Daily noon–11pm. Moderate

A decent café-restaurant, opposite the village church, offering tasty local dishes such as *sopa de trigo* – cracked wheat soup with broad beans, potatoes and greens – and homemade cake, along with omelettes and salads.

WEST OF FUNCHAL

PONTA DO SOL

Café-Restaurante Poente
Map 6, I9.
Tues–Sun noon–11pm.
Moderate
Perched on top of a dramatic rocky outcrop overlooking the water, the café is a great spot for a drink or a snack, especially at sunset. For a full meal, the restaurant over the road is set back from the sea with less spectacular views, but serves decent fish and seafood.

RIBEIRA BRAVA

Restaurante Água Mar
Map 7, B6. Avda Luis Mendes
℡ 291 951 148

Daily 6am–2am. Expensive
Right on the beach just beyond the bridge over the river and with a sea-facing terrace, this is the most romantic dining spot in town and the best place to sample the local fresh fish; tasty giant prawns, too, but seafood veers on the expensive side.

Casa dos Grelhadas
Map 7, E4. Largo dos Herédias
Tues–Sun 11am–3pm & 7–11pm. Moderate
Specializes in grills, as its names suggests, with dishes such as *frango na brasa* (barbecue grilled chicken) and *leitão* (suckling pig). Outdoor tables are set on an attractive raised terrace overlooking a little square near the Ethnographical Museum.

NORTHERN AND CENTRAL MADEIRA

FAIAL

A Chave Restaurante
Map 8, H4.
Daily 10am–midnight.

Moderate–expensive
Situated opposite the church, this place does sizzlingly good fish and meat dishes and has a lovely terrace garden, complete with a

small fish pond and distant sea views.

A Ponte Velha
Map 8, H4.
Tues–Sun 11am–11pm.
Moderate
Named after its position by the old bridge over the Ribeira Sêca, this place is quiet during the week, but pulls in Madeirans at weekends thanks to its excellent grills.

PORTO MONIZ

Marydoce
Map 6, G1.
Daily 8am–midnight.
Inexpensive
An all-purpose affair (bakers, *pastelaria*, café, pizzeria and restaurant), with a back terrace facing the sea and a menu that features pizzas, octopus and grilled chicken.

Polo Norte
Map 6, G1.
Daily 9am–11pm. Inexpensive
Smallish place offering good-value Madeiran fare overlooking the car park

behind the *Orca Residencial* (see p.238). There's a bustling first-floor dining room and a roof terrace with slightly obscured sea views.

Restaurante Cachalote
Map 6, G1.
Daily noon–5pm. Expensive
Porto Moniz's most high-profile restaurant, open for lunch only, and built on the rocks right next to the eastern sea pools. There's even a mock tunnel inside connecting two of the varied rooms, one of which has space for 600 diners – it only gets remotely full when tour coaches pass by. The cuisine includes fish bouillabaisse, lobster and the usual Madeiran dishes.

Restaurante Orca
Map 6, G1. Sítio das Poças
Daily noon–3pm & 7–11pm.
Moderate
A large, smart dining room overlooking the sea pools, offering decent fish, seafood and Madeiran specialities. Service is crisp and there are usually as many locals as tourists.

NORTHERN AND CENTRAL MADEIRA

RIBEIRO FRIO

Victor's Bar
Map 8, F7.

Daily 9am–7pm. Moderate
Cosy, wood-lined dining
room with a log fire; the
reasonable menu offers trout
from the local farm, as well
as other grilled fish and
meats.

SANTANA

Quinta Furão
Map 8, G2. Achada do
Gramacho
☏ 291 570 154
Daily noon–3.30pm & 7–9pm.
Expensive
This restaurant, bar, *adega*
and shop lies just below the
hotel of the same name (see
p.239), 4km west of Santana.
The slightly formal restaurant
offers expensive but unusual
dishes, such as Santana cheese
with yoghurt and honey,
watercress soup and lamb
with honey and thyme, as
well as a good range of
wines. But the main
attraction is the superb view

over the cliffs from the front
terrace, which overlooks
Ponta de São Lourenço in
the distance.

Restaurante O Colmo
Map 8, G3.

Daily noon–3pm & 7–10pm.
Moderate
On the main road opposite the
post office, this is the liveliest
place to eat in Santana, with a
few outdoor tables and a busy
bar and restaurant area at the
back. Tasty dishes include
interesting starters such as
goats cheese with honey,
hearty tomato soups with egg
and *lapas*.

SÃO JORGE

Casa de Palha
Map 8, E1.

Daily 9am–11pm
Café-restaurant set in a
traditional, straw-thatched
wooden building and serving
light meals and local produce,
such as honey cake and
Madeira wine.

SÃO VICENTE

Ferro Velho
Map 6, L3. Rua da Fonte Velha
Daily 8am–6pm.
Moderate–expensive

Sitting next to the post office in the heart of the historic centre, this place sucks in tourists thanks to its bougainvillaea-shaded outdoor patio, though the menu of fish and meat dishes is somewhat limited and overpriced. Inside the decor is decidedly pub-like, with an array of international soccer scarves on the walls.

O Virgílio
Map 6, L3. Calhau
Daily 8am–midnight.
Inexpensive

This attracts slightly more locals than the neighbouring restaurants on this stretch on the seafront, with inexpensive grilled meats and fish served inside or on the veranda.

Restaurante Calamar
Map 6, L3. Juncos-Fajã da Areia
Daily 8am–10pm. Inexpensive

This cavernous – and often deserted – hotel restaurant five minutes' walk east of the bridge on the seafront has a terrace facing the sea and the lido. The reasonable menu includes superbly cooked dishes such as *arroz de lapas* (rice and limpets), *arroz de marisco,* beef stroganoff and a range of *bacalhau* dishes; the trout is excellent.

SEIXAL

Restaurante Brisa Mar
Map 6, I3.
Daily 8am–10pm. Moderate

This smart place is the best place to eat in Seixal, with a large dining area, snappy service and views over the harbour; the fresh fish is the thing to go for. There's also a downstairs café for inexpensive snacks and drinks, along with a few outdoor seats and table soccer.

PORTO SANTO

CALHETA

Restaurante Pôr do Sol
Map 9, B7.
℡ 291 984 380
Daily 10.30am–11pm.
Moderate–expensive

This bar-restaurant offers the best – and priciest – beachside food on the island, with an outdoor terrace offering great views over the beach, Ilhéu de Baixo and the distant outline of Madeira. There's a good range of meat dishes, though it is best known for its fresh fish and seafood such as *caldeirada* (fish casserole) and superb *feijoada de marisco* (bean and seafood stew). You don't have to splash out on a full meal either; the attached bar does drinks, ice creams and snacks such as octopus sandwiches. Phone ahead and the restaurant will pick you up from your hotel and drive you back again afterwards.

CAMACHA

Bar Torres Restaurante
Map 9, F2.
Mon–Fri 7pm–midnight.
Moderate

Open only during the week, this restaurant serves hearty meat and chicken dishes grilled on a giant outdoor barbecue. You can eat in the cosy indoor dining room or on a terrace shaded by vines. There's also a good bar attached (see p.300).

Estrela do Norte
Map 9, F2.
Daily 10am–4pm & 7pm–2am.
Moderate

People from all over the island visit this highly rated *churrascaria* for its superior if slightly pricey grilled meat and fish served in a modern, barn-like, stone-clad room with wooden benches. There are a few outdoor seats on a gravel forecourt or under a covered porch.

CAMPO DE BAIXO

Restaurante Mar e Sol
Map 9, D5.
Daily 10am–midnight. Moderate
Though the food and service is nothing special, the outdoor terrace on a raised bit of dune is superbly positioned, overlooking a wide swathe of beach. Moderately priced specialities include tuna steaks, *fragateira* (fish stew) and other fish dishes.

VILA BALEIRA

Arsênios
Map 9, F5. Avda Dr Manuel Gregório Pestana
Daily 11am–2am. Inexpensive
On the main road opposite the Pingo Doce supermarket, this wood-beamed place is popular with families thanks to a menu featuring 50 types of pizza to eat in or take away, along with filling pasta dishes, salads, fish and meat.

Baiana
Map 9, F5. Rua do Dr Nuno S.

Teixeira 9
Daily 10am–2am. Moderate
The best place in town for a full meal, this airy, wood-ceilinged restaurant just east of the main square is always busy. There are superb starters such as cheeses, olives and spongy *bolo de caçao* with garlic butter. Moderately priced main courses include barbecued chicken, grilled prawns and steaks with egg on top. Fresh fish usually includes *bodião* (parrot fish), *badejo* (coal fish) and octopus. Leave room for the tasty desserts and milkshakes.

Bar Gaivota
Map 9, E5. Rua Goularte Medeiros
Daily 10am–midnight, until 4am from May–Sept. Moderate
Plonked atop a sand dune right on the beach, this café-restaurant is slightly spoiled by naff piped music and a flouncy canopy over the terrace which fails to screen out the heat. Otherwise the fish, meat and seafood is good value, considering the superb position.

PORTO SANTO

Esplanade de Mar

Map 9, E5. Alameda Infante D. Henrique

Daily 10.30am–4am.

Inexpensive

Right by the jetty, this simple restaurant serves a good range of well-priced seafood, fish and meat, along with light snacks such as *pregos* (beef in a roll), soup and sandwiches. There's a small back patio and indoor seating facing the beach.

O Forno

Map 9, E5. Rampa da Fontinha

Daily 11am–11pm. Moderate

Good-value place with a modern decor of wood and chrome tables and chairs, offering traditional barbecue-grilled *espetada*, chicken and meats, along with home-baked bread. The entrance is opposite the campsite on the main south coast road.

Drinking and nightlife

Madeira has an awful lot to offer visitors, but a wild **nightlife** is not one of them. Though Funchal has a fair share of clubs and good bars, elsewhere only Machico and Porto Santo can boast anything vaguely lively after dark. Because of the dearth of nightlife, many of the larger hotels lay on their own entertainment programmes: aimed squarely at the more mature set of visitors, they usually consist of dire musicians doing cover versions of ancient hits or gentler classical or jazzy sounds. Other themed nights may include quizzes, games evenings or marginally more authentic displays of fado or folk music.

For more information about seeing live music
and dancing in Madeira, see p.353.

Unless this sort of entertainment appeals, the best thing to do is to head to one of the bars or cafés listed below and to make the most of Madeira's range of inexpensive and fiery drinks, with the island's stunning scenery more than making up for the lack of disco lights.

Virtually every village in Madeira has at least one bar or café, usually open from around 8am to 10pm, often later in the larger resorts. Outside Funchal, **cafés** often double up as the local shop and are frequented by people of all ages. The most basic will serve coffee and simple food such as sandwiches; the larger ones will serve a range of alcoholic drinks and full meals. In rural areas, **bars** remain a largely male domain, but though single women travellers may feel uncomfortable, there is usually no reason to feel unwelcome. In Funchal and the larger resorts, there is a more bohemian range of cafés and bars, many playing the latest sounds or showing live soccer on TVs in the corner. As in mainland Portugal, there is often little to distinguish between a café and bar; you can usually get a coffee, beer or a glass of wine in both.

Many of the major hotels have their own bars and cafés. Catering firmly to tourists, there is usually nothing much to distinguish them; the best ones are listed below.

There is not much of a local **clubbing** scene in Madeira, and the tourist market has yet to cater for visitors into a vibrant night out. However, the advantage of such limited options is that the clubs have very much a local and laid-back feel, and though sounds and fashions are pretty contemporary, strict dress codes certainly do not apply.

NON-ALCOHOLIC DRINKS

Water in Madeira is perfectly safe to drink. Still bottled water (*água sem gas*) and fizzy water (*água com gas*) are widely available in all cafés, restaurants, bars and most shops. Porto Santo has its own mineral water that is said to have miraculous healing powers – though it is not sold commercially and is only available from springs on the island – but it is

GAY MADEIRA

Madeira's gay scene is on the muted side. Most of the island has a conservative attitude to homosexuality, though in Funchal people are more open-minded. Indeed *Reid's* hotel had something of a reputation as a gay social centre in the early twentieth century, while Funchal's annual carnival kicks off with a transvestite night (see p.66). There are no specifically gay clubs or bars, though in Funchal, *Café do Teatro* on Avenida Arriaga (see p.281) is a popular gay hangout.

not advisable to drink standard tap water in Porto Santo as it is desalinated and tastes revolting.

Along with the usual international soft drinks, look out for fresh **fruit juices**: *sumo de laranja* (orange juice) and *sumo de maça* (apple juice). A pleasant bottled or tinned local drink is *brisa maracujá* – fizzy passion fruit juice.

In common with much of Europe, **tea** (*chá*) tends to be drunk black or *com limão* (with lemon). *Chá de limão* is tea flavoured with lemon rind. Ask for *chá com leite* if you want it with milk. Though tea is popular in Madeira, it is nowhere near as in demand as **coffee**, without which Madeirans seem incapable of functioning. Coffee is invariably fresh and of good quality, but comes in various forms. The most popular type is *uma bica,* a small, strong espresso. *Uma carioca* is a weaker *bica* with more water in it and *um garoto* is a *bica* with a little milk. *Um galão* is a tall milky coffee in a glass, often little more than flavoured milk; ask for it *escuro* (dark) if you want it to taste of coffee. If you want a plain coffee with milk, ask for *uma café grande com leite* or *uma chinêsa com leite.*

BEER AND SPIRITS

The local **beer** (*cerveja*) is Coral, a fairly strong and very

BEER AND SPIRITS

drinkable lager. The company also make Tónic, a dark beer. Ask for *um imperial* for a half glass of beer, or *uma caneca* for a large glass (half-litre). Other very drinkable beers from mainland Portugal are Sagres, Cristal and Superbock. International imports are more expensive.

For something stonger, the island specializes in some fairly lethal **spirits**, many of them derived from the sugar or tropical fruit industries. *Aguardente* is a firewater distilled from sugar cane and forms the basis of some even stronger tipples. *Branquinha* is a type of *aguardente* with a stick of sugar cane still in the bottle. *Poncha* is *aguardente* mixed with brandy, lemon and honey. *Maracujá* is a sweet liqueur made from passion fruit, and is said to have passionate side effects too. *Ginja* is the local cherry liqueur, while *licor de castanha* is a distillation of the local chestnuts. Less powerful but refreshing is *sidra* – **cider** – usually found in mountain bars. Portuguese spirits include the pleasant Maciera brandy and gin, though the Portuguese gin is less strong than international variants.

WINE

Wine has been produced on the island since the first settlers arrived in the fifteenth century, and without it it is unlikely that Madeira would have achieved anything like the degree of wealth it now enjoys. It was soon discovered that the wines improved with age. In 1999, two bottles of Madeiran wine were discovered by archaeologists during excavation work near Spitalfields Market in London dating back to 1670. The contents were sampled and declared "fresh and lively". Sailors also found the wine to be rich in vitamins and a handy way to ward off scurvy, so boats stocked up with it on their way to the New World and the East. But it was only with the accidental discovery of what is now known as Madeira wine (see box on p.286) that the wine trade on Madeira really took off – today's Madeiran grapes nearly all go towards the production of Madeira wine.

Nowadays in Europe, Madeira wine is about as fashionable as acrylic underpants, but it does have a burgeoning market in the USA and Japan. Generally written off as a sweet cross between sherry and port, there are actually several types of Madeira. Most Madeira is made with the red **Tinta Negra Mole** grape, introduced from France and known as a "chameleon" grape as it takes on the qualities of different grapes depending on the altitude it grows at. Other grapes include the famous **Malvasia** or Malmsey, which can be white or red, making a sweet, rich, dark wine with burnt caramel, nutty taste. The white **Bual** grape gives a more fruity, medium-sweet, golden-coloured wine more suitable as a dessert wine. The amber coloured **Vedelho** is a medium dry wine which is often chilled, and can be drunk with a meal. **Sercial** is dry and soft, a pale golden wine with a lemony edge which makes a good aperitif. You will also come across **Rainwater Madeira**, a pale, medium dry blend, so called because it is said to taste as soft as rainwater. Lesser varieties include **Bastardo**, a rather heavy, sweet wine; and the dry, fresh **Terrantez**.

Wines also come with the following terms. **Vintage** wines are from a single harvest and remain in oak casks for at least twenty years. **Reserve** is a blended wine of at least five years of age, **Special reserve** is the same but at least ten years old, while **Extra reserve** is the same but at least fifteem years old. But the majority of Madeira is younger **Finest** (a blended three-year-old wine) or **Bulk/Granel** (about eighteen months old and often sweetened with caramel).

If you buy a bottle of Madeira, you should leave it to breathe before serving like conventional wine. Bual and Malmsey should be served at room temperature, but Sercial

WINE

●

MADEIRA WINE

Legend has it that in around 1687, a barrel of **wine** was left forgotten in a corner of a ship for two lengthy sea journeys. When a sailor was allowed to drink the "spoiled" wine, he discovered to his amazement that it was delicious. It seems that the slow warming of the barrel as the ship passed to and from the tropics had helped mature the wine. After verifying his findings, wine merchants, keen to have more of the stuff, asked captains to store wine barrels on their boats as ballast and wines became known as *vinho da roda* – wines of the round routes.

Various methods were then tried to recreate the warming effect of the sea journeys. Local wine producers began building shelves behind their window shutters to store wine so it could be heated by the sun; these are still evident in older houses today. Some people even tried storing wine in trenches filled with hot horse manure for six months. In the eighteenth century, an abbot managed to heat wine on a larger scale in a greenhouse (*estufa*). This *estufa* process became very popular, with wine put in oak barrels stacked in tiered attics.

Flushed with success, merchants tried further ways to improve the wines. From around the 1720s, brandy was added to the wine, a trick probably learnt from the exporters of port from Porto. The brandy was believed to stabilize the wine during transportation. Though unfortified wines continued to be produced, by the nineteenth century the popular fortified wines

and Verdelho should be slightly cooled. Older Madeiras may need decanting if they leave a deposit.

Those looking for non-fortified wines will be hard pushed to find the young, local produce (see box on p.112). Instead, restaurants almost invariably stock more expensive **Portuguese wines** from the mainland, which is no bad thing, as Portuguese wines have a growing reputation.

had become the norm. Nowadays French brandy is added to halt the fermentation process and improve the longevity of the wine, and today's fortified Madeiras are around 17 percent proof.

Fortified Madeira was hugely popular and was sold throughout the world. It is said that American Independence was toasted with a glass of Madeira, and British soldiers returning home after the war increased the demand for it in Britain, where it became fashionable in the late eighteenth century. It is also said to have been the favourite drink of George Washington.

Despite pests and climactic problems that decimated many of the harvests – persuading Madeiran farmers to diversify into other products – vines for Madeiran wine remain the mainstay of the island's economy.

Today's Madeiras are stored in are stored in large vats which are still called *estufas*, where they are kept at temperatures of 40–50°C for three to six months. This gives the wines a warm, slightly smoky taste. The wine is then cooled and stored for about a year and a half before it is transferred into American oak barrels. These barrels are not tightly sealed as air actually improves the Madeira.

Madeira remains fairly unique in its ability to improve with age. Some Madeirans are said to buy a good Madeiran wine and have a glass of it once a year to celebrate their wedding anniversaries, with no noticeable spoiling evident in the open wine.

Some of the best are the rich, fruity reds from the Dão and Bairrada region near Coimbra; the full-blooded red and lemony white Ribatejo, Arruda and Liziria wines from the Ribatejo district; or the earthy reds and tangy whites from Reguengos and Borba in the Alentejo. Finally, young *vinho verdes* from the Minho in northern Portugal are deliciously light and refreshing.

WINE

FUNCHAL

THE CITY CENTRE

Adega A Cuba
Map 2, E3. Rua do Bispo 28
Daily 8am–10pm
Wood-ceilinged *adega* (wine lodge) filled with giant wooden barrels which double as table and chairs. Popular in the evenings when students come for cold sangria and inexpensive meals (see p.252).

A Lua
Map 2, C3. Rua da Carreira 78
Mon–Fri 7am–9pm, Sat 7am–6pm
Characterful, traditional stand-up café, with windows stuffed full of wine, biscuits and *bolo de mel* cakes. Also serves fresh bread.

Café Concerto
Map 2, C4. Jardim de São Francisco
Daily 8am–11pm
Small kiosk café offering milkshakes, sandwiches, pastries and fresh fruit juices, including kiwi, mango and papaya; also full lunches, *poncho* and wine. The piped music is naff, otherwise the setting is perfect: in the leafy municipal gardens next to the park auditorium.

Café da Praça Columbo
Map 2, E4. Praça Columbo
Daily 8.30am–9pm
Modern stand up café–bar kiosk, with outdoor tables spreading out onto the attractive square opposite the Museu Cidade do Açucar. Good fresh juices and coffee; also Guiness and Coral beer on tap.

Café do Teatro
Map 2, C4. Avda Arriaga
Daily 8am–midnight
Small café–bar in one corner of the town theatre, with shaded outdoor tables. Attracts tourists and local arty types for drinks and sandwiches.

Café Funchal

Map 2, E4. Rua Dr José
António Almeida

Daily 8am–11pm

One of a cluster of high-
profile cafés on this
pedestrianized street. Open-
fronted, with a counter full of
cakes, and shaded outdoor
seating under a blue canopy;
a great spot to watch the
world go by.

Cervejaria Beerhouse

Map 2, C5. Porto de Funchal

Daily 10am–11pm

Cervejaria above the marina
with tent-like canopied roof.
Does its own home-brewed
unfiltered beer – you can see
the metal brewing casks at
the back. Also does good
food (see p.256) and has
superb views over the city.

Dó Fá Sol

Map 2, D4. Galerias São
Lourenço

Daily noon–4am

With its entrance and an
outdoor terrace just below
Avenida do Mar near Palácio
de São Lourenço, this is one
of Funchal's trendier places,
with a sleek, wood floor, a

long bar and neat lighting.
Attracts a young clientele,
expecially when there's a live
band (usually at weekends),
but doesn't get going till late.

Esplanada Mar

Map 2, E4. Avda do Mar

Daily 9am–11pm

One of several kiosk bars
with outdoor tables on the
seafront; this one is right
opposite the entrance to the
town beach. Drinks and
snacks are a bit on the pricy
side, but worth it for the sea
views.

Golden Gate

Map 2, D4. Avda Arriaga 21

Mon–Wed & Sun 8am–midnight,
Thurs–Sat 8am–2am

This has been a fashionable
meeting place since the
nineteenth century, when it
was a hotel bar. You can get
everything from morning
coffee and croissant to ice
creams, alcohol and full meals
(see p.253). Substantially
remodelled in 1998, its decor
nevertheless retains a period
feel, with lots of mirrors,
ceiling fans and wicker chairs.
There's also a first-floor

FUNCHAL

289

balcony and a few outside tables.

O Leque

Map 2, E3. Praça do Município 7

Mon–Fri 8am–midnight, Sat 8am–6pm

This café's outdoor tables on the lovely town square are hard to resist, overlooking the swirling mosaic pavements and central fountain. Reasonably priced drinks, snacks and lunches.

Pastelaria Ancora

Map 2, E3. Travessa do Forno 7

Mon–Sat 7am–11pm, Sun 7am–3pm

Tiny *pastelaria* with attractively positioned outdoor tables on a pedestrianized corner of the shopping zone near the Sé; a favourite with locals.

Pastelaria Boutique Zarco

Map 2, C4. Rua Serpa Pinto 31

Mon–Sat 7am–8pm

Little stand-up *pastelaria* near the Museu Barbeito Cristovão Colombo with superb range of fresh breads, pastries and biscuits with barely a tourist in sight.

Pastelaria Penha d'Águia

Map 2, E3. Rua de João Gago 6–8

Mon–Fri 8.30am–7.30pm, Sat 8.30am–1.30pm

Just round the back of the Sé, this is one of the best places in central Funchal for pastries, with a long stand-up counter groaning with chocolates, cakes, big croissants, biscuits, mini pizzas, sandwiches and *sonhos* ("dreams"): cake balls dipped in dark honey.

Pátio

Map 2, D3. Rua da Carreira 43

Mon–Sat 8am–10pm

Superb spot in the courtyard of the photogenic photographic museum (see p.66), where you can enjoy drinks and ice creams surrounded by plants beneath a wrought-iron balcony. Also adjoins a restaurant (see p.255).

Prince Charles

Map 2, C3. Rua da Mouraria 54

Daily 7am–11pm

Handy drinks stop between the aquarium and the Museu da Freitas, attracting a largely local clientele

Snack Bar da Sé

Map 2, E4. Rua António José de Almeida 4

Daily 9am–11pm

Small café with appealing outdoor tables – some under cover – on an attractive pedestrianized street near the Sé. Serves good, moderately priced soups, light meals and drinks.

Trintas

Map 2, D5. Marina do Funchal

Daily 3pm–2am

Bills itself as a disco-pub, and is certainly the liveliest and trendiest spot in the marina, with pulsing music and a wide TV screen in one corner often showing live soccer.

ZONA VELHA AND EAST OF THE CENTRE

Alfama Bar

Map 2, H4. Rua da Santa Maria 160

Mon–Sat 8am–midnight, Sun 6pm–midnight

Cosy, darkened bar with stone arched ceiling and wooden bench-like seats, a good night-time drinks spot in the heart of the Zona Velha.

Arco Velho

Map 2, G4. Rua Dom Carlos I 42

Daily 8am–midnight

Lively café in the Zona Velha; especially busy on a Sunday morning when locals gather here to read the Sunday papers over coffee and drinks. There's an outdoor terrace and a small *pastelaria* section doing a decent range of pastries. See also restaurants on p.257.

Marcelino

Map 2, H4. Travessa da Torre 22a

Daily 10pm–2am

Fado house just round the corner from *Arsénio's* (see p.257), and less well known. Certainly a better bet if you don't want a full meal with the fado experience.

O Fresquinho

Map 2, F3. Mercado dos

Lavradores, Rua Brigadeiro
Oudinot
Mon–Fri 8am–8pm, Sat
8am–2pm
The most appealing of the
market's café-bars, set in the
front of the upper floor with
a stand-up bar area and a few
tables set to the side
surrounded by plants and
hemmed in by stalls selling
fruit and plucked chickens.

Qualifrutas
Map 2, F3. Rua da
Cooperativo Agricula
Mon–Sat 8am–8pm
Fruit shop which doubles as a
café specializing in fruit and
milkshakes, along with cakes
and sandwiches; there's
upstairs seating or, best of all,
outdoor tables under the
arcades of the attractive Praça
do Carmo square.

WEST OF THE CENTRE AND HOTEL ZONE

Bar Santa Catarina
Map 2, B5. Avda do Infante 22
Daily 7am–midnight
Unpromisingly positioned café

on a busy road at the foot of a
modern shopping centre
opposite Quinta Vigia, but this
does a mean range of pastries
and superb *batidas* (fruit
shakes), including pineapple,
mango and custard apple.

Casino da Madeira
Map 2, A6. Avda do Infante
Daily 8pm–4am
Predictably over-the-top,
glitzy and generally naff floor
shows and in-house disco as
side shows to the serious
business of card playing and
chucking money into slot
machines.

Esplanade do Lago
Map 2, B5. Parque de Santa
Catarina
Daily 9am–8pm
Tranquil spot by the park lake
and next to the children's play
area, where you can enjoy
coffees, ice creams or pastries
surrounded by palms,
bamboos and flowering trees.

Harry's Bar
Map 2, A6. Rua Imperatriz
Dona Amélia 69
Daily 12.30pm–midnight
English-style pub with a

FUNCHAL

lovely patio filled with plants and *azulejos*, despite being loomed over by towering *Carlton Park Hotel*.

O Molhe

Map 2, B7. Estrada da Pontina, Forte de Nossa Senhora da Conceição

Café Tues–Fri noon–3pm & 7pm–midnight; bar Tues–Thurs 7pm–midnight, Fri & Sat 7pm–2am

Superbly positioned café right at the top of Loo Rock jutting out from the harbour – reached by a lift. The sea views are exhilarating and the prices not too outrageous. The bar is made up of cosy rooms tucked inside the fort. The place puts on live salsa and jazz sessions most weekends and is more popular with young locals than tourists. There's also a restaurant (see p.263).

Petit Fours

Map 3, E7. Estrada Monumental 188, Loja 4

Daily 8am–8pm

Risk crossing the busy road just down from *Reid's Hotel* for a modern place offering great croissants, fresh bread and pastries, with a few tables set out on a patio inside the neighbouring shopping centre.

Pub No. 2

Map 3, E7. Rua da Favila 2

Daily 11am–2am

Unoriginal name but charismatic low wood-beamed bar with two wood-panelled rooms. There's a small outside terrace, live soccer on the TV and a healthy mix of locals and tourists of all ages.

Reid's Palace Hotel Cocktail Bar

Map 3, D7. *Reid's Palace Hotel*, Estrada Monumental 139

Daily 10am–1am

Dress up for the evening and check your bank balance before mixing it with the rich and famous – and fellow star spotters – at the renowned hotel's bar.

Reid's Palace Hotel Tea Lounge and Terrace

Map 3, D7. *Reid's Palace Hotel*, Estrada Monumental 139

☏291 717 171

Teas daily 3–6pm

FUNCHAL

Not cheap at 3800$00/€19, but a seriously large traditional English tea, consisting of sandwiches, tea and cake, at the world-famous hotel, served on the sea-facing terrace. The best way to mix it with the elite, but reservations (24 hours in advance) are essential.

Salsa Latina
Map 2, A6. Rua Imperatriz Dona Amélia 101
Daily 11am–2am
Bills itself as a night-time hotspot, with a glitzy terrace and occasional live Latino music, but caters mostly to the 30-somethings; more Romford than Rio.

Vespas
Map 2, B6. Avda Sá Carneiro 60

☏ 291 231 202
Tues–Sat midnight–6am
Funchal's best-known nightclub, set in a suitably gritty-looking former warehouse opposite the entrance to the harbour. All the latest sounds, a decent light show and a relaxed, young crowd, though it can seem on the empty side outside weekends.

www.cyber Café
Map 2, C4. Avda Infante 6
Ⓔ cybercafé@netmadeira.com
Mon–Fri 8am–2am, Sat 8am–2pm & 8pm–2am
Cyber-café (800$00/€4 per hour), but also a lively student bar in its own right, attached to the Escola Profissional Cristovão Colombo.

AROUND FUNCHAL

CAMACHA

Snack Bar O Relógio
Map 3, H4. Achada
Daily 9am–10pm
The ground floor café has a phenomenally long list of drinks including local liqueurs, spirits and Madeira wine, though most people pop in for a coffee or Portuguese pastry.

CÂMARA DE LOBOS

Ammar à Boia
Map 3, B6. Rua Nossa Senhora da Conceição 8–10

Daily 3pm–4am

One of the town's liveliest and trendiest bars, with doors at the back opening up to reveal views over the harbour. There's good music and the usual range of local and international drinks.

Bar Adega Regional
Map 3, B6. Rua João de Deus 2

Mon–Sat 9am–1pm & 2–4pm, Sun 4pm–midnight

A chance to down some drinks with the local fishermen, with local *poncha* being the speciality.

CURRAL DAS FREIRAS

Bar Central
Map 3, B2.

Daily 9am–9pm

The best place in town to head for inexpensive drinks amongst a more local clientele – probably as it faces away from the best views – with old men playing cards out the back.

ESTREITO DE CÂMARA DE LOBOS

Adega da Ginginha
Map 3, B5. Rua da Achada 13

Daily 7am–midnight

A traditional old *adega* with wood beams hung with plastic grapes and walls lined with barrels; the best place in town to sample inexpensive local wines and cider.

LEVADA DOS TORNOS

Hortensia Gardens Tea House
Map 3, G5. Caminho dos Pretos 89, São João Latrão

Daily 9am–6pm

Signposted off the *levada* to the right, this place boasts lovely gardens, a couple of terraces and an attractive interior with superb views over Funchal. It also offers a wide range of Portuguese food along with home-baked bread, tea and scones.

AROUND FUNCHAL

295

Jasmine Tea House
Map 3, G5. Caminho dos Pretos 40
Daily 10am–6pm

Well-known English-run tea house which cashes in on its position on the *levada* walk. Reached by a series of steep steps, it seems to have been beamed in from some South of England coastal town, complete with corny wall signs, framed cartoons and a patio garden with ornamental fountain. Dishes include tea and scones, some good broth-like soups and an impressive range of fruit and herbal teas.

MONTE

Café do Parque
Map 3, E4. Largo Da Fonte
Daily 9am–6pm

Café-cum-souvenir shop right on the main square, serving hot and cold drinks and snacks. There's a roof terrace, though the best tables are those outside on the square itself.

Snack-Bar Alto Monte
Map 3, E4. Travessa das Tilias
Daily 8am–9pm

Just above the main bus stop on Largo da Fonte – with its entrance on Travessa das Tilias – this is the best spot in Monte for a light meal, offering good salads and superb home-made bread sandwiches with an interior lined with old prints of Monte and the disused railway. Most people choose the outside terrace with great views over Funchal – there is even an old British telephone box in one corner of the terrace.

EASTERN MADEIRA

CANIÇAL

Bar Clube O Caniçal
Map 4, F2. Junto à Lota
Daily 8am–10pm

The liveliest spot in Caniçal – though hardly heaving – with the usual range of drinks and ice creams, and outdoor tables facing the sea. It's right next to the Museu da Baleia.

CANIÇO

The Village Pub
Map 4, B7.

Tues–Sun noon–2am

Some 300m out of Caniço on the road to Caniço de Baixo, this is a British-style pub set in an old white Madeiran house. Attractions include Guinness, cider and all-day British breakfasts, which you can enjoy on the outside terrace or inside surrounded by traditional English pub decor.

MACHICO

Bar Azul Central da Cidra
Map 5, D5. Rua General António Teixeira de Aguiar 52

Daily 7am–midnight

A cavernous local, traditional bar which is half given over to selling handicrafts, with wickerwork, tacky ceramics and other local souvenirs.

La Barca Discoteca
Map 5, C7. Praceta 25 de Abril
☏ 291 963 387

Fri–Sat midnight–4am

The town's only disco, so expect the locals to be on familiar terms. It would hardly set Ibiza alight, but the music's pretty good and the atmosphere friendly.

Café O Publico
Map 5, D6. Largo Dr António Jardim d'Oliveira

Daily 8am–2am

Right on the main square, with outdoor tables and a local clientele usually propped against the bar sampling the lethal local spirits that eye you from behind the bar.

O Dedal Retrosaria
Map 5, D7. Rua do Mercado 13

Daily 8am–2am

Lively cocktail bar opposite the tourist office. The music clicks in only when there's nothing of interest on the TV, which takes pride of place behind the bar.

EASTERN MADEIRA

O Doce D'Avo

Map 5, D7. Mercado Municipal

Daily 7am–midnight

A small *gelataria* and *pastelaria* for cakes and ice creams by the market building, with outdoor tables facing a dusty five-a-side soccer pitch for live entertainment.

Pastelaria O Galã

Map 5, D7. Rua General António Teixeira de Aguiar 3

Daily 8am–midnight

The best central place in Machico to sample Portuguese pastries, cakes and ice creams with the locals. It's just up from the tourist office.

SANTA CRUZ

Café Alameda

Map 4, D5. Rua da Praia

Daily 7am–2am

This attractive café with wrought-iron chairs and marble table tops sits on the seaside promenade beneath palms and facing the colourful beached fishing boats, and offers the usual range of drinks, snacks and pastries.

THE WEST COAST

JARDIM DO MAR

Joe's Bar

Map 6, E6.

Fri–Wed 11am–10pm

A tiny place selling fresh fruit juices at the western end of town by the local shop.

RIBEIRA BRAVA

Herédia Bar

Map 7, E4. Largo dos Herédias

Tues–Sun 9am–11pm

A pleasant café–bar with outdoor tables set on an attractive square to the north of town. A good spot for a drink or light snack.

Pastelaria Concord
Map 7, C7. Rua Gago
Coutinho e Secadura Cabral
Daily 6am–2am
One of the best places on the seafront for ice creams, croissants and snacks served inside or on the attractive esplanade facing the sea.

NORTHERN AND CENTRAL MADEIRA

FAIAL

Pub Kredo
Map 8, H4.
Mon–Fri & Sun 11am–11pm,
Sat 6pm–midnight
Situated just below the church, this is a surprisingly trendy little bar with a bright yellow interior and a few outdoor tables.

SÃO VICENTE

Estoril Bar Pastelaria
Map 6, L3. Sítio de Igreja
Daily 7am–10pm
Right opposite São Vicente's historic church, with outdoor tables on the pedestrianized square, this is the perfect spot to enjoy pastries, inexpensive snacks or drinks.

Pub O Corvo
Map 6, L3. Rua da Fonte Velha
Daily 8am–2am
Any modicum of nightlife to be had in São Vicente can be found here, a British-style pub with an old still in one corner and bank notes pinned to one wall. There are low stools inside and a TV often showing live sport in one corner, with a couple of outdoor tables.

PORTO SANTO

CABEÇO DA PONTA

- - - - - - - - - - - - - - - - - -

Bar João do Cabeço
Map 9, C6. Sítio do Cabeço
Daily 6pm–2am

On the main road between the *Luamar* and the *Hotel Dom Pedro*, this traditional stone building with a clay roof attracts a young clientele for drinks and snacks such as *chouriço* (sausage), *caldo verde* (cabbage soup), *pregos* (beef in a roll) and *camarão* (shrimps). There are wooden seats with rock and pop music inside and a covered terrace outside.

Tia Maria
Map 9, D6. Ribeira Salgado
Daily 11am–8pm

Right on the beach between Cabeço da Ponta and Campo de Baixo, this café-bar is built in traditional stone with an outdoor terrace facing the sands – a great spot for a snack or a sunset beer. It also does pricey meals in high season.

CAMACHA

- - - - - - - - - - - - - - - - - -

Bar Torres Restaurante
Map 9, F2. Camacha
Daily 9am–4am

This attractive wood-lined bar is a local favourite, with a table football game in one corner and a huge outdoor terrace shaded by vines and passion plants. There's also an attached restaurant (see p.278).

VILA BALEIRA

- - - - - - - - - - - - - - - - - -

Apolo 14
Map 9, E5. Rua do Dr Nuno S. Teixeira 3
Daily 9am–11pm.

Locals usually prop up the bar in this small bar–restaurant on the main square, with Coral beer on tap and walls lined with crusty bottles of wine, but families also pop in for coffee, ice creams or inexpensive meals served at a couple of indoor tables.

PORTO SANTO

Bar Gel Burger

Map 9, E5. Largo do Pelourinho
Daily 8am–2am

With outside tables sprawling out onto the main square beneath palm trees, this is the liveliest café in town, offering everything from morning coffee and croissants to light meals, pastries, cakes, ice creams and drinks.

Bar O Golfinho

Map 9, F5. Rua João Gonçalves Zarco
Tues–Sat 6am–midnight, Sun 6am–7pm

At the southern end of Rua João Gonçalves Zarco facing the town beach, this little snack bar with a wooden terrace plays some lively sounds and serves reasonably priced drinks and snacks.

Big Boy

Map 9, E5. Rua João Santana
July–Sept daily 11pm–4am; Oct–June Sat & Sun only 11pm–4am

Just to the east of Vila Baleira's main square, this place is generally more frequented by tourists than locals. Music and atmosphere is a bit hit or miss.

Café and Bar Torre Praia

Map 9, E5. Rua Goularte Medeiros
Café daily 10am–6pm; bar daily 9pm–midnight

The *Hotel Torre Praia*'s beachside café is a bustling place serving reasonably priced sandwiches, burgers, ice creams and drinks. Lively Latin sounds and a palm-leaf-covered terrace facing the waves. The bar is on a raised platform above the hotel and offers great views.

Challenger

Map 9, F5. Rua D. Estevão de Alecastre
July–Sept daily 11pm–4am; Oct–June Sat & Sun only 11pm–4am

Situated to the northeast of town out by the cemetery, this place is usually livelier than its rival *Big Boy* (see above) – it's a larger, glitzier venue hosting theme nights such as karaoke. Definitely the in place for locals.

PORTO SANTO

301

Shopping

On an island where the majority of goods have to be imported, it is not surprising that Madeira hardly stands out as a shoppers' paradise. The best-value items are those produced locally, which means mainly **arts and crafts** – notably wicker (see p.107), embroidery and tapestry (developed originally by Germans in the 1930s as a means of diversifying from embroidery). Madeira also has a tradition for inlaid wood, and many shops sell decorative chess and draughts boards, wooden boxes and trunks. Excellent-value **local food** can also be purchased round the island in shops and at the various **markets**, the best of which are reviewed in the text: popular purchases include *bolo de mel* (see p.251), jars of honey and *pastéis de nata* (Portuguese custard tarts). **Madeira wine** (see p.286) is another worthwhile purchase, and Funchal has several *adegas* where you can sample the produce before you buy.

For details of supermarkets in Madeira and Porto Santo, see p.328.

Traditional **shopping hours** are Monday to Friday 9am to 1pm and 3pm to 7pm and Saturday 9am to 1pm. Large shopping centres and tourist shops tend not to close for lunch and stay open until 10pm Monday to Saturday, some of them on Sundays too. The following represent a selection of the best places to get these products and things you may need during your stay.

BOOKS AND NEWSPAPERS

O Kiosque
Map 2, E3. Rua do Bispo 16, Funchal
Mon–Fri 9am–7pm, Sat 9am–1pm
Tiny newspaper kiosk selling English newspapers.

Pátio Livraria Inglesa
Map 2, D3. Loja 1 & 2, Rua da

Carreira 43, Funchal
Mon–Fri 10am–noon & 2–7pm, Sat 10am–1pm
Tiny English-language book kiosks attached to courtyard of photographic musuem (see p.66), packing in a fine range of books on Madeira, novels, children's books, cards and academic textbooks.

CLOTHES SHOPS

Barros & Abreu Irmãos Peles e Botas
Map 2, H4. Rua do Portão de São Tiago 22–23, Zona Velha, Funchal
Mon–Fri 9am–1pm & 3–7pm, Sat 9am–1pm
A traditional family workshop where typical Madeiran *cordovo* (goatskin boots) are made to measure on the premises at very reasonable rates.

Hat shop
Map 2, H4. Rua Santa Maria 237, Zona Velha, Funchal
Mon–Fri 8.30am–1pm & 2.30–7pm
Unmarked and unnamed workshop where one man churns out traditional boaters and other hats by hand.

Mango
Map 2, E3. Rua Queimada de Cima, Funchal

Mon–Fri 10am–7pm, Sat
10am–1pm

Popular Spanish clothes chain
offering inexpensive, bright
and well-made clothes.

Marcus
Map 2, F3. Rua Dr Fernão

Ornelas 16, Eastern Funchal
Mon–Fri 9am–1pm & 3–7pm,
Sat 9am–1pm

Fashionable shop stocking
Ralph Lauren, Hugo Boss
and other designer menswear
labels.

FOOD AND DRINK

Adegas de São Francisco
Map 2, D4. Avda Arriaga 28,
Funchal
Mon–Fri 9am–7pm, Sat
10am–1pm

Funchal's oldest and largest
wine lodge (see p.60), which
represents the leading
Madeira wine companies.
This is the place to get expert
advice and to enjoy some free
samples, though in terms of
buying wines, it's usually
cheaper to visit a local
supermarket.

Bio-Logos
Map 2, C3. Rua Nova de São
Pedro 34, Funchal
Mon–Fri 9am–8pm, Sat
9am–2pm

Funchal's main health-food

shop, filled with health
products (dried beans, pulses,
vitamins and the like) and
books. There's also an upstairs
vegetarian canteen (see
p.253).

Fabrica Santo António
Map 2, E3. Travessa do Forno
27–29, Funchal
Mon–Fri 9am–1pm & 2–7pm,
Sat 9am–1pm

Wonderful bakery piled high
with homemade cakes,
biscuits, preserves and
croissants.

Mercado dos Lavradores
Map 2, F3. Rua Brigadeiro
Oudinot, Funchal
Mon–Thurs 7am–4pm, Fri
7am–8pm, Sat 7am–2pm

FOOD AND DRINK

Funchal's atmospheric main market on three levels (see p.83): a good place to stock up on food for a picnic or if you're self-catering.

Nova Lojinha dos Cafés
Map 2, F3. Rua Dr Fernão Ornelas, Funchal
Mon–Sat 9am–7pm
Aromatic coffee shop on the corner with Rua do Visconde Anadia, selling freshly ground coffee beans.

Pingo Doce
Map 2, F3. Anadia Shopping, Rua do Visconde Anadia, Funchal
Daily 9am–10pm
Huge all-purpose supermarket in the basement of a shopping centre, selling international and local food produce, including well-priced olive oils and wines.

HANDICRAFTS

Bar Azul Central da Cidra
Map 5, D5. Rua General António Teixeira de Aguiar 52, Machico
Daily 7am–midnight
A cavernous bar selling handicrafts, with wickerwork, tacky ceramics and other local souvenirs.

Casa do Turista
Map 2, D4. Rua do Conselheiro José Silvestre Ribeiro 2, Funchal
Mon–Fri 9.30am–1pm & 2.30–6.30pm, Sat 9.30am–1pm
Part museum, part handicrafts shop, set inside a period building just back from the seafront (see p.55). The nineteenth-century decor is impressive, but the effect is spoilt by the sheer quantity of "traditional" produce on offer – ceramics, embroidery, bags, wicker, dolls, silver, quilts, tiles, maps, guides, Madeira wine and liqueurs, all of very mixed quality and at varied prices. There's a small terrace at the back with a mock post office-cum-bar front and a traditional bedroom, perhaps the best part of an interesting

HANDICRAFTS

place that doesn't quite work.

Mercado dos Lavradores
Map 2, F3. Rua Brigadeiro Oudinot, Funchal
Mon–Thurs 7am–4pm, Fri 7am–8pm, Sat 7am–2pm
Along with food (see above), Funchal's main market has a number of handicrafts stalls selling wickerwork, embroidery and woolly jumpers, usually at cheaper prices than shops in town.

O Relógio
Map 3, H4. Achada, Camacha
Mon–Fri 8.30am–8pm, Sat & Sun 8.30am–9.30pm.

Camacha is Madeira's main centre for wicker, and this is the main outlet, with a vast array of wicker products, along with other Portuguese handicrafts including ceramics, mats, rugs and wines.

Universal Store
Map 2, F2. Rua de João de Deus 14a, Funchal
Mon–Sat 9am–7pm, Sun 11am–1pm
Handicrafts emporium set in a former Protestant church. Prices aren't particularly cheap but it offers a wide range of everything from wines to embroidery, leather belts, pottery and children's toys.

TOYS AND SOUVENIRS

Clube Desportivo Nacional
Map 2, E4. Rua do Esmeraldo 46, Funchal
Mon–Fri 9am–12.30pm & 2–6pm
Club shop for Funchal's second football team, Nacional, with lots of archive newspaper reports and a

souvenir section selling club colours, scarves and pennants.

Imaginarium
Map 2, F3. Anadia Shopping, Rua do Visconde Anadia, Funchal
Mon–Sat 10am–10pm, Sun 10am–2pm
Small, modern building in the

Anadia Shopping centre, stocking imaginative and solid-looking plastic toys, including inexpensive buckets, spades, toy trains and cars.

Quinta da Boa Vista
Map 3, F6. Rua Lombo da Boa Vista, Funchal

Mon–Sat 9am–5.30pm

Orchid farm that packages its flowers for visitors, delivering them to your hotel on the day of your departure. You can also buy orchid seedlings in sealed glass jars. Its orchid gardens are open to the public (see p.92).

TOYS AND SOUVENIRS

Sports and outdoor activities

With its wide open spaces and extensive coastline, Madeira is perfect for outdoor enthusiasts, and there are countless activities that can be enjoyed either individually or as part of a group. Madeira is something of a **walkers**' paradise, with thousands of kilometres of footpaths along the coast and penetrating the dramatic mountainous interior, many of them on *levadas* (see box on p.311). Despite its rocky coastline, there are plenty of opportunies for **swimming**, too. In recent years, Madeira has also been heavily promoting alternative and **adventure sports** in a bid to throw off its image as a destination for the elderly, and its valleys, dramatic terrain and deep Atlantic waters make it ideal for everything from sailing, surfing and diving to canyoning and mountain biking. If you are interested in any of these, make sure you use one of the companies recommended by the tourist office or those below, as there are a few companies that operate with unqualified staff.

ADVENTURE SPORTS OPERATORS

Eurofun

Map 2, B5. Centro Comercial Olimpo, Loja 206d, Avda do Infante, Funchal

ⓣ 291 228 638, ⓕ 291 228 620. Guided walks, jeep safaris, sailing and bike rental.

Mar da Aventura

Map 3, C7. Praia Formosa, Funchal

ⓣ 291 776 818.

On the main road above Praia Formosa, this place offers jet skiing, waterskiing and canoeing.

Terras de Aventura & Turismo

Map 3, D7. Caminho do Amparo 25, Funchal

ⓣ 291 765 827, ⓕ 291 761 018. Guided walks, mountain bike tours, canyoning, canoeing, jeep safaris, jet skiing and waterskiing.

WALKING

Despite its diminutive size, Madeira offers a surprisingly diverse range of **walks** in stunning scenery – from coastal paths to woodland trails and dramatic mountain passes. Many of the walks are along well-marked paths, used by locals to pass from village to village before the road network was constructed.

Some of the best walks on the island are detailed in this guide – there is an index of them on p.375. These details were accurate when the book went to press, but conditions can change – landslides during the winter months can wipe out sections of walk, as can road-building – so it is a good idea to check that the walk is still manageable with the local tourist office or your hotel before you set off.

All the walks in this guide can be tackled by anyone who is vaguely fit, but before you set off it is vital to be properly prepared. Paths can cross extremely precipitous terrain and weather conditions can change quickly, reducing visibility and making the paths extremely slippery. As a result, you

WALKING

should take the following precautions before you set off:

• Ask your hotel, the tourist office or local people for the latest weather forecast. If they say bad weather is imminent, do not attempt a walk.

• Tell someone – your hotel or a local contact – where you are going so that they can call a rescue party if you do not return. If you have a mobile phone, give them your number (see p.40).

• Wear suitable footwear, ideally walking shoes or boots. Do not attempt a walk if you do not have shoes with adequate grip.

• Take a warm top and a waterproof. It can be cold in the mountains and rain is always possible.

• Many of the paths pass through tunnels, so a torch is always useful. A whistle can also come in handy if you need to attract attention.

• Take bottled water with you. You can refill the bottle from the *levadas* at high levels, though low-level *levadas* may be contaminated.

• Wear a high-factor sun cream. Because of the altitude you can get burned even when it does not feel particularly warm.

If you are unsure about setting off on a walk alone, consider taking a **guided walk**. Most hotels organize a weekly walking programme, and the companies listed on p.309 offer half- or full-day walks. Two companies specializing in walks are **Turivema**, Estrada Monumental 187, Funchal (map 3, D7; ℡291 763 898, ⓦwww.madeira-levada-walks.com), who offer expert commentary on the flora and fauna you pass, and **Natura**, also in Funchal (℡291 236 015, ⓕ291 238 652). Prices for all companies start from around 6000$00/€30 per person for a day's walk, including transport to and from your hotel and sometimes a picnic lunch.

WALKING

LEVADAS

The most famous walking trails on Madeira are the levadas – irrigation canals that have been constructed ever since the Portuguese first colonized the island to channel water from the mountains to lower-lying agricultural land. Some of the *levadas* have been hacked into the side of sheer-sided slopes, and they often run through tunnels. Initially the work was done by slaves imported from Portugal's former colonies in Africa, but nowadays high-tech machinery does the job. The most recent *levadas* have been constructed with an astonishing degree of engineering accuracy, along carefully plotted gradients so that the water flows gently down to where it is needed. Water flow is carefully regulated by a system of sluices operated by the *levadeiros* – men whose job it is to ensure that different farmers get an equal amount of water to their land and who keep the *levadas* clean and flowing.

As well as bringing water to farmers, the canals have proved to be ideal walkways, with an astonishing network of over 2000km winding across the island at gentle gradients. Slowly tourists have begun to exploit the *levadas* for leisure, realizing they offer an ideal route into some of Madeira's most dramatic, unspoilt terrain. Today *levada* walking has become big business, with several tour companies offering guided *levada* walks round the island. Though this has had the inevitable effect of removing the solitude from some of the walks, it has had the advantage of encouraging the local government to improve signposting and to provide dangerous sections of *levadas* with new fencing.

CYCLING AND MOUNTAIN BIKING

With its arduous gradients and narrow roads, Madeira does not lend itself to casual **cycling**. However, it is possible to

CYCLING AND MOUNTAIN BIKING

cycle along some footpaths and *levadas*, as well as across the inland plain known as Paúl da Serra. The relatively flat island of Porto Santo is much more cycle-friendly and nearly all the main hotels rent out bikes; see p.241 for details.

In June, Madeira hosts the Portugal Mountain Biking Cup, when some of the country's top cyclists visit the island. July sees the Round Island Cycling race on Porto Santo, with a similar event round Madeira in September.

Mountain biking is surprisingly popular, despite the apparently impossible gradients of much of the island. **Bike rental** costs around 2200$00/€11 per day, slightly less for longer hire periods. In addition to the companies listed on p.309, try Joyride, Centro Comercial Olimpo, Loja 210, Avda do Infante, Funchal (map 2, C5; ☎291 234 906). A good way to see some of the best of the island – mostly by exploring unpaved roads and *levadas* – is to take a half- or full-day organized mountain bike **tour**. Tours can be arranged by Terras de Aventura & Turismo (see p.309), with full-day rides from Pico do Ariero to Caniço and half-day rides from Camacha to Santo da Serra. Prices are 7800$00/€39 for full-day tours and 5400$00/€27 for half-day trips.

HORSE-RIDING

Despite its potential for some superb **horse-riding**, opportunities for visitors to Madeira are limited. If you want to brush up on your riding skills or learn to ride, the Associação Hípica da Madeira, Quinta Vale Pires, Caminho dos Pretos, São Gonçalo (map 3, G5; ☎291 792 582), signed off the EN102-1 Funchal–Camacha road, offers individual lessons at 3000$00/€15 per person, or a course of ten lessons at the *quinta* for 12,000$00/€60; lessons last around 20 minutes for beginners and 50 minutes for experienced riders.

HORSE-RIDING

JEEP SAFARIS AND HELICOPTER TOURS

Jeep safaris are a good way of getting to see the mountainous interior of Madeira – indeed, four-wheel drive jeeps are the only way to get down many of the unmade roads that still link many of the remoter valleys. Routes covered usually include from Funchal east to Caniço, Santa Cruz and Santo de Serra or north to Pico do Ariero, Encumeada and Santana; some of the trips are off-road. Prices for full-day trips start at around 7000$00/€35 per person. In addition to the companies listed on p.309, the Funchal-based travel agent **Intertours**, Avda Arriaga 30, 3° (map 2, D4; ⊤291 228 344), can arrange jeep safaris.

Madeira is host to two famous rallies, details of which can be found on p.30 and p.31.

An even more dramatic ways of seeing the spectacular scenery of the island – if you have the funds – is to take a **helicopter tour**. HeliAtlantis (⊤291 232 882, Ⓕ291 232 804) offers spectacular ten-minute rides over the island, departing from just below Parque da Santa Catarina in Funchal (map 2, C5), for around 10,000$00/€50.

SWIMMING

Along with hotel **swimming pools**, there are various lido complexes dotted round the island, with outdoor pools and access to the sea. **Lidos** can be found in the Hotel Zone (see p.80) and the Zona Velha (see p.88) in Funchal, at Santa Cruz (see p.125) and at Caniço de Baixo (see p.123). An increasing number of places also have man-made **sea pools**, where walls have been built round sections of the harbour for safe sea swimming. These can be found in Calheta (see p.151) in the west of the island and at Porto da Cruz (see p.142), Ponta Delgada (see p.173) and Seixal (see p.169) in the north. There are also natural sea pools at Porto Moniz (see p.166). In addition, nearly every coastal village has some sort of **beach** or jetty that you can swim off, as long as you don't mind large stony beaches – take extreme care, however, when the weather is rough as the large Atlantic waves can easily dash you against the rocks or drag you out to sea. The best places for safe **sea swimming** are in Machico (see p.129), which has a sheltered, stony town beach, and Prainha, a lovely little sandy bay on the Ponta de São Lourenço (see p.134).

DIVING

Many of the larger hotels can arrange **scuba diving**, usually in the protected coastal waters off Caniço de Baixo and Machico. To **hire equipment**, you will need to show a diving certificate, log book and sometimes a medical certificate. Basic equipment hire starts at around 6000$00/€30 per day. Most places also arrange four- to five-day internationally recognized PADI **diving courses** for beginners, starting off in swimming pools before progressing to sea dives, though most courses will set you back around 70,000–90,000$00/€350–450. Once in the sea, you can swim face to face with moray eels, conger eels, squid, octopus, monkfish, tuna, parrot fish and Atlantic rays and mantas. Madeira's main diving centres are listed below.

DIVING CENTRES

Atalaia Club
Map 4, B7. *Hotel Roca Mar*,
Caniço de Baixo
ⓣ291 934 330, ⓕ291 933 011.

Baleia Diving Center
Map 5, B8. *Hotel Dom Pedro Baia*, Machico
ⓣ291 965 751, ⓕ291 966 889,

Ⓔ dp.baia@mail.telepac.pt; see also box on p.130.

Manta Diving Center
Map 4, B7. *Lido Hotel Galomar*, Caniço de Baixo
Ⓣ 291 935 588 or 291 934 566, Ⓦ www.mantadiving.com;
May–Oct only.

Moser
Map 9, F5. Rua João Gonçalves Zarco 5, Vila Baleira, Porto Santo
Ⓣ 291 982 162, Ⓕ 291 982 163.

Scorpio Divers
Map 3, D7. Complexo Balnear Lido, Funchal Ⓣ 996 861 846.

SURFING AND OTHER WATERSPORTS

Madeira was discovered as a **surfing** destination by intrepid Portuguese and Brazilian surfers during the 1990s, and now hosts an annual leg of the World Surfing Championships, usually in January or February in Jardim do Mar. A European surfing competition takes place in Paúl do Mar in September. Other good places to surf are São Vicente, Feijã da Areia and Ponta Delgado. Madeira's deep Atlantic waters supply superb breakers, and the main attraction is the challenge of the big riders – three-metre-high waves which crash onto the basalt rock of the sea bed; there are no sandy beaches to cushion you here, so extreme care and skill is required. As yet, there is no surfing association and there are no surf shops on Madeira either, so surfers are advised to take their own board repair kits as the rocky floor easily takes chunks out of the boards. For more information, contact the main tourist office (see p.48).

The Atlantic also offers ideal conditions for **windsurfing** – a native Madeiran won the 1996 World Windsurfing Championship – and many of the major hotels in Funchal rent out windsurfing equipment, as does the Club Naval do Funchal, Marina do Funchal (map 2, D5; Ⓣ 291 224 602). Board hire costs around 3000$00/€15 an hour.

SURFING AND OTHER WATERSPORTS

For other watersports, such as **jet-skiing** and **water-skiing**, Praia Formosa (see p.133) is the place to go: jet skis cost around 3600$00/€18 for 15min or 9000$00/€45 per hour, while waterskiing will set you back 5600$00/€28 for 15min or 10,600$00/€53 for an hour.

CANOEING AND CANYONING

Canoeing is a popular sport in Madeira, and if you don't mind riding a few breakers to get into the open water, it can be a great way to see the coastline. The sheltered waters around Praia Formosa (see p.81) are a good place to start, with canoe hire from 600$00/€3 an hour for one person, 800$00/€4 an hour for two people. In Porto Santo, canoe hire is offered by the **Club Naval do Porto Santo** in Vila Baleira (map 9, F5; ☏291 985 190, ℻291 982 585).

Canyoning involves descending remote river valleys – often by jumping or swimming into rock pools. Terras de Aventura & Turismo (see p.309) arrange canyoning around Ribeiro Frio; half-day excursions cost around 10,000$00/€50.

SEA FISHING

Those in the know rate the deep off-shore waters around Madeira as some of the best in the world for big game **fishing**, especially Atlantic blue marlin, which can weigh over 1000lbs (in season June–Sept). Other fish include blue eye tuna (June–Sept), blue shark, hammerhead shark, barracuda, bonito and wahoo (April–Oct), and Manta rays (Aug–Oct). Listed below are some of the charter boat companies that can arrange **fishing trips**, including equipment hire. Most offer half-day trips from around 20,000$00/€100 per person and full-day trips from around 30,000$00/€150 per person, or you can charter a boat for around 80,000\$00/€400 for four hours.

FISHING TRIP OPERATORS

Costa do Sol
Map 2, D5 Marina do Funchal, Funchal
ⓣ291 934 330, ⓕ291 933 011.

Katherine B
Map 3, E5. Quinta das Malvas, Rua da Levada de Santa Luzia 124, Funchal
ⓣ291 220 334, ⓕ291 229 896, ⓦwww.madeira-web.com /sportfishing.

Madeira Big Game Fishing
Map 2, D5. Actividades Náuticas Limitada, Marina do Funchal, Funchal
ⓣ & ⓕ 291 227 169.

Missiltour
Map 4, B7. Vista do Mar 4, Garajau-Caniço ⓣ291 933 414.

Nautileste
Map 5, D8. Largo da Praça, Machico ⓣ & ⓕ 291 965 248.

Nautisantos
Map 2, D5. Marina do Funchal, Funchal ⓣ291 231 312.

Turipesca
Map 2, D5 Marina do Funchal, Funchal ⓣ & ⓕ 291 231 063.

DOLPHIN- AND WHALE-WATCHING

Historically, Madeira had a flourishing whaling industry, but now whaling is prohibited and its waters offer a safe haven for sea mammals such as whales and dolphins. **Whales** rarely go near Funchal's coastline, though they can be seen in deeper water, while **dolphins** are far more common closer to the shore.

Katherine B, Travessa das Virtudes 23, S. Martinho, Funchal (map 3, D6; ⓣ291 752 685, ⓕ291 752 689, ⓦwww.fishmadeira.com), arranges twice-weekly trips from

Funchal marina along the west coast to see striped, spotted and bottle-nosed dolphins with the chance to swim with them – they occasionally spot sperm whales too. Trips cost around 15,000$00/€75 per person, usually departing at 2.30pm and returning around 5.30pm.

FOOTBALL

The Madeirans are **football** mad, though there aren't too many places on the island that are flat enough to have a decent game. The British are said to have introduced the sport in the nineteenth century, the first game apparently

MARÍTIMO

Marítimo (ⓦ www.csmaritimo-madeira.pt) are not only Madeira's most successful football team but also one of the leading sides in Portugal. Founded in 1910, the Funchal side developed rapidly and by the 1925–26 season had won the Portuguese championship. In those days the championship took the form of a knock-out competition, but after World War II it changed to a league format, effectively excluding Marítimo because it took two days for the team to reach mainland Portugal by boat. As a result, until Madeira's airport opened in 1965, the team played away from the island only when it went on tours of Portugal and Portugal's former colonies in Africa.

When the airport opened Marítimo joined the Portuguese second division and within eight years won promotion to the first division. Relegation quickly followed, though they returned as second division champions in 1976–77, a feat celebrated by crowds of 20,000 people. They were promoted as second division champions again in 1981–82 and have remained in the top league since.

being played at Camacha (see p.105). Nowadays, almost every town of any note has its own football team fighting it out for glory in the local league – enthusiastic and enjoyable, if rather low-key affairs – while the better teams play in the lower divisions of the Portuguese national league. However, Madeira does boast one team of real quality: **Marítimo** (see box below).

TENNIS

Most of the major hotels have their own **tennis** courts, though public ones are in short supply. In Funchal, the best

The 1990s represented a golden age for Marítimo. They qualified for the UEFA Cup in 1992–93 and in 1994–95, when they went out narrowly to Juventus 1–3 on aggregate in the second round. That same year they reached the final of the Portuguese cup, losing 2–0 to Sporting. Their last foray into Europe was in 1998 when they beat Leeds 1–0 in Funchal to draw 1–1 on aggregate; Leeds finally won on penalties in a game that ended virtually at midnight. In 2001, they reached the Portuguese cup final again, this time losing 2–0 to Porto. Today the team is truly international, with players from eastern Europe, Spain, Argentina and Africa outnumbering the handful of local Madeiran representatives.

Marítimo play at the Barreiros Stadium on Rua do Dr Pita in Funchal (map 3, D6; city bus #8 or #45), a small venue (its capacity is 9000), with a friendly, family atmosphere. Games usually take place on Sunday afternoons, or Tuesday, Wednesday or Friday evenings; they are rarely sold out, unless one of the big Portuguese teams – Benfica, Sporting or Porto – is in town. **Tickets** cost 2500–4000$00/€12.50–20 and can be bought from the stadium on match days or in advance from the Museu de Marítimo (see p.86) or the União club shop (see p.306).

TENNIS

public courts are at Quinta Magnolia on Dr Pita (map 3, D6; daily 9am–7pm; ☏291 763 237; bus #5, #6, #8 or #45 from opposite the Marina). Courts can be booked at the main gate for just 300$00/€1.50 per hour, though they get snapped up quickly especially in summer, so it's best to arrive early.

Funchal hosts two major tennis tournaments: the Madeira International Tennis Tournament in September and the Inocêncio de Freitas Tournament in late November.

GOLF

Madeira's boasts two quality **golf** courses in spectacular positions. Inexperienced golfers can have lessons at either course, though only Palheiro Golf allows inexperienced golfers onto the greens. If you plan to play a lot of golf, it is worth asking the clubs below for the names of hotels whose guests get a discount on the fees listed below.

Every year – usually in March – the Clube de Golf Santo da Serra hosts the PGA Tour Madeira Island Open, which attracts top golfers from around the world.

GOLF COURSES

Clube de Golf Santo da Serra
Map 4, C3. Santo António da Serra
☏291 550 100, ⓕ291 552 367, ⓔgolf.santoserra @mail.telepac.pt.

Designed by Robert Trent Jones, the course is rated one of the most spectacularly situated in Europe, at 670m above sea level, just outside Santo Da Serra (see p.136). There are superb views over

GOLF

Machico, Ponta do São Lourenco and the Ilhas Desertas on clear days. The par-72 18-hole course is some 6000m in total. You do not need to be a member but you do need to show a handicap certificate or permission-to-play letter from a golf club. T-shirts, trainers, shorts and jeans are prohibited. A round costs 11,500$00/€57.50.

Palheiro Golf
Map 3, G6. Balancal, S. Gonçalo ⓣ291 792 116, ⓕ291 792 456. Designed in 1993 by Cabell Robinson, this spectacularly sited 18-hole par-71 golf course was part of the estate founded by the Count of Carvalhal, now owned by the Blandy family, one of Madeira's biggest wine producers, and offers superb views over Funchal. Measuring 6015m, the course is famed for its fast greens and the challenging position of trees from the old estate. There is a resident English golf pro who can offer lessons. There are also putting greens and practice nets. You do not need to have a handicap certificate, though inexperienced golfers can only play after 2pm. A round costs 12,000$00/€60.

Madeira for kids

With its lack of beaches and traditionally older visitors, Madeira has a somewhat unjustified reputation for not being suitable for **children**, and indeed, for those whose children are only happy with buckets and spades on a big sandy beach, then Porto Santo is certainly a better option. However, for older children who enjoy outdoor activities, there's no shortage of things to do at any time of the year. As on mainland Portugal, children are welcomed everywhere and, while you're unlikely to find specific facilities such as baby-changing areas, the locals will do their best to accommodate children's requirements.

HOTEL FACILITIES

The larger package **hotels** generally have good facilities for children, though it is worth establishing what is available before you book. Most places have shallow children's swimming pools and many have children's play areas and – for older kids – games rooms with table tennis, pool, darts and the like. Some of them – though by no means all of them, especially in Funchal – also have their own grounds with lawned areas. Some hotels also offer babysitting and the smarter ones may even have creche facilities and special kids' programmes, designed to take the children off your hands while you relax. Hotel entertainment programmes tend to be of the rather tacky variety aimed at older visitors, but nearly all hotels also have satellite television, so if all else fails you can usually find something suitable on one of the channels.

EATING AND DRINKING

Madeira is well geared to northern European tastes, and most **restaurants** can offer pasta dishes and often pizzas. *Espada* can also bear more than a passing resemblance to fish and chips. All places can do a range of ice creams and desserts. Most restaurants have outside tables, often in pedestrianized zones, which are ideal for kids wanting to run around. The Zona Velha and the marina in Funchal are good destinations, while the centres of Machico and São Vicente are also traffic free.

International-brand baby foods, nappies and baby products are all widely available in supermarkets and chemists.

You can get the brand-name fizzy **drinks** from any shop, café or restaurant, though you may prefer to buy the natural fruit juices, ranging from apple and orange to more exotic kiwi fruit and passion fruit – the last is also sold in bottled or tinned form, either still or fizzy. For those with babies, **fresh milk** – *leite do dia* – can usually only be bought from larger supermarkets. Smaller shops tend to stock only long-life milk.

PARKS AND PLAYGROUNDS

Nearly every town or village that you are likely to visit will have some sort of children's **playground**, usually in the village square, the park or on the seafront. Madeira's various

parks and gardens are also great for smaller kids to let off steam in. In Funchal, the main Jardim de Santa Catarina (see p.75) is the best place to head for, complete with duck ponds and a great children's play area at the top of the park. The Jardim Botânico (see pp.89–91), Blandy's Gardens (see pp.100–103), the gardens at Monte (see pp.97–98) and the park at Santo António da Serra (see p.138) are also good places for children to explore – the last has a mini zoo and a crazy golf course. Madeira also has some fantastic **picnic spots**: the one at Queimadas (see pp.179–182) is particularly popular with Madeiran families and is one of the most beautiful spots on the island. A close second is the ranger's hut at Rabaçal (see p.156).

SPORTS AND ACTIVITIES

Older kids into sports will find plenty to do in Madeira. Those who enjoy **walking** will certainly be interested in the *levada* walks (see p.311). Most companies offering organized walking tours have no age restriction on their walks, though they will advise parents on which ones are potentially strenuous and hazardous for smaller children. **Swimming** is also possible throughout the island: along with hotel pools, many of the resorts have lido complexes or safe sea pools, and you can also swim in the sea from several beaches (see p.313 for details). Many companies in Funchal can also arrange **adventure sports**, ranging from snorkelling and scuba diving to watersports such as canoeing and windsurfing (see p.316 and p.315). Some of the larger hotels hire out **mountain bikes**, though the only places that are really flat enough to do any serious cycling is on the Paúl da Serra (see p.159). You will also find outdoor **table tennis** tables dotted in public places all over the island, though you will need to provide your own bats and ball. For details of other sports, see Chapter 11.

Kids of all ages love the **cable car** (see p.95) up from Funchal to Monte and the **toboggan run** back down again (see p.99). **Boat trips** from Funchal's harbour (see p.55) are also popular, though be careful if your kids are prone to seasickness, as the sea can get rough. You can also go dolphin- and even whale-watching (see p.317). In the north of the island, you can take a hair-raising cable-car ride down the cliff just south of Santana (see p.179), though the service only runs three days a week. Non-vertigo sufferers may also enjoy the **lift ride** down the sheer cliffs above Fajã das Padres (see p.115).

SIGHTS

Sights that will appeal specifically to kids are a bit thin on the ground. In Funchal, the aquarium in the **Museu Municipal** (see p.68) may be of passing interest, while the walls and ramparts of the Fortaleza de São Tiago are also good for exploring. The **Vagrant "Beatles Boat"** (see p.54) is also very popular with children who can sit at its mini boats in a mock harbour and explore the main boat, now turned into a café–restaurant. Outside Funchal, Caniçal's **Museu da Baleia** (see p.133) is a small educational museum about the whaling trade and moves towards marine conservation. The **Grutas de São Vicente**, just outside São Vicente (see p.171) are a series of underground caves, which you can visit on regular tours. Finally, a spot Madeiran families make special efforts to go to is the bizarrely situated jungle-themed restaurant, *Jungle Rain*, on the high moors of Paúl da Serra, where you can eat surrounded by mock jungle noises and plastic animals (see p273).

Directory

ADDRESSES In the larger towns, addresses in Madeira follow the Portuguese convention of having the street name followed by the building number. A house or building number followed by, for example, 4° shows it is on the fourth floor. However, in smaller villages the address may simply consist of the name of the house, café or hotel without any street name, or with a general area name such as *Sítio da Igreja*, roughly meaning "in the place where the church is".

AIRLINES TAP Air Portugal, Avda do Mar 10 (map 2, E4; ⓣ 291 239 210, ⓕ 291 239 211; airport ⓣ 291 524 362); British Airways, Rua São Francisco 6 (map 2, D4; ⓣ 291 229 113, ⓕ 291 232 942; airport ⓣ 291 524 539); GB Airways (airport ⓣ 291 524 539); Portugália (airport ⓣ 291 524 510).

AIRPORT INFORMATION
ⓣ 291 220 064 (Madeira);
ⓣ 291 980 640 (Porto Santo).

AMERICAN EXPRESS Top Tours, Rua Brigadeiro Couceiro, Funchal (map 2, A6; Mon–Fri 9.30am–1pm & 3–6.30pm; ⓣ 291 742 611).

CINEMAS Funchal: Cine Max, Avda Arriaga 75 (map 2, C4; ⓣ 291 231 933); Cine Santa Maria, Rua Dom Carlos I 27 (map 2, xx; ⓣ 291 237 900); Cinema Dom João, Loja 42, Rua Dom João 6 (map 3, E6; ⓣ 291 742 504); ITI-Cinecasino, Avda Infante (map 2, A5; ⓣ 291 229 800). Funchal's main theatre, the Teatro Municipal Baltazar Diaz (see p.59), Avda Arriaga (map 2, D4; ⓣ 291 220 416), also occasionally shows art-house films.

CONSULATES See p.17.

CONTRACEPTION Condoms are available from pharmacies. Automatic condom vending machines are often found outside pharmacies.

CRIME Madeira remains remarkably crime free, though it pays to take basic precautions against pick-pocketing, especially in crowded areas such as Funchal's market and on public buses. Most places have a local police station if you do need to report a theft; make sure you get a police report form in order to claim for the loss on your insurance policy.

ELECTRICITY The current is 220 volts AC. Most plugs take two-point round pins as in continental Europe. UK appliances work with an adaptor, but North American appliances will also need a transformer.

EMERGENCIES Call ⊤ 112 for police, ambulance or fire brigade.

GAY SCENE See box on p.283.

HOSPITALS Hospital Cruz Carvalho, Avda Luís Camões, Funchal (map 3, D6; ⊤ 291 705 600); Hospital dos Marmeleiros, Estrada dos Marmeleiros, Funchal

(map 3, E5; ⊤ 291 705 730).

INTERNET See p.41.

LAUNDRY All the main hotels offer laundry facilities. Otherwise try Bem Limpa, Loja 2, Caminho Amparo bloco 2, loja 2 (map 3, D6), or Lavandaria Técnica Limpeza, loja 1, Avda Arriaga 133 (map 2, C5).

LOST LUGGAGE ⊤ 291 524 913 (airport).

PHARMACY Funchal: Farmacia Inglesa, Rua da Câmara Pestana 23–25 (map 2, D4); central pharmacy with English-speaking staff who can sell medicines and drugs often only available on prescription in the UK. Porto Santo: Rua Cristovão Colombo and Rua D Estévão Alencastre, Vila Baleira (map 9, E5). Both are open Mon–Fri 9am–1pm & 3–7pm, Sat 9am–1pm.

PHOTOGRAPHY There are several photographic shops and supermarkets stocking regular, monochrome and slide film. Central options include Foto Continental, Gal. São Lourenço lj27, Avda Arriaga 8 (map 2, D4), and Belafoto, with branches in

DIRECTORY

327

Avda Calouste Gulbenkian (map 2, B4) and in the Anadia Shopping centre on Rua Visconde Anadia just up from the main market (map 2, F3).

POLICE To report a theft or any crime, go to the main station on Largo de São João in Funchal (map 3, D6), or call ☎ 291 222 022. On Porto Santo, the main police station is on Sítio das Matas in Vila Baleira (map 9, E5), or phone ☎ 291 982 423. In an emergency, dial ☎ 112.

POST OFFICE Funchal's main post office is on Avenida Calouste Gulbenkian, next to the SAM bus terminal (map 2, B4; Mon–Fri 8.30am–6.30pm). The city's most central post office is on Avenida Zarco (map 2, D3; Mon–Fri 8.30am–8pm, Sat 9am–1pm). The main post office in Vila Baleira is on Avenida Vieira de Castro, oppo-site the tourist office (map 9, E5; Mon–Fri 9am–6pm, Sat 9am–1pm).

SUPERMARKETS Madeira's biggest and best supermarket is Pingo Doce. There are several branches round the town, such as opposite the Lido (map 3, D7)

and at Anadia Shopping on Rua Visconde Anadia just up from the main market (map 3, F3; open daily 9am–10pm). There are also branches in Machico, on Rua General António Teixeira de Aguiar (map 5, D5), and Vila Baleira on Porto Santo, on the junction of Avda Dr Manuel Gregório Pestana Júnior and Rua Bartolomeu Perestrelo (map 9, F5). An alternative in Vila Baleira is Super-Zarco, on the junction of Rua Bartolomeu Perestrelo and Rua Dr Nuno Silvestre Teixeira (map 9, F5).

TIME Madeira follows GMT (late Sept to late March) and BST (late March to late Sept). This is 5hr ahead of Eastern Standard Time and 8hr ahead of Pacific Standard Time.

TIPPING As on the Portuguese mainland, large tips are not expected. Service charges are normally included in hotel and restaurant bills. If you are partic-ularly pleased with the service of a porter, maid or waiter, leave ten percent of the bill.

TOILETS There are public toi-lets in most towns. You should tip attendants.

CONTEXTS

History	331
Wildlife and the environment	347
Music	353
Books	357
Language	360
Glossary of Portuguese terms	366

History

Considering its remote location in the heart of the Atlantic, Madeira has been buffeted surprisingly often by events not only in Portugal but also in the rest of mainland Europe and the New World – a political football that has been kicked or swiped at by everyone from Britain and Spain to France, Germany, Brazil and even South Africa.

Early sightings

The first official record of Madeira was in 1351, when an island called "Isola della Lolegname" (Wooded Island) appeared on a Genoese map, which also recorded Porto Santo as Porto Séo, though the Genoese seem not to have landed here. However, it is likely that traders were aware of the islands even before this time. In around 50AD, the **Roman** writer Pliny referred to "Purple Islands" close to the "Fortunate Islands" (the name used for the Canaries), and in the second century AD, **Greek** geographer Ptolemy referred to an Atlantic island called Erythia (Red Island). It is possible that the colours red and purple refer to the distinctive red sap of the native dragon trees, which was used by the ancients as dye. The **Moors**, who occupied Iberia from the eighth century, also referred to Atlantic islands,

which they called El Ghanam (Cattle), though the prove-
nance of this name is unclear, as there would have been no
native animals on the island. From then on, Madeira pops
up in sailor's myths, which refer to a strange, misty island
believed to mark the end of the world or even Atlantis.
One of these legends relates how in the fourteenth century
the island was occupied by an Englishman, **Robert
Machim**, and his lover Anne d'Arfet (see p.126), who were
shipwrecked there, though versions of this dramatic tale are
as inconsistent and unverified as the Robin Hood myths.

Portuguese discoveries

Though some still subscribe to the Machim theory,
Madeira was officially discovered by Portuguese explorers in
1418. At this time, Portugal was developing into the most
important maritime power on earth (along with Spain).
Portugal's maritime expansion came about largely after a
treaty with Castile (in 1411), which allowed the kingdom
to turn its attention to overseas exploration, initially as a
series of crusades but increasingly for economic gain. The
biggest single influence was **Prince Henry the
Navigator**, the third son of João I. The prince was head of
a powerful religious order, known as the Order of Christ,
and he set about using the resources of the order to fund a
School of Navigation in Sagres, the westernmost tip of the
Algarve. Under the auspices of this school, cartographers
and navigators developed techniques for the newly designed
caravels to set off into the unknown. Unsurprisingly,
Portugal's earliest explorations were of the Atlantic islands:
they initially settled in the Canary Islands, enslaving the
local Berber population, but continued to search for new
territories.

In 1418, Henry sent **João Gonçalves** and **Tristão Vaz
Teixeira** to explore the coast off Guinea in Africa. João

Gonçalves was a seasoned explorer, better known as **Zarco**, "the one-eyed", as he had lost an eye fighting against the Moors in Ceuta for Henry (see box on p.57). The two explorers were blown off course and soon spotted "vapours rising from the mouth of hell" – what they thought was the end of the world. On closer inspection they found a densely wooded island, which they named Ilha da Madeira (Island of Wood). Reluctant to visit the strange, mist-shrouded larger place, they took shelter in nearby Porto Santo. The following year, however, they returned to the islands with another explorer, Bartolomeu Perestrello. Perestrello stayed on Porto Santo, while Zarco and Teixeira went on to Madeira, landing at Machico (see p.126).

First settlers

Madeira was first colonized in 1425 and, during the same year, the island – along with Porto Santo – was declared a province of Portugal. The province was initially divided into three **administrative zones** run by three "captains" – appropriately the people who had helped discover the islands: Zarco, Teixeira and Perestrello. Zarco was the overall governor, and though he initially set up his government in Câmara de Lobos, he soon moved to Funchal. Teixeira was based at Machico and Perestrello at Porto Santo. In 1440 Machico was declared Madeira's first capital.

The first **settlers** set about clearing the wooded slopes, burning much of the native lauraceous forest, certainly on the lower slopes – it is said the burning of the trees was so intense that fires raged for seven years. One beneficial side-effect of this burning, however, was that all the ash made the soil extremely fertile.

When the land had been cleared, **wheat** was planted to supply Lisbon with corn; it was shipped to the capital by Genoese merchant bankers. However, the colonizers were

FIRST SETTLERS

keen to make money from a more lucrative crop, and in 1460 they planted **sugarbeat** cuttings from Sicily. (At that time, sugar was a very expensive commodity – honey was used as a sweetener and only the wealthy used sugar for cooking.) The plantations were worked by slaves imported from North Africa, who also began to cut the first **levadas** (see p.311). The water from these was used not only to irrigate the plantations but also to power water mills to process the cane. With the slaves' labour, Funchal grew prosperous and many people made their fortunes: Funchal's coat of arms is still five sugar loaves. One of the successful early sugar merchants was Christopher Columbus, who lived in Madeira and Porto Santo during the 1470s and 1480s after marrying the governor of Porto Santo's daughter (see p.199).

In 1497, the king of Portugal, **Manuel I** abolished the captaincy system and unified the island, naming Funchal its capital. The town gained a charter in 1508, and Zarco and his descendants continued to rule the island until the Spanish occupation of 1580.

Growth and vulnerability under the sugar trade

As the fifteenth century came to a close the **sugar trade** continued to be highly lucrative, with Flemish traders in particular using Madeira as a port of call. A spin-off from the trade with Flanders was art, and many superb works of Flemish art still reside in the Museum of Sacred Art in Funchal (see p.64). By the start of the sixteenth century, Funchal had 5000 residents, many of them slaves or foreign traders involved in the sugar trade. The town was rewarded with a cathedral to reflect its growing importance, and the Sé in Funchal was consecrated in 1516.

The downside of all this wealth was that Madeira and Porto Santo became increasingly attractive targets for passing pirates, especially in view of their lack of effective defences. As a result, forts were built in the sixteenth century to protect towns from attack and lookouts were posted on high points to warn of approaching hostile vessels. However, this was not enough to prevent sporadic violent raids. In 1566, around one thousand French pirates looted the island over a period of 16 days, taking valuables from the mansions and churches as well as killing 300 Madeirans. Later, in 1620, a British pirate, John Ward, also attacked, taking 1200 people prisoner to sell as slaves in Tunisia.

Spanish rule

By 1580, events on the mainland had begun to have a dramatic influence on Madeira's development. Following the lead of Spain, Portugal had set up the **Inquisition** in 1531, forcing the expulsion or conversion of the Jewish population that had traditionally controlled the country's financial institutions. Without their financial expertise, Portugal's economy began to fail, and to compound the country's problems, Portugal's kings were still obsessed with overseas crusades. Following the defeat of Dom Sebastião in a disastrous crusader attack in Morocco in 1578, his successor, Cardinal Henriques, tried to pay ransoms to buy back many of those captured in the battle. When he, too, died without an heir, Portugal – as well as being financially crippled – was without a king and ripe for takeover.

Philip II of Spain saw his opportunity and, after defeating various rivals' claim to the Portuguese throne at the battle of Alcantara in 1581, he was crowned Felipe I of Portugal. In 1582 Madeira was sent a Spanish governor, and the Spanish set about improving the island's defences, constructing more forts, including the **Forteleza de São Tiago** in Funchal and the **Pico do Castelo** fortifications on Porto Santo. Less beneficial was their obstruction of

Madeira's fledgling wine trade, which was seen as a potential threat to its own. Instead, the **timber trade** was encouraged – many boats in the Spanish Armada were constructed with Madeiran wood.

Spain's rule, however, was short lived. When, following the ineffectual reign of Felipe II, Felipe III attempted to recruit Portuguese troops to put down a rebellion in Catalonia, it was the last straw for the resentful Portuguese. In 1640, the palace in Lisbon was stormed and the **Duke of Bragança** was crowned João IV. Portugal has remained an independent country ever since.

The development of the wine trade

During the early part of the seventeenth century, Madeira's sugar trade began to flounder in the face of cut-price competition from Brazil and the British-controlled West Indies, forcing the islanders to look to alternative sources of revenue. The main beneficiary of this was the **wine trade**, which had recovered after the Spanish left.

As wine-making techniques improved over the course of the seventeenth century (see pp.284–287), so did the stability and quality of the wine which was exported to England, mainland Portugal and Brazil. As a result, more and more of Madeira's sugar plantations were dug up, and replaced with vines, which became the island's main crop.

It was not until the middle of the century, however, that the wine trade really took off. Portugal's position as a trading nation had been greatly weakened by Spain's occupation of Madeira and the mainland, with the Dutch and British grabbing many of the markets Portugal had lost. In an effort to halt Britain taking even more of Portugal's overseas markets, João IV struck a deal with British merchants, allowing them special concessions on exports. In 1658, the **British Factory** was formed in Madeira, a powerful association of merchants, who were now able to exert considerable influence over the island's wine-based economy.

In 1660, the English banned wine exports to their colonies from all places other than English ports, but in 1663 Madeira was excluded from the ban. As a result, English companies could export Madeiran wines directly to English colonies, giving Madeiran merchants a virtual monopoly on wine exports to the New World. The exclusion followed hot on the heels of Charles II of England's marriage to Catherine of Bragança in 1662, after which the English were granted increased trading rights in Portugal.

The marriage also almost saw Madeira lose its Portuguese sovereignty. It is said that Catherine's mother, Dona Luisa, considered giving Madeira, along with Bombay and Tangier, as part of the royal dowry. Legend has it that the scribe asked to write down the agreement was Madeiran and, reluctant to lose his island, persuaded the queen to withhold Madeira unless absolutely necessary. Dona Luisa agreed.

The eighteenth century

Thanks in large part to its flourishing wine trade, Madeira enjoyed a spell of peace and prosperity during the first half of the eighteenth century. Its trade routes were secured by the powerful Portuguese navy and, safe from pirate attack, Funchal's defensive walls were pulled down in the 1750s, though ironically Loo Rock was attacked by none other than Captain Cook in 1768 after he was enraged by an apparent insult to the British flag.

However, Madeira remained prone to disaster. In 1748, much of Funchal was ravaged by an **earthquake**, which destroyed several important buildings, including the original bishop's palace – now the Museu de Arte Sacra – and most of the original Alfândega Velha, Funchal's custom's house.

THE EIGHTEENTH CENTURY

A few years later, in 1755, mainland Portugal was devastated by its own earthquake, after which the **Marquês de Pombal** – a powerful right-hand man to the king – set about reconstucting the country, shaking up its institutions at the same time. One of his initiatives was to expel the Jesuits from the country. The Jesuits, who had established a college in Funchal in 1569, owned many of Madeira's vineyards, and when they were expelled in 1759, their estates were broken up and sold off privately, which opened up the land to more wine producers.

A period of instability followed during the lead up to the American War of Independence (1777–82). In 1767 there was a failed uprising against the king, and in 1773 the rural workers, most of whom worked for wine companies, tried petitioning the king for a fairer income, again unsuccessfully. This instability was exacerbated by the war itself, which cut down demand for Madeiran wine in America, as well as reducing imports of cereal, which had traditionally come from America. With the island's population increasing, the islanders faced extreme poverty.

By this stage the British Factory – now acting as a sub-colonial government for the resident British community and funded by a levy on goods imported from England and on wine shipping – had become a powerful economic force and had sufficient funds to help finance a British church, cemetery and hospital. The contrast between the wealth of the Factory, which in effect controlled Madeira's wine trade, and the harshness of life for workers on the wine estates not surprisingly aroused resentment in the local population against the British community.

The Napoleonic Wars

The British and Portuguese alliance had been broadly advantageous economically to both countries through the eighteenth century, but during the **Napoleonic campaigns**, Portugal became increasingly dependent on its traditional ally. The French had threatened to invade Portugal unless it agreed to support France's blockade of Britain's ports, but as Portugal relied on Britain for so much of its exports, it refused, and Napoleon's General Junot attacked Lisbon in 1807.

Britain quickly set about trying to defend Portugal. The Portuguese royal family was evacuated to Brazil, and Generals Beresford and Wellesley were put in charge of the campaign against the French. A garrison of British troops had been based in Madeira briefly in 1801 in case of a French invasion but, after Lisbon's occupation, a larger garrison of troops arrived under Beresford. From 1807 to 1814, several thousand soldiers were based in Monte, Camacha and Santo da Serra, constituting a virtual British occupation of the island, which the Madeirans resented. Beresford pulled out half the garrison in 1808, realizing the island was relatively safe, but the other troops remained until Napoleon was defeated. Ironically, Napoleon himself actually called in on Madeira en route to exile in St Helena in 1815 (see p.74).

Natural disasters and diversification

During the remainder of the nineteenth century, life for Madeira's wealthy was extremely comfortable, most of them living a grand lifestyle in their *quintas*. In contrast, Madeira's poor in particular remained susceptible to **natural disasters** and **disease**. In 1803, floods in Funchal destroyed part of the town and killed 600 people. As a result, new channels were built in the capital to control the flows (they still dissect the town today) and, much later, in 1895, a breakwater was built between the mainland and Loo Rock (it was extended in the 1930s to form today's harbour).

Following the end of the Napoleonic wars, Madeira's wine trade, the mainstay of its economy, also began to suffer, as Spain and France re-emerged as major wine exporters. In 1838, the powerful British Factory was forced to close down after a disastrous dip in the wine trade, caused by a combination of recession and poor crops. Then, in 1852 and again in 1873, the whole island's wine crop was devastated by pests and disease. As a result, **banana cultivation** and **sugar-refining** were stepped up in an attempt to diversify the economy; **embroidery** – introduced by a British woman, Elizabeth Phelps – and **basket-making** also took off to help buffer the economy against crop failure. Meanwhile, the local vines were crossbred with American varieties to form hybrids which were more resistant to pests.

Also in 1852, a **cholera epidemic** wiped out 7000 people. Although food and clothing was sent from London to help Madeira's poor, and the Funchal to Câmara de Lobos road was built in an attempt to reduce unemployment, all these disasters persuaded many Madeirans to emigrate to Portugal's other colonies and, later, to Venezuela and South Africa – the latter has more people of Madeiran descent than the population of Madeira itself.

Rebellion and the development of tourism

After the Napoleonic wars, with the Portuguese royal family remaining in exile in Brazil, the Portuguese army staged a coup and set up a new liberal constitution. Dom João finally returned from Brazil in 1821 and accepted the new constitution but, following his death five years later, João's younger son, Dom Miguel, declared himself absolute monarch of Portugal. This move set so-called **Miguelites** at odds with **Liberals**, who approved the new constitution. In 1828, Miguelites arrived on Madeira with 1000 troops to help put down a Liberal rebellion. Though backed by a group of British troops, the Liberals were defeated and imprisoned or sent into exile, many of them escaping to Britain. In 1834, however, Dom Miguel's older brother, Pedro IV, who also wanted to keep the new liberal constitution, returned from Brazil to claim back the throne, supported not only by the Liberals but also the British. Dom Miguel was finally defeated in the same year at the battle of Evora-Monte.

Portugal remained split between Liberals and the old absolutists for much of the nineteenth century, but nevertheless Madeira enjoyed economic stability. By the mid-nineteenth century, wealthy Brits began stopping off in Madeira en route to or from British colonies, staying at *quintas* and private manors. Luxury hotels were founded to cater for them, the first of which was *Reid's* in 1891 (see pp.78–80). The resident Brits also continued to have a positive effect on the island's economy, founding wicker and embroidery industries and cultivating gardens. They also invented the Monte toboggan ride, when a Brit wanted a fast way to get into town from his hilltop *quinta*. Monte soon became the main destination for visiting tourists, and a railway was built between Funchal and Monte in 1893 (the service was unfortunately cancelled in 1939 after a series of steam-boiler explosions).

The birth of the republic and World War I

As the century ended, the growing **Republican movement** on the mainland led to the eventual assassination of the Portuguese king Dom Carlos in Lisbon in 1908. Two years later, the last king of Portugal, Dom Manuel, was forced into exile, and in 1910 Madeira became part of the newly proclaimed republic of Portugal.

Meanwhile, Germany had become an important trading partner with Madeira. As well as importing Madeiran wine and embroidery, it also began to take over the freight shipping industry. In 1905, perhaps envious of the privileged existence of the British in Madeira, Germany offered to pipe water from the mountains to Funchal in exchange for being able to establish further trading preferences. The Madeirans were tempted until it was reported that the Germans actually planned to open a then illegal gambling casino.

With the outbreak of **World War I**, however, the fledgling German trading alliance was quickly destroyed. In 1916, Lisbon impounded German ships on the Tagus, and as a result Germany declared war on Portugal. Madeira subsequently confiscated all German property at England's request. In retaliation, Funchal was twice bombarded by German submarines, a traumatic experience for the islanders, who later erected a statue of the Madonna near Monte to commemorate the war.

Salazar and World War II

The war and the continually changing governments on the mainland meant Portugal and Madeira's economies were weakened. In 1926, a military coup in Portugal led to **Dr António Salazar de Oliveira** becoming minister of finance, then prime minister – and virtual dictator – from 1932. Salazar called his quasi-fascist state the "New State": it was a severe and repressive regime, decidedly inward looking, with the belief that Portugal could survive by trading with its former colonies without the need for the rest of the world. The regime put down a small uprising in Madeira in 1931 after a new law gave virtual monopoly of trade to select local mill owners, which led to two local banks going out of business; many people lost their savings instantly. A strike was followed by a military coup, which led to **General Sousa Dias** being declared Madeira's ruler, but troops from Lisbon were dispatched to the island to restore the status quo. Salazar saw Madeirans as little more than third-class citizens and the little income that was generated by the island went largely into central government's coffers. Resentment of the regime simmered until the dictator's demise in 1968.

World War II largely bypassed a neutral Madeira, though the island did put up 2000 British refugees from Gibraltar. However, the war did adversely affect the economy, and agriculture continued to rely on ancient methods, with the rural population living on or close to the poverty line; Porto Santo had no electricity until 1954. Things did not really improve until the 1960s, when farmers began to earn a living by planting Chinese dwarf bananas. Forms of **banana** – mainly plantain – had been grown in Madeira since the first settlers, but this new crop proved so commercially successful that they began to threaten the wine trade. To counter this the government decided to introduce subsidies in the 1970s to save the traditional vines.

Tourism and modernization

Until the 1950s, most travellers to Madeira arrived by boat, with a few affluent travellers able to arrive by flying boat. It was not until 1960, when an **airport** was built in Porto Santo – initially a NATO airport – and 1964, when Madeira's airport opened, that more tourists started to arrive.

Another boost to tourism came with the downfall of Salazar's dictatorship in 1968, when the Portuguese leader was crippled after a bizarre accident involving a collapsed deckchair. His successor, **Marcelo Caetano**, continued his policies, but the wars in Portugal's former colonies were leading to a growing resentment amongst the armed forces. In 1974, a coup was organized under Major Otelo Saraiva de Carvalho, and a peaceful **revolution** in Lisbon ushered in a new democracy in Portugal and Madeira.

Initially, Portugal's politics were in turmoil. A backlash against the right-wing Salazar led to a huge growth in support for the communists on the mainland. Scared of their influence, a right-wing separatist group, **Frente de Liberação Madeirense**, set itself up on the island, declaring independence from Portugal. The group perpetrated isolated acts of terrorism, but these came to an end two years after the 1974 revolution, when Madeira was declared an autonomous political region with its own government and parliament. The **Região Autónoma da Madeira** – known as RAM – was able to pass new laws and deal with issues relating directly to Madeira and Porto Santo. In addition to the regional parliament, Madeira was also allowed five representatives from its 50 regional seats to represent Madeira in the Portuguese parliament in Lisbon.

The island's first leader was the PSD (Social Democratic) **Dr Alberto João Jardim**, who has continued to govern into the twenty-first century. With the new government, modernization of the island slowly commenced. Tenants were allowed to buy the land they had farmed for years, though the downside of this was that many quickly sold up to property developers and many of the vineyards disappeared under new housing developments. Entry to the EU in 1986 saw more funds pour in and Madeira's economy grew rapidly, in tandem with the economic growth on the mainland.

Madeira today

Over the past decade, modernization has continued apace. In 1996, a new **south-coast highway** greatly increased access to Madeira's southern shores, cutting journey times dramatically and opening up villages that had been almost cut off from the capital. In addition, much of Funchal was spruced up in preparation for the **millennium festivities**, and the year 2000 also saw the connection of the airport road with the south-coast highway and the opening of a giant runway extension.

Although most of the improvements to infrastructure have taken place round Funchal, the regional government is trying to encourage tourism and trade away from the capital. Tunnels have improved access to several villages in the south, north and east, tourist resorts and hotels are increasingly growing up all over the island and a huge Free Trade Zone has been developed near Caniçal in the east of the island. This port and industrial zone has been given tax-free status until 2011 in an attempt to lure in foreign industry.

João Jardim won the local government elections for the sixth time in 2000. Seen as the people's president, Jardim remains unpopular on the Portuguese mainland for his out-spoken views but is seen as a hero on Madeira for sticking up for the islanders' rights – though his critics say he has pushed things too far in getting things done. Certainly some projects – such as the road tunnel from Jardim do Mar to Paúl do Mar on the south coast – seem extravagant in the extreme.

While Portugal and especially the EU continues to pump millions into improving the island's economy, there are strings attached, and the Madeiran government has promised to increase dramatically the number of hotel beds on the island in a bid to attain economic self-sufficiency. Many locals wonder if the island's infrastructure will be able to support the planned increase in tourist visitors, and there is concern about how the economy will cope when EU funds finally dry up.

The **population** of Madeira has remained stable for quite some time at around 250,000, a third of whom live in Funchal. Madeirans are worried that their island could easily be overrun by incoming tourists or by returning emigrants, especially from South Africa, Brazil and Venezuela, many of whom want to retire or start up new businesses in Madeira. Although such entrepreneurs have brought business to the island, many incomers are viewed with suspicion and locals are scathing of the so-called "Venezuelan" homes – over-the-top and usually extremely tacky mansions – built to show off the wealth of the owners.

Nevertheless, Madeirans are also aware of the importance of tourists and remain extremely courteous and friendly to visitors. However, their friendliness could be put firmly to the test if the expected new wave of tourists comes flooding in.

Wildlife and the environment

With its rich volcanic soil and warm, moist climate, Madeira has forged a reputation for a fantastic array of vivid **plant life**, which seems to grow from every nook and crevice in the mountains, valleys and even the waste ground in the towns – a reputation which stretches back to when Captain James Cook visited Madeira in 1768 and 1772 with a team of specialist botanists to describe the island's fauna and flora. The island also supports a vivid range of non-native species, including many that are endangered in their natural habitat. By contrast, neighbouring Porto Santo is far more arid and lacks Madeira's floral range.

Madeira and Porto Santo's remote Atlantic position has restricted native **animal life**; most of the islands' wild animals were introduced by colonizers. Birdlife, however, is far more diverse with an array of colourful and rare species on both islands.

Native flora

Though Madeira's exotic, imported flora is often more spectacular, the most important plants on the island are the **native species of Macaronesia** (those found only on Madeira, the Azores and the Canaries), such as the lauraceous forests and unusual dragon trees. The importance of the native flora to the development of Madeira is clear from the names the early settlers used for their new home: *madeira* means wood, reflecting the densely forested island they discovered, while *funcho* – which gave its name to Funchal – means fennel, which grew profusely in the area. The red sap from the **dragon trees** – dense, spiky succulents – probably contributed to even earlier references to a "purple" and "red" island (see p.331). During the first two hundred years of colonization, the trees were wiped out in the wild on both Madeira and Porto Santo to exploit the dye, but they are slowly being reintroduced in parks and gardens round both islands.

Madeira was so heavily wooded that the early Portuguese settlers had to burn many of the trees in order to cultivate the land. Despite the burning, however, most of the upper slopes from around 300m to 1300m in altitude – especially in the north of the island – remain virgin, primary forest. Much of it consists of **lauraceous forest**, one of the earth's last great concentration of laurel trees, which once flourished throughout the Mediterranean and eastern Africa. Nowadays only pockets survive in North Africa, the Canary Islands and on Madeira, where the forests are considered to be so important that in 1999 they were declared a UNESCO World Heritage Site. The lauraceous forest consists of three types of laurel: the Laurus Azonica, the Til tree and Vinhático, also known as Madeiran mahogany because it is so hard. The lauraceous forest and other plants such as juniper, shield ferns and oil-trees are protected also by the Parque Natural da Madeira, which covers sixty percent of the island.

Above the tree line, the soil is more barren, supporting familiar plants such as gorse, thistles, wild thyme, oregano and broom, along with local species, such as the yellow-flowering Pride of Madeira, rock cress, house leeks, with their weird interlocking leaves, the smelly-flowered groundsell and the ancient, twisted heather trees, whose roots do not burn and which are used to make briar wood pipes. The climate also produces familiar species, but at a bizarre scale, such as giant buttercups and tiny geraniums.

Non-native flora

In addition to native species, a wide range of the world's most beautiful **cultivated flora** thrives in Madeira's parks and gardens, many introduced from ships calling on the island on the way back from South Africa, Australasia, Asia and South America. In addition, wealthy landowners, such as the Count of Carvalhal, specially ordered English and Australian trees, as well as plants from New Zealand, Hong Kong and Brazil – you can see many of these plants at the Count of Carvalhal's Palheiro gardens (see pp.100–103). The tradition of importing plants continues today: *Reid's Palace Hotel*, for example, is undertaking a garden restoration scheme in the hotel grounds with the aim of forming one of the best gardens on the island.

Today, species as diverse as amaryllis, poinsettias, jacaranda, mimosa, tulip trees, frangipani, agapanthus, bird-of-paradise, camellias, kapok and magnolias provide a riot of colour at one time of the year or other. Begonias, bougainvillaea, hibiscus, oleanders and morning glory flower pretty much all year round, while more familiar plants, such as rhododendrons, azaleas, hydrangeas, red-hot pokers, cedars, oaks and chestnut trees, thrive on the cooler upper slopes.

NON-NATIVE FLORA

The island also supports tropical **fruits**, such as kiwis, figs, bananas, custard apple and passion fruit, and it is famed for its vineyards and orchid gardens. In addition the island has become something of a refuge for **endangered plant species**, with Funchal's Jardim Botânico (see pp.89–90), the Jardins Tropicais do Monte Palace in Monte (see pp.97–98) and the various orchid gardens in Funchal (see p.91 & p.92) being important breeding grounds for species whose natural habitats are under threat.

Despite the current level of environmental protection, a lot of damage has been done during the near 600 years of human activity on the island. By the early twentieth century, many of the slopes – especially in the south of the island – were severely **deforested**. To avoid the potential flood damage and soil erosion this would cause, an extensive planting programme of **eucalyptus** was undertaken on Madeira, though Porto Santo missed out on the reforestation scheme and remains severely eroded. Eucalyptus is a fast-growing tree that smells nice to humans but appalling to mosquitoes. Unfortunately, it was soon discovered that this natural mosquito repellent soaks up an enormous quantity of water from the soil, which is left virtually devoid of nutrients, a downside that was only realized towards the end of the twentieth century. In addition, they are extremely flammable, and forest fires have caused further havoc to the landscape ever since the eucalyptus were planted. The eucalyptus woods are gradually being replaced by less environmentally damaging alternatives, which are also now being planted on Porto Santo, but this is a slow process.

Wildlife

The other damaging effect of human occupation on Madeira was the introduction of **animals**, which until the first settlers arrived had been practically non-existent due to Madeira's isolated position in the middle of the Atlantic. The only wild animals on the island – rabbits, rats, ferrets and mice – have all been introduced by man, along with their pets and cattle, whose grazing has to be carefully controlled to prevent soil erosion.

The only native mammals are **bats**: the tiny pipistrelle, the long-winged lesser noctule and the grey long-eared bat. The **Madeiran wall lizard** is the native animal most likely to be encountered, a harmless, varying-coloured lizard, which is unusual in that it takes nectar from flowers rather like a bee. Otherwise there are few other lizards and a surprisingly limited variety of insects, the only one of any note being the **black wolf spider**, a poisonous creature found on the neighbouring Ilhas Desertas.

While animals were unable to establish themselves on Madeira or Porto Santo, **birds** had an easier time, with few natural predators. The rarest of the native species is the *columba trocaz*, better known as the long-toed wood pigeon, which lives in Madeira's remoter laurel forests. Another rare species is the Madeira petrel, which survives in the highest mountains in the middle of the island. Some two hundred other species of bird are resident or visit Madeira, including buzzards, kestrels, petrels, egrets, hoopoes and canaries.

Like the animal life, **sea life** round Madeira and Porto Santo is also surprisingly limited, partly because of the over-fishing of the waters, and partly because of the depth of the sea. Many of the surviving species are protected in the waters of the Garajau Nature Reserve, a marine park off Caniço (see p.123). The Ilhas Desertas also have protected status and form a safe haven for **monk seals**, almost wiped out by fishing and rated as one of the ten most threatened animal species on earth; these have been adopted as the symbol for Madeira. More common are **dolphins**, which can be seen on organized boat trips from Funchal harbour (see p.317). **Whales** are also occasional visitors to Madeira, which once had a thriving whaling industry based at Porto Moniz and Caniçal (see p.133). **Fish** tend to be deepwater species, such as scabbard fish, tuna and barracuda, while fishermen have also hauled in blue marlin, swordfish, blue and hammerhead sharks, bonito and wahoo (see pp.316–317). Other species include moray eels, squid, octopus and parrot fish, which you can encounter in superbly clear water on one of the numerous available diving trips (see p.317).

Music

As on mainland Portugal, **folk music** has always played an important part in Madeira's social and cultural life, and traditional folk continues to be played at festivals throughout the year (see pp.28–32). Tourist restaurants and hotels also often lay on folk-music nights, along with **fado**, the melancholy Portuguese music that became hugely popular in mainland Portugal and to a lesser extent Madeira from the late nineteenth century onwards. **Classical music** has also always been popular among Madeira's elite, and is sometimes performed at a few low-key venues round the island, along with jazz and rock. Live performances are usually by local groups, though famous international groups do sometimes perform in Funchal during the Musical Weekends.

Folk music and dance

Madeira has developed several strands of its own distinctive **folk music**. One of the more popular sounds is the **charamba**, in which two groups of singers take it in turns to sing gently teasing lyrics at the expense of the other group. *Charamba* is accompanied by the *braguinha* – a local variant of the ukulele – along with a wash-board-like rasping *raspadeira*. You'll also spot the distinctive *brinquinho*, a pole with bobbing decorative dolls wearing traditional costume, who jingle bells and castanets as they are moved up and down. A variant of the charamba is the **desfaio** – basically an amusing rhyming narrative of local events, from village gossip to local news.

Folk music is performed at many of the local festivals throughout the year and restaurants in Funchal's marina often hire folk bands to perform outside on the harbour, giving a free performance to anyone around.

Madeiran **folk dancing** has had something of a renaissance over the last ten years or so, largely thanks to the big hotels, which often hire folk-dancing groups to provide evening entertainment. The best known Madeiran group is the Grupo Folclórico da Camacha, who often go on European tours – though they also perform round the island and in their native Camacha (see p.107). Many of the dances traditionally grew up to help lessen the burden of tiring agricultural labour, such as dances which reflect lugging heavy loads on the performers' backs or stamping dances to reflect treading the grapes. The most extreme of these is the Dance of Ponta do Sol, or *baile*, in which dancers shuffle as if in chains in slow circles with their heads bowed, a reflection of early slaves.

Fado

Fado is a very Portuguese sound that grew up in Lisbon in the nineteenth century, though its derivatives are thought to be partly influenced by sounds introduced by African and Brazilian immigrants from Portugal's colonial days. The music first received recognition in the 1830s, when a working-class Lisbon fado singer, Maria Severa, started a controversial relationship with the Count of Vimiosa. Fortunately the music struck more of a chord with the public than the scandalous affair, and fado went on to become hugely popular, both when sung spontaneously in bars and more formally in music halls.

Fado music tends to be an emotional lament, its popular themes being love, death, destiny, bullfighting and *fado* (fate) itself. Part of the reason that the Portuguese take it so seriously is because of its role during the Salazar dictatorship of the twentieth century. During the 1930s, fado was popular in the theatre and in variety shows, but Salazar decided all fado should be censored and only sung in approved fado houses. Fado singers went along with this up to a point, singing approved lyrics when they thought it prudent, and unapproved lyrics at other times. There was also an unofficial fado scene, with uncensored performers singing spontaneously in clubs and bars.

The greatest fado singer to date has been **Amália Rodrigues**, who achieved international recognition from the 1950s onwards. Her death in 1999 – which sparked off three days of national mourning – seemed an appropriate end to the twentieth century, regarded as the golden age of fado.

In Madeira, fado has played less of a part historically but features in specialist restaurants and clubs, often aimed squarely at tourists. The fado singers usually get going late, after people have finished their meals. The singer is traditionally accompanied by one or two Portuguese guitars – originally introduced to Portugal via the British community in Porto – and one or two violas. The audience is expected to remain quiet while the performance takes place. Fado can be an acquired taste: at its best it can be deeply moving and infectious, at its worst a drawling bore – even worse are the warm-up singers often hired to perform while people eat. The big stars to look out for are Camané, Helder Moutinho, Carlos do Carmo, Maria da Fe, Cristina Branco and Misia, though their performances in Madeira are rare.

FADO

Classical music

Classical music has always been popular amongst Madeira's upper classes, but the island has produced no composers of note. Apart from the Musical Weekends summer music festival and the Meeting of the Regional Philharmonic Bands in Ribeira Brava in October, when international performers come to the island, performances of classical music are limited to local or student orchestras, which can be hit or miss. The best performances are usually saved for the Teatro Municipal Baltazar Diaz, Avenida Arriaga, in Funchal (map 2, C4; ℡ 291 220 416), and occasionally for the Sé cathedral (see p.62); smaller chamber music groups are booked up by many of the major hotels. Look out, too, for occasional performances in the open-air amphitheatre in the gardens of Jardim de São Francisco (see p.60), which are highly atmospheric.

Books

Surprisingly Madeira has failed to inspire much fiction, though it has produced the poet **Francisco Alvares de Nóbrega** (1773–1807), known as Little Camões, whose works unfortunately are not available in English. Another writer of Madeiran descent is **John dos Passos** (1896–1970), one of the most important modernist American authors of the twentieth century, best known for *Manhattan Transfer* – a lyrical, fragmented look at New York in the 1920s – and *Three Soldiers*, a look at the devastating effects of war on three soldiers returning to the States after World War I. However, there is a good range of non-fiction books, covering all aspects of Madeira's history, culture and geography.

Where two publishers are given for the books listed below, they refer to the UK and US publishers respectively. Books published in one country only are followed by the publisher and UK, US or Portugal; if a book has the same UK and US publisher, only the publisher's name is given. University Press has been abbreviated to UP.

History

J. and S. Farrow, *Madeira* (Robert, UK). Good background information on the island, with an especially detailed section on history.

Desmond Gregory, *The Beneficent Usurpers* (Associated UP; Fairleigh Dickinson UP). A somewhat dry account of Britain's influence on Madeira's history, though not all would agree with the author's assertion that the British were beneficent.

H.J. Weaver, *Reid's Hotel – Jewel of the Atlantic* (Souvenir Press Ltd, Portugal). Rather like the hotel itself, the prose is old-fashioned and slightly dry, but it forms an entertaining chronology of the great hotel's history and its illustrious visitors through anecdotes, photographs and memorabilia.

Food and wine

Alex Liddell, *Madeira* (Faber & Faber). A detailed study of Madeira wine, tracing its development, which is inextricably linked to the history of the island itself. At times illuminating but generally a bit of a slog unless you're a keen wine buff.

Don Glen Sands, *Madeira Wine at Home* (Empresa do Bolhão, Portugal). Solid background information on all aspects of the island's wine; there is also a range of local recipes.

Flora and fauna

António Da Costa and Luis de Franquinho, *Madeira – Plants and Flowers* (Francisco Ribeiro & Filhos, Portugal). An exhaustive account of the island's plant life; this one is highly illustrated so useful for species identification.

Rui Vieira, *Flowers of Madeira* (Francisco Ribeiro & Filhos, Portugal). Portuguese publication – in English – containing comprehensive information on the local flora.

Walking

Discovery Walking Guides, *Madeira – A Warm Island Guide* (UK). Independently produced pamphlet and map detailing 18 short walks, mostly in the south of the island. Not a bad choice for those into manageable walks within striking distance of Funchal.

Raimundo Quintal, *Levadas and Footpaths of Madeira* (Francisco Ribeiro & Filhos, Portugal). Local knowledge of Madeira's walkways; not particularly well written but with some good background information.

Pat and John Underwood, *Landscapes of Madeira* (Sunflower Books, UK). The essential book for keen walkers, with over 40 walks throughout Madeira (but not Porto Santo) described in painstaking detail – though it takes time to tune into the confusing geography of the book and the maps are so detailed as to make the simplest walk look daunting.

Language

There has been a resident British community on Madeira for hundreds of years, and most Madeirans – certainly those in the tourist industry – have a very good knowledge of English. However, knowledge of Portuguese is useful, especially in rural areas, and a few choice words of the language will get you a good reception whereever you are.

If you have some knowledge of Spanish, you won't have much problem reading **Portuguese**. Understanding it when it's spoken, though, is a different matter: pronunciation is entirely different and at first even the easiest words are hard to distinguish. Even so, it's well worth the effort to master at least the rudiments; once you've started to figure out the words it gets a lot easier very quickly.

A useful word is **há** (the H is silent), which means "there is" or "is there?" and can be used for just about anything. Thus: *Há uma pensão aqui?* (Is there a pension here?), *Há uma camioneta para…?* (Is there a bus to…?), or even *Há um quarto?* (Do you have a room?). More polite, and better in shops or restaurants, are **Tem**…? (pronounced *taying*), which means "Do you have…?", and **Queria**… (I'd like…). And of course there are the old standards "Do you speak English?" (*Fala Inglês?*) and "I don't understand" (*Não compreendo*).

Pronunciation

The chief difficulty with **pronunciation** is its lack of clarity – consonants tend to be slurred, vowels nasal and often ignored altogether. The **consonants** are, at least, consistent:

C is soft before E and I, hard otherwise, unless it has a cedilla – *açucar* (sugar) is pronounced "assookar".

CH is somewhat softer than in English; *chá* (tea) sounds like "shah".

J is pronounced like the "s" in pleasure, as is G, except when it comes before a "hard" vowel (A, O and U).

LH sounds like "lyuh" (*batalha*).

NH sounds like "nyuh"; *vinho* sounds like "veenyoo".

Q is always pronounced as a "k".

S before a consonant or at the end of a word becomes "sh", otherwise it's as in English – *cais* is pronounced "kaish", Sagres is "Sahgresh".

X is also pronounced "sh"– *caixa* (cash desk) is pronounced "kaisha".

Vowels are worse – flat and truncated, they're often difficult for English-speaking tongues to get around. The only way to learn is to listen: accents – Ã, Ô, or É – turn them into longer, more familiar sounds. When two vowels come together they continue to be enunciated separately except in the case of **EI** and **OU** – which sound like "a" and long "o" respectively. **E** at the end of a word is silent unless it has an accent, so that *carne* (meat) is pronounced "karn", while *café* sounds much as you'd expect. The **tilde over Ã or Õ** renders the pronunciation much like the French "-an" and "-on" endings, only more nasal. More common is **ÃO** (as in *pão*, bread – *são*, saint – *limão*, lemon), which sounds something like a strangled yelp of "Ow!" cut off in midstream.

BASIC PORTUGUESE WORDS AND PHRASES

sim; não	yes; no
olá; bom dia	hello; good morning
boa tarde	good afternoon
/noite	/night
adeus,	goodbye, *até*
logo	see you later
hoje	today
amanhã	tomorrow
por favor	please
/se faz favor	
tudo bem?	Everything all right?
está bem	it's all right /OK
obrigado/a*	thank you
onde; que	where; what
quando;	when;
porquê	why
como;	how;
quanto	how much
não sei	I don't know
sabe . . .?	do you know...?
pode . . .?	could you . . .?
desculpe;	sorry;
com licença	excuse me
aqui; ali	here; there
perto; longe	near; far
este/a;	this;
esse/a	that
agora;	now;
mais tarde	later
mais; menos	more; less

grande;	big;
pequeno	little
aberto;	open;
fechado	closed
senhoras;	women;
homens	men
lavabo/quarto	toilet/
de banho	bathroom
banco;	bank;
câmbio	change
correios	post office
(dois) selos	(two) stamps
sou Inglês	I am English
/Inglesa	
Americano/a	American
Irlandês	Irish
/Irlandesa	
Australiano/a	Australian
Canadiano/a	Canadian
Escocês	Scottish
/Escosesa	
Galês/ Galesa	Welsh
Como se	What's your
chama?	name?
(Chamo	(My name
me . . .)	is . . .)
Como se diz	What's this
isto em	called in
Português?	Portuguese?
O que é isso?	What's that?
Quanto é?	How much is it?

* *Obrigado* agrees with the sex of the person speaking – a woman says *obrigada*, a man *obrigado*.

Getting around

Para ir a. . .?	How do I get to. . .?
esquerda	left
direita	right
sempre em frente	straightahead
Onde é	Where is
a estação de camionetas?	the bus station?
a paragem de autocarro para . . .	the bus stop for . . .
Donde parte o autocarro para . . .?	Where does the bus to . . . leave from?
A que horas parte?	What time does it leave?
(chega a . . .?)	(arrive at . . .?)
Qual é a estrada para. . .?	Which is the road to . . .?
Para onde vai?	Where are you going?
(Vou a)	(I'm going to)
Está bem, muito obrigado/a	That's great, thanks a lot
Pare aqui por favor	Stop here please
bilhete (para)	ticket (to)
ida e volta	round trip

Accommodation

Há uma pensão	Is there a pension
aqui perto?	near here?
Queria um quarto	I'd like a room
É para uma noite	It's for one night
(semana)	(week)
É para uma pessoa	It's for one person
duas pessoas	two people
Posso ver?	May I see/look around?
Está bem, fico com ele	OK, I'll take it

continues overleaf

from previous page

Quanto custa?	How much is it?
É caro, não o quero	It's expensive, I don't want it
Há um quarto mais barato?	Is there a cheaper room?
Com duche	With a shower
(quente/frio)	(hot/cold)
chave	key

Days and months

domingo	Sunday	março	March
segunda-feira	Monday	abril	April
terça-feira	Tuesday	maio	May
quarta-feira	Wednesday	junho	June
quinta-feira	Thursday	julho	July
sexta-feira	Friday	agosto	August
sábado	Saturday	setembro	September
		outubro	October
janeiro	January	novembro	November
fevereiro	February	dezembro	December

Phrasebooks

Numerous Portuguese **phrasebooks** are available: one of the most user-friendly is the *Rough Guide Portuguese Phrasebook*, set out dictionary-style for easy access, with English–Portuguese and Portuguese–English sections, cultural tips for tricky situations and a handy menu reader. For teaching yourself Portuguese, the BBC's *Get By in Portuguese* is excellent.

Numbers

1	um	19	dezanove
2	dois	20	vinte
3	três	21	vinte e um
4	quatro	30	trinta
5	cinco	40	quarenta
6	seis	50	cinquenta
7	sete	60	sessenta
8	oito	70	setenta
9	nove	80	oitenta
10	dez	90	noventa
11	onze	100	cem
12	doze	101	cento e um
13	treze	200	duzentos
14	catorze	500	quinhentos
15	quinze	1000	mil
16	dezasseis	2000	dois mil
17	dezassete	1,000,000	um milhão
18	dezoito		

Glossary of Portuguese terms

Achada a flat area of volcanic soil

Adega tavern, wine cellar

Albergaria inn

Azulejo decorative, glazed ceramic tile

Boca mountain pass

Cabo coastal headland, cape

Caminho path, way

Capela chapel

Centro Commercial shopping centre

Correios (CTT) post office

Cruz cross

Cruzamento crossroads

Dias úteis weekdays

Dom, Dona Sir/madam; usually applied to the names of kings and queens

Estádio stadium

Estalagem inn, usually in rural area

Estrada (main) road

Faja flat area of land suitable for building on, formed after a landfall

Farmácia chemist

Festa festival or carnival

Fonte fountain or spring

Fortaleza fort

Grutas caves, grotto

Horário timetable

Igreja church

Jardim gardens

Largo small square

Levada irrigation canal

Manueline maritime-influenced architectural style, named after Manuel I (1495–1521)

Mercado market

Miradouro viewpoint

Nossa Senhora Our Lady – the Virgin Mary

Paragem bus stop

Parque park

Parque de Campismo campsite

Pastelaria patisserie, cake shop

Pául marshland

Pico mountain peak

Piscina swimming pool

Poio terrace

Ponte bridge

Pousada government-run guest-house

Praça (town) square

Praia beach

Quinta farm estate

Ribeiro stream

Rio river

Romaria religious festival or pilgrimage

Sé cathedral

Serra mountain range

Common Portuguese signs

Aberto open

Ar condicionado air conditioned

Desvio diversion (on road)

Dormidas private rooms

Elevador lift

Entrada entrance

Fecha a porta close the door

Fechado closed

Incluído IVA (price) includes VAT

Obras roadworks

Paragem bus stop

Perigo/Perigoso danger/dangerous

Pré-pagamento pay in advance

Proibido estacionar no parking

Quartos private rooms

Saída exit

Turismo tourist office

INDEX

25 Fontes 158

A

accommodation................... 219–227
  Boaventura 237
  Calheta 233
  Camacha 227
  Caniçal 228
  Caniço 228
  Caniço de Baixo 229–230
  Estreito de Câmara de Lobos 127
  Funchal 219–227
  Garajau....................................230–231
  Jardim do Mar 233–234
  Machico 231–232
  Paúl da Serra 234
  Paúl do Mar 234
  Pico do Arieiro 237
  Ponta Delgada 237
  Porto da Cruz...............................232
  Porto Moniz 238
  Porto Santo 241–244
  Praia Formosa 226
  Prazeres 234–235
  Ribeira Brava 235–236
  Santa Cruz 232
  Santana 238–239
  Santo António da Serra 233
  São Jorge....................................239
  São Vicente 240
  Serra de Agua 236
Achada do Teixeira 182
addresses.....................................326
adventure sports operators 309
airlines 326
airport 127
airport information.........................326
American Express office 326
apartments 219
Arco da Calheta 149
Art and Minerals Museum (Monte)....98
azulejos...................................70–71

B

Baia de Abra.................................136
Balancal Palheiro Golf 103
Balancal Palheiro Golf 321
Balcões 185
banks 27–28
bars 281–301
beaches 314
Bica da Cana 160
bicycle rental................................312
bike tours 312
Blandy's 100–103
Boaventura 174
Boca da Encumeada 161
Boca do Risco 141

books 357–359
British Factory 336–338
bus services 33–34

C

Cabanas 174
cable car
Monte..95
Santana......................................179
Cabo Girão 114
cafés..................................281–301
Caldeirão do Inferno 181
Caldeirão Verde 181
Calhau 170
Calheta 150–151
Camacha 104–108
Câmara de Lobos 108–112
camping 216–217
Canhas..149
Caniçal 132–133
Caniço 122
Caniço de Baixo 122
canoeing......................................316
canyoning....................................316
car rental......................................35
car-rental companies 36
Casa Museu Cristóvão
Colombo 198–200
children..322
Christmas 32
Churchill, Winston 110
cinemas 326
classical music 356
Clube de Golf Santo da Serra 137, 320
coach tours 38
Columbus week 31
Columbus, Christopher 59, 62, 199
consulates 17
contraception................................327
costs 26
crime 327
Cristo Rei 159
Curral das Freiras 118–119
currency 25
cycling 311–312

D

directory 326–328
diving 314, 315
in Caniço de Baixo 123
in Machico 130
doctors..19
dolphin-watching 317–318
dos Passos, John 147, 357
drinks 281–287
driving...35
earthquake 337
eating 245–252
Eira do Serrado............................117
electricity 327
embassies (Portuguese) 17
emergencies 327
Estreito da Calheta 151
Estreito de Câmara de Lobos 112
Ethnographical Museum 145–146

E

euro 25
exchange rates 26

F

fado 354–355
Faial 183–184
Fajã dos Padres 115–116
festivals..29
fish 352
fishing 316–317
fishing-trip operators....................317
Flemish art 64–65
flights
from Australia and New Zealand ..13–16
from Britain and Ireland..................3–8
from Canada 11
from North America......................9–12
from the USA 10
flora 348–350
flower festival 30
folk music 353–354
food 250–252

food terms 246–247
football 318–319
Funchal 45–91
  accommodation 219–227
  Adegas de São Francisco 60–61
  Antiga Alfândega 52
  aquarium 68
  arrival 48
  Avenida Arriaga 58
  Avenida do Mar 52
  azulejos 70–71
  Banger's Tower..........................54
  Barbeito Wine Lodge 80
  Barreirinha Lido 86
  bars 288–294
  Beatles' Boat 54
  boat trips 55
  British Cemetery 73
  bus services 49
  cable car 86, 95
  cafés...............................288–294
  Câmara Municipal........................63
  Capela de Santa Catarina................75
  Capela do Corpo Santo 86
  carnival 66–67
  Casa do Turista.........................55
  Casa Museu Frederico De Freitas ..68–69
  casino..................................76
  Columbus, Christopher..............59, 62
  Convento de Santa Clara 69–71
  driving.................................50
  English Church 73–74
  Flemish art 64–65
  Fortaleza do Pico 73
  Forte de São Tiago 87–88
  harbour.................................77
  history..............................46–48
  Hospício da Princesa 76
  Hotel Zone 80
  IBTAM (Institutue of Embroidery, Tapestry
    and Craftsmanship)...................85
  Igreja de Santa Maria Maior 88
  Igreja do Carmo 83–84
  Igreja do Colégio.......................64
  information 48–49
  Instituto do Vinho da Madeira 63

Jardim Botânico (botanical
  garden) 89–91
Jardim de Santa Catarina 75
Jardim de São Francisco 60
Jardim Orquídea (orchid garden)........91
lido 80
Loiro Parque (parrot park) 91
Loo Rock 77
marina 54
market 83
Mercado dos Lavradores 83
Monumento João Gonçalves Zarco ..59
Museu Barbeito Cristovão Colombo ..59
Museu Cidade do Açúcar (sugar
  museum)..............................62
Museu de Arte Contemporânea ..87–88
Museu de Arte Sacra 64–65
Museu de Electricidade 82
Museu de Francisco Franco 84
Museu de História Natural...............90
Museu do Club Sport Marítimo...........86
Museu Municipal do Funchal 68
Palácio da Justiça 63
Palácio de São Lourenço 56
Praça do Município......................63
Praia Formosa 81
Quinta da Boa Vista 92
Quinta das Cruzes 72
Quinta Magnolia 78
Quinta Vigia 75
Reid's 78–80
restaurants 252–264
Ribeira de João Gomes 81
Rua da Carreira 66
Rua de Santa Maria 89
Rua Dr Fernão Ornelas 83
Scottish Kirk 60
Sé (cathedral) 62
seafront 52
shops 303–307
taxi services 50
Teatro Municipal Baltazar Diaz 59
tickets and passes 49
transport...............................49
Universidade de Madeira 64
Vicente Gomes da Silva 66–68

Wine Museum 63
Zarco (João Gonçalves) 57
Zona Velha 86–89

G

Garajau 121–122
gay scene 283
glossary 366–368
golf 320
golf courses 103, 137, 320
government rest houses 218
Grutas de São Vicente 171–172
guesthouses 218
guided walks.................................310

H

health and insurance......................18
helicopter tours.............................313
Henrique e Henrique wine lodge 109
history 331–346
holidays 28–29
Homem em Pé 182
horse-riding 312
hospitals.................................19, 327
hotel price codes 214
hotels 215

I

Ilhas Desertas 53
information 22
insurance 19
internet 24
internet cafés 41

J

Jardim do Mar......................152–153
Jardim, Dr Alberto João 344
Jardins Tropicais do Monte
    Palace 97–98
jeep safaris 313
João Carlos Abrue Collection 146

K

kids..322

L

Lamaceiros 167
language 360–365
laundry 327
lauraceous forest...................348–349
Levada da Central da Janela..166–167
Levada da Serra Choupana 104–105
Levada do Caldeirão Verde 180–181
Levada do Norte 113
Levada dos Tornos 102–103
Levada Nova...............................153
levadas 311
Lido Galo Mar (Caniço de Baixo)....123
Loo Rock 77
Lorano 140
lost luggage 327

M

Machico 126–131
Madalena do Mar 147–148
Madeira wine 284–287
Madeiran cuisine 250–251
Manueline architecture 150
maps 23
Marítimo 318–319
meals 248–252
media 42
medical matters 18
mobile phones 40
money 25
Montado do Barreiro.....................191
Monte 94
motorbike rental 37
mountain biking 312
Museu de Arte Sacra 64–65
Museu da Baleia (whaling
    museum) 133
music 353–356

N

Napoleonic Wars....................338–339
New Year's Eve 32
newspapers 42
nightlife 281–282
Nossa Senhora de Fátima..............172
Nossa Senhora de Piedade 135
Nossa Senhora do Monte 96–97

O

O Relógio (Camacha) 106–108
Ovil 160

P

packages 5
palheiros 178
Parque do Monte 96
Parque do Santo da Serra 138
Parque Ecológico do Funchal 191
Paúl da Serra 159–161
Paúl do Mar 154–155
Penha de Águia 184
petrol 35
pharmacy 327
photography 327
phrasebooks...................................364
picnic spots 324
Pico das Pedras 182
Pico do Arieiro 185–190
Pico do Facho......................131–132
Pico dos Barcelos 116–117
Pico Ruivo.............................182–183
playgrounds 323–324
Poço de Neves 185
Poiso 190–191
police 328
politics 344
Ponta de São Lourenço 133–136
Ponta Delgada 172–173
Ponta do Pargo 155–156
Ponta do Sol.........................146–147
population.......................................345

Portela 138
Porto da Cruz 139–142
Porto Moniz 164–168
Porto Santo 193–209
  Porto Santo 192–209
  history 193
  getting there 194–195
  ferry 194
  flights 195
  bus services 195
  public transport 195
  taxis 195
  tours...196
  walking tours 196
  car rental 196
  scooter rental 196
  bike rental 196
  carriola (pony and trap)....................196
  information 197
  tourist office 197
  banks 197
  Internet.......................................197
  Vila Baleira 198
  Casa Museu Cristóvão
    Colombo.............................198–200
  Columbus, Christopher...................199
  boat trips 201
  beach..201
  Camacha 202
  Fonte da Areia 202
  Pico do Castelo 203
  Pedragal.....................................203
  Pico Branco 203–204
  Terra Chã 203–204
  Serra de Dentro 204
  Serra de Fora 204
  Portela 205
  Capela de Nossa Senhora
    da Graça 205
  Campo de Baixo..........................206
  Pico de Ana Ferreira 206
  Capela de São Pedro 206
  Cabeço da Ponta 206
  Ponta da Calheta 207
  Ilhéu de Baixo.............................207
  Ilho de Ferro 207, 208

Miradouro das Flores 207–208
Morenos...208
Adega das Levadas......................208
Ponta da Canaveira 208
Campo de Cima 208
Quinta das Palmeiras (botanical
    garden)....................................209
accommodation 241–244
restaurants 278–280
bars 300–301
nightlife 300–301
cafés.................................300–301
Portuguese embassies abroad 17
Portuguese language 360–365
Portuguese tourist offices abroad 23
post office.....................................328
postal services 39–40
pousadas 236–237
Praia 175–176
Praia dos Reis Magos 124
Prainha 134
Prazeres 153
private rooms 218
public holidays 29

Q

Queimadas 179–182
Quinta do Palheiro Ferreiro 100–103
Quinta Furão................................176
Quinta Splendida (botanical
    garden) 122
quintas 216

R

Rabaçal 156–159
radio...42
Reid's 78–80
restaurants 252–280
    Calheta......................................272
    Camacha 264–265
    Câmara de Lobos......................265
    Caniçal 267
    Caniço 267–268

Caniço de Baixo 268
Curral das Freiras 265–266
Estreito de Câmara de Lobos.......266
Faial 274–275
Funchal.................................252–264
Garajau...269
Jardim do Mar 272
Machico 269–270
Madalena do Mar 272
Monte...266
Paúl da Serra 273
Paúl do Mar 273
Pico dos Barcelos.........................266
Ponta do Pargo 273
Ponta do Sol 274
Portela 270
Porto da Cruz 270–271
Porto Moniz 275
Porto Santo 278
Ribeira Brava 274
Ribeiro Frio 276
Santa Cruz 271
Santana 276
Santo António da Serra 271
São Jorge 276
São Vicente 277
Seixal 277
revolution.......................................343
Ribeira Brava 144–146
Ribeira Seca do Machico 141
Ribeiro Frio 184
Risco Waterfall 158
Rocha do Navio Teleférico.............179

S

Salazar 342
Santa Cruz 124–125
Santana 177–179
Santana houses 178
Santo António da Serra..........136–138
São Jorge......................................175
São Vicente...........................169–171
sea pools 314
Seixal 169
Serra de Água...............................161

shopping..............................302–307
sightseeing tours...........................38
Spanish rule 335–336
sport..................................308–321
sugar trade 334
supermarkets 328
surfing...315
swimming 313–314

T

taxi services 37
telephones 40–41
television..42
tennis 319–320
Terreiro da Luta............................98–99
time..328
tipping 328
toboggan run (Monte) 99–100
toilets...328
tourist offices
   abroad 23
   in Madeira................................22
tours...38
transport...33

V

Vale Paraíso 104
vegetarian food...........................252
Vila Baleira 198
villas...219
visas and red tape 16

W

walking..309
walks
   Achada do Teixeira to
     Pico Ruivo..........................182–183
   Cabeço da Ponta to Ponta da
     Calheta (Porto Santo) 207
   Levada da Central da Janela
     (near Porto Moniz)...............166–167

Levada da Serra Choupana (Vale
   Paraíso to Camacha)............104–105
Levada do Caldeirão Verde (Queimadas
   to Caldeirão Verde) 180
Levada do Paúl (Rabaçal to
   Cristo Rei) 159
Levada dos Tornos (Monte to
   Funchal) 102–103
Levada Nova (Prazeres to Ponta do
   Pargo)..153
Lorano to Machico 140–141
Pedragal to Pico do Castelo (Porto
   Santo)..202
Pico Branco and Terra Chã (Porto
   Santo)...............................203–204
Pico do Arieiro to Pico Ruivo....188–189
Pico do Arieiro to the Buzzard's
   Nest...190
Ponta de São Lourenço 134–135
Prazeres to Paúl do Mar 154
Queimadas to Pico das Pedras........182
Rabaçal to 25 Fontes 158
Rabaçal to Risco waterfall...............158
Ribeiro Frio to Balcões 185
Ribeiro Frio to Portela.....................185
São Jorge a Quinta Furão 176
water 18
watersports...........................315–317
websites...24
whale-watching................................318
whales 352
wicker trade 107
wildlife....................................347–352
windsurfing 315–316
wine......................................284–287
wine festival 31
wine production 112–113
wine rally..31
Wladislaw II....................................148
World War I.....................................342

Z

Zarco (João Gonçalves)....57, 332–333

ROUGH GUIDES: Travel

Amsterdam
Andalucia
Australia
Austria
Bali & Lombok
Barcelona
Belgium &
  Luxembourg
Belize
Berlin
Brazil
Britain
Brittany & Normandy
Bulgaria
California
Canada
Central America
Chile
China
Corfu & the Ionian
  Islands
Corsica
Costa Rica
Crete
Cyprus
Czech & Slovak
  Republics
Dodecanese
Dominican Republic
Egypt
England
Europe
Florida
France
French Hotels &
  Restaurants 1999
Germany
Goa
Greece

Greek Islands
Guatemala
Hawaii
Holland
Hong Kong
  & Macau
Hungary
India
Indonesia
Ireland
Israel & the Palestinian
  Territories
Italy
Jamaica
Japan
Jordan
Kenya
Laos
London
London Restaurants
Los Angeles
Malaysia, Singapore &
  Brunei
Mallorca & Menorca
Maya World
Mexico
Morocco
Moscow
Nepal
New England
New York
New Zealand
Norway
Pacific Northwest
Paris
Peru
Poland
Portugal
Prague

Provence & the
  Côte d'Azur
The Pyrenees
Romania
St Petersburg
San Francisco
Scandinavia
Scotland
Sicily
Singapore
South Africa
Southern India
Southwest USA
Spain
Sweden
Syria
Thailand
Trinidad & Tobago
Tunisia
Turkey
Tuscany & Umbria
USA
Venice
Vienna
Vietnam
Wales
Washington DC
West Africa
Zimbabwe & Botswana

ROUGH GUIDES: Mini Guides, Travel Specials and Phrasebooks

MINI GUIDES

Antigua
Bangkok
Barbados
Big Island of Hawaii
Boston
Brussels
Budapest
Dublin
Edinburgh
Florence
Honolulu
Lisbon
London Restaurants
Madrid
Maui
Melbourne
New Orleans
St Lucia

Seattle
Sydney
Tokyo
Toronto

TRAVEL SPECIALS

First-Time Asia
First-Time Europe
More Women Travel

PHRASEBOOKS

Czech
Dutch
Egyptian Arabic
European
French

German
Greek
Hindi & Urdu
Hungarian
Indonesian
Italian
Japanese
Mandarin Chinese
Mexican Spanish
Polish
Portuguese
Russian
Spanish
Swahili
Thai
Turkish
Vietnamese

ROUGH GUIDES:
Reference and Music CDs

REFERENCE
Classical Music
Classical:
   100 Essential CDs
Drum'n'bass
House Music

World Music:
   100 Essential CDs
English Football
European Football
Internet
Millennium

ROUGH GUIDE
   MUSIC CDs
Music of the Andes
Australian
   Aboriginal
Brazilian Music
Cajun & Zydeco
Classic Jazz
Music of Colombia
Cuban Music
Eastern Europe
Music of Egypt
English Roots
   Music
Flamenco
India & Pakistan
Irish Music
Music of Japan
Kenya & Tanzania
Native American
North African
Music of Portugal

Jazz
Music USA
Opera
Opera:
   100 Essential CDs
Reggae
Rock
Rock:
   100 Essential CDs
Techno
World Music

Reggae
Salsa
Scottish Music
South African
   Music
Music of Spain
Tango
Tex-Mex
West African Music
World Music
World Music Vol 2
Music of Zimbabwe

AVAILABLE AT ALL GOOD BOOKSHOPS

100

Essential

CDs

Eight titles,
one name

ROUGH GUIDES

Will you have enough stories to tell your grandchildren?

©2000 Yahoo! Inc.

Yahoo! Travel

DO YOU
YAHOO!
?

Rough Guides
on the Web

www.travel.roughguides.com

We keep getting bigger and better! The Rough Guide to Travel Online
now covers more than 14,000 searchable locations. You're just a click
away from access to the most in-depth travel content, weekly
destination features, online reservation services, and an outspoken
community of fellow travelers. Whether you're looking for ideas for
your next holiday or you know exactly where you're going, join us online.

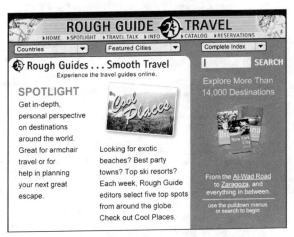

You can also find us on Yahoo!® Travel (http://travel.yahoo.com) and
Microsoft Expedia® UK (http://www.expediauk.com).

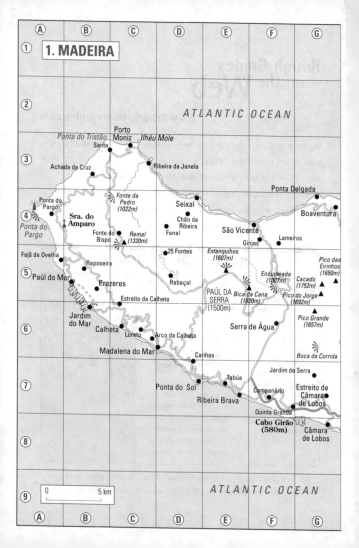

1. MADEIRA

ATLANTIC OCEAN

Ponta do Tristão
Porto Moniz
Ilhéu Mole
Santa
Achada da Cruz
Ribeira da Janela
Ponta Delgada
Ponta do Pargo
Fonte da Pedro (1022m)
Seixal
Boaventura
Sra. do Amparo
Chão da Ribeira
São Vicente
Ponta do Pargo
Fonte do Bispo
Remal (1320m)
Fanal
Ginjas
Lameiros
Fajã da Ovelha
25 Fontes
Estanquinhos (1607m)
Pico das Eirinhos (1650m)
Raposeira
Rabaçal
Endumeada (1007m)
Cacado (1752m)
Paúl do Mar
Prazeres
PAÚL DA SERRA (1500m)
Bica da Cana (1620m)
Pico do Jorge (1692m)
Estreito da Calheta
Pico Grande (1657m)
Jardim do Mar
Calheta
Loreto
Arco da Calheta
Serra de Água
Madalena do Mar
Canhas
Boca da Corrida
Tabúa
Jardim de Serra
Ponta do Sol
Campanário
Estreito de Câmara de Lobos
Ribeira Brava
Quinta Grande
Cabo Girão (580m)
Câmara de Lobos

0   5 km

ATLANTIC OCEAN

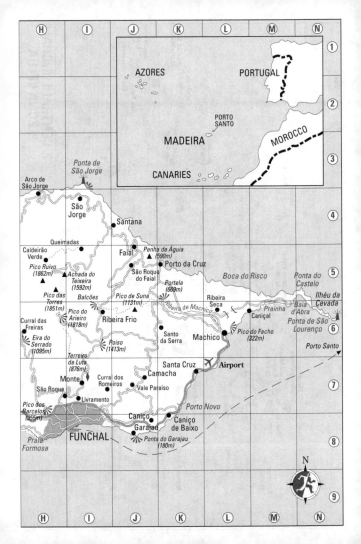

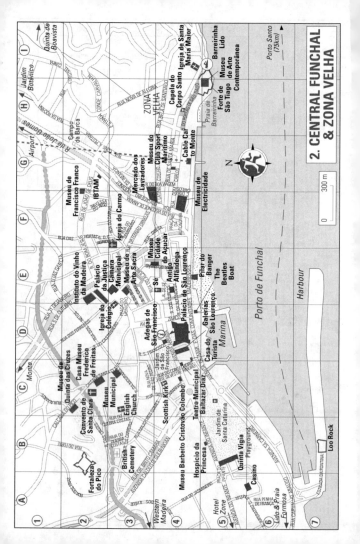

2. CENTRAL FUNCHAL & ZONA VELHA

0 — 300 m

Quinta de Boavista

Jardim Botânico

Porto Santo (75km)

Museu de Arte Contemporânea

Barreirinha Lido

Museu

Forte de São Tiago

Praia de Barreirinha

Igreja de Santa Maria Maior

Capela do Corpo Santo

Cable Car to Monte

ZONA VELHA

Museu Clip Sport Marítimo

Museu de Electricidade

Mercado dos Lavradores

Museu da Cidade

Museu do Açucar

Igreja do Carmo

IBTAM

Museu de Francisco Franco

Airport

R de João Gomes

Instituto do Vinho da Madeira

Palácio da Justiça

Câmara Municipal

Museu de Arte Sacra

Sé

Igreja do Colégio

Antigo Alfândega

Pilar do Banger

The Beatles Boat

Palácio de São Lourenço

Galerias São Lourenço

Casa do Turista

Adegas de São Francisco

Marina

Porto de Funchal

Harbour

Museu da Quinta das Cruzes

Casa Museu Frederico de Freitas

Convento de Santa Clara

Museu Municipal

English Church

British Cemetery

Scottish Kirk

Museu Barbeito Cristovão Colombo

Teatro Municipal Baltazar Dias

Hospício da Princesa

Jardim de Santa Catarina

Quinta Vigia

Casino

Western Madeira

Hotel Zone

Playground

Loo Rock

Lido & Praia Formosa

Monte

Fortaleza do Pico

Quinta de Boavista

N

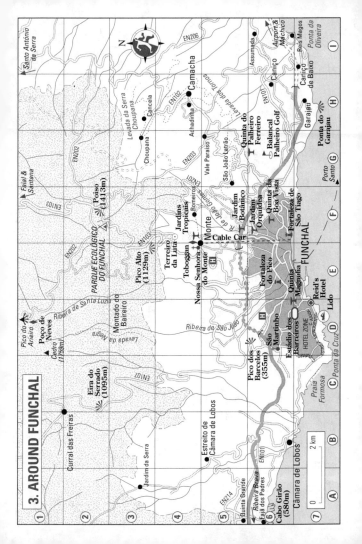

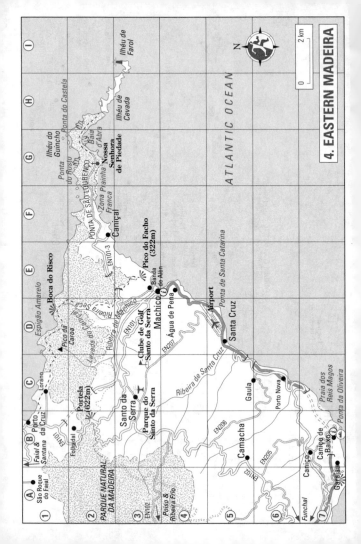

4. EASTERN MADEIRA

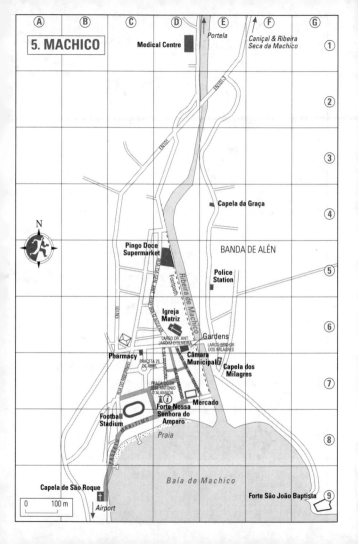

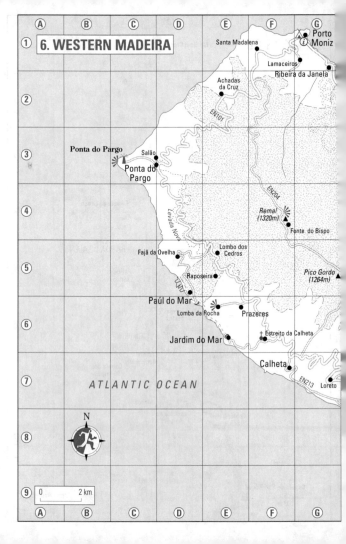

6. WESTERN MADEIRA

Santa Madalena

Porto Moniz

Lamaceiros

Ribeira da Janela

Achadas da Cruz

EN101

Ponta do Pargo

Salão

Ponta do Pargo

EN204

Remal (1320m)

Fonte do Bispo

Levada Nova

Fajã da Ovelha

Lombo dos Cedros

Pico Gordo (1264m)

Raposeira

Paúl do Mar

Lomba da Rocha

Prazeres

Jardim do Mar

Estreito da Calheta

Calheta

ATLANTIC OCEAN

EN213

Loreto

N

0   2 km

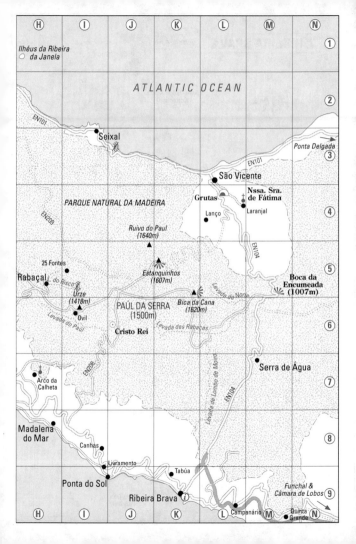

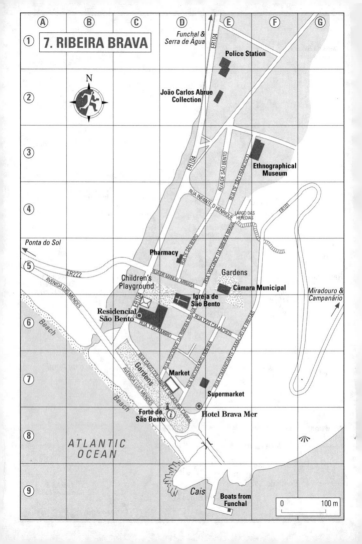

7. RIBEIRA BRAVA

Funchal & Serra de Água

Police Station

João Carlos Abrue Collection

Ethnographical Museum

Ponta do Sol

Pharmacy

Children's Playground

Gardens

Câmara Municipal

Igreja de São Bento

Residencial São Bento

Miradouro & Campanário

Beach

Gardens

Market

Supermarket

Forte de São Bento

Hotel Brava Mer

ATLANTIC OCEAN

Beach

Cais

Boats from Funchal

0   100 m

N

ER104

ER222

AVENIDA LUIS MENDES

RUA DE SÃO BENTO

RUA DE SÃO FRANCISCO

RUA INFANTE D HENRIQUE

LARGO DAS HEREDIAS

ER101

RUA DR MANUEL ARRIAGA

RUA DR PESTANA JUNIOR

RUA VISCONDE DA RIBEIRA BRAVA

RUA DOS CAMACHOS

RUA 1 DE DEZEMBRO

RUA GAGO COUTINHO

RUA VISCONDE DA RIBEIRA BRAVA

RUA COMANDANTE CAMACHO DE FREITAS

RUA NOVA DA RIBEIRA BRAVA

AVENIDA LUIS MENDES

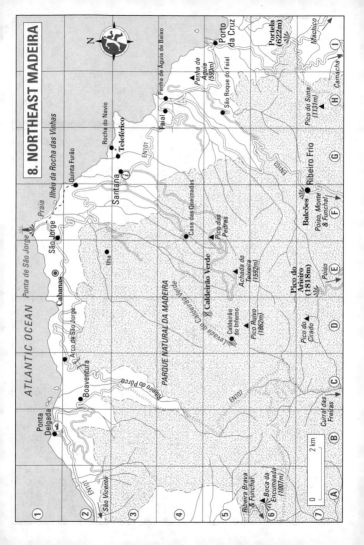

8. NORTHEAST MADEIRA

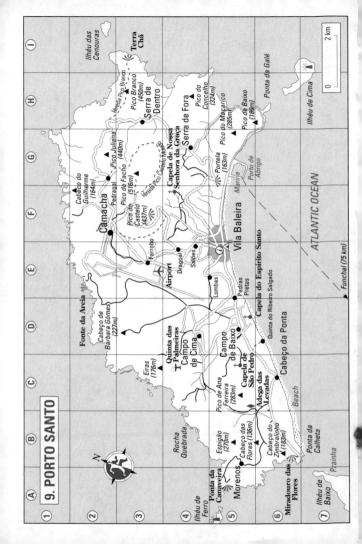

9. PORTO SANTO

Ilhéu das Cenouras

Terra Chã

Pico Branco (450m)

Vereda Pico Branco

Serra de Dentro

Pico Juliana (440m)

Cabeço do Guilherme (164m)

Pedregal

Pico do Facho (516m)

Vereda Pico Castelo Miho

Camacha

Pico do Castelo (437m)

Capela de Nossa Senhora da Graça

Serra de Fora

Pico do Concelho (324m)

Pico do Maçarico (285m)

Pico da Baixo (189m)

Portela (163m)

Porto de Abrigo

Marina

Vila Baleira

Farrobo

Airport

Dragoal

Sabões

Lombas

Pedras Pretas

Capela do Espírito Santo

Quinta do Ribeiro Salgado

Fonte da Areia

Cabeço de Barbara Gómes (227m)

Quinta das Palmeiras

Campo de Cima

Eiras (176m)

Campo de Baixo

Capela de São Pedro

Cabeço da Ponta

Pico de Ana Ferreira (283m)

Adega das Levadas

Beach

ATLANTIC OCEAN

Funchal (75 km)

Ponta da Galé

Ilhéu de Cima

Rocha Quebrada

Espigão (270m)

Cabeço das Flores (136m)

Morenos

Cabeço do Zimbralinho (183m)

Ponta da Canaveira

Ilhéu de Ferro

Miradouro das Flores

Ponta da Calheta

Prainha

Ilhéu de Baixo

N

0   2 km